MUNICH

FODOR'S TRAVEL PUBLICATIONS

are compiled, researched, and edited by an international team of travel writers, field correspondents, and editors. The series, which now almost covers the globe, was founded by Eugene Fodor in 1936.

OFFICES
New York & London

Fodor's Munich

Editor: Thomas Cussans
Executive Editor: Richard Moore
Contributors: Robert Brown, Andrea Dutton, Pamela Vandyke Price
Drawings: Beryl Sanders
Maps: Swanston Graphics
Cover Photograph: Jason Hailey/FPG International

Cover Design: Vignelli Associates

Fodor's 89

Munich

Reprinted from *Fodor's Germany 1989*

FODOR'S TRAVEL PUBLICATIONS, INC.
New York & London

ISBN 0–679–01675–9

MANUFACTURED IN THE UNITED STATES OF AMERICA

10 9 8 7 6 5 4 3 2 1

CONTENTS

FOREWORD

Munich is one of the great cities of Europe: vibrantly modern, culturally and historically rich, packed with excellent hotels and restaurants. It's also a city that has long had a love affair with tourism, and indeed the large numbers of special deals available to visitors—for travel, museums, hotels, restaurants, and the like—make it delightfully easy to visit. Easy on your pocketbook as well as on your travel planning.

Of course, much the same could be said for many of the great cities. But Munich is special.

It has a proud history as one of the major cultural centers of the German-speaking world. With time out for wars and their subsequent chaos, Munich has always been prosperous and lively, with the arts flourishing over several centuries. It is also the center of a great deal of imaginative industry—with optical and precision instruments, printing, and publishing, cars and chemicals well to the fore. Munich is the capital of one of Germany's most individualistic regions, Bavaria, and shares in the area's vibrant chronicles that stretch back to well before the Middle Ages. It is a city for the rich, for the middling rich, and for the visitor who watches every pfennig like a hawk, for the business traveler who daren't be out of reach of the telex machine, and for the student who wants to grab a bite at the Oktoberfest snack bar. In short, it has all the best elements of Germany rolled into one attractive parcel.

* * * *

While every care has been taken to assure the accuracy of the information in this guide, the passage of time will always bring change, and consequently the publisher cannot accept responsibility for errors that may occur.

All prices and opening times quoted in this guide are based on information available to us at press time. Hours and admission fees may change, however, and the prudent traveler will avoid inconvenience by calling ahead.

Fodor's wants to hear about your travel experiences, both pleasant and unpleasant. When a hotel or restaurant fails to live up to its billing, let us know and we will investigate the complaint and revise our entries where the facts warrant it.

Send your letters to the editors of Fodor's Travel Publications, 201 E. 50th Street, New York, NY 10022. European readers may prefer to write to Fodor's Travel Publications, 30–32 Bedford Square, London WC1B 3SG, England.

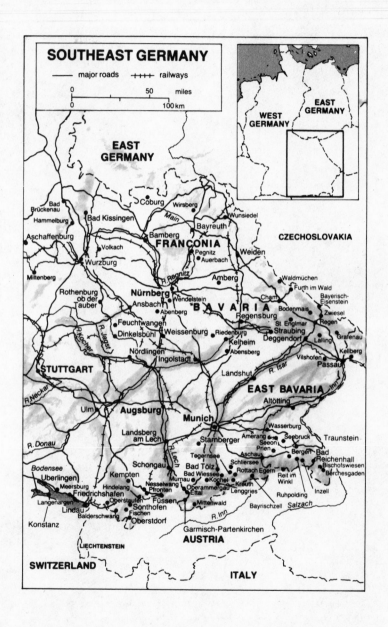

FACTS AT YOUR FINGERTIPS

Planning Your Trip

SOURCES OF INFORMATION. The major source of information for all aspects of travel to Germany is the German National Tourist Office. It produces a wealth of tourist literature, the bulk of it free and all of it useful. It is a strikingly efficient organization and should be the first place you contact when planning your vacation.

Their addresses are:

In the U.S.: 747 Third Ave., New York, NY 10017 (212–308–3300); 444 South Flower St., Suite 2230, Los Angeles, CA 90071 (213–688–7332).

In Canada: P.O. Box 417, 2 Fundy, Place Bonaventure, Montreal, H5A 1B8 (514–878–9885).

In the U.K.: 61 Conduit St., London W.1 (01–734 2600).

WHEN TO GO. The main tourist season in Germany runs from May to late October, when the weather is naturally at its best. As well as many tourist events, this period has many hundreds of folk festivals. The winter sports season in the Bavarian Alps runs from Christmas to mid-March.

Prices are generally higher during the summer, so you may find considerable advantages visiting during the low season. Tourist offices can provide lists of hotels offering special low-price inclusive weekly packages *(Pauschalangebote)*. The other major advantage of off-season travel is that crowds, which in the major tourist destinations are often otherwise thick on the ground, are very much less in evidence.

However, there are a number of disadvantages. First, the weather, which during the summer is normally delightful throughout the country, is pretty miserable in the winter. Secondly, many major tourist attractions close down.

Climate. The German climate is generally temperate and mild. Winters, as we say, are often quite gloomy, though, away from the Alps, never particularly cold; rather they are dull and mostly wet. Summers, however, are usually excellent and warm, though be prepared for cloudy and wet days from time to time. The south is normally quite a bit warmer than the north, but as you get nearer the Alps, summers are much shorter lived, starting in May. Spring and fall are often delightful, though they, too, can be wet.

1

The only real exception to the above is the strikingly variable weather in southern Bavaria caused by the *Föhn,* an Alpine wind that gives rise to very clear but rather oppressive conditions.

Average afternoon temperatures in degrees Fahrenheit and centigrade in Munich:

	Jan.	Feb.	Mar.	Apr.	May	June	July	Aug.	Sept.	Oct.	Nov.	Dec.
F°	33	37	45	54	63	69	72	71	64	53	42	36
C°	1	3	7	12	17	21	22	22	18	12	6	2

National Holidays 1989. January 1 (New Year's Day); March 24, 27 (Easter); May 1 (Labor Day); May 4 (Ascension); May 15 (Pentecost Monday); May 25 (Corpus Christi, southern Germany only); June 17 (German Unity Day); November 1 (All Saints); November 22 (Day of Prayer and Repentance); December 25 and 26 (Christmas).

WHAT TO PACK. The golden rule is to travel light; generally, try not to take more than you can carry yourself. Not only are porters more or less wholly extinct in Europe these days (where you can find them they're very expensive anyway), the less luggage you take the easier checking in and out of hotels becomes. Similarly airports (increasingly the number-one nightmare of all modern travel) become much easier to get through, and if you only take one piece of luggage, the less risk there is of your luggage being lost en route, and, in theory anyway, the less time you need to wait for it to appear when you get off the plane. Remember also that there are strict regulations governing the amount of luggage you can take with you on the plane. Each passenger is allowed two pieces of luggage, neither of which must exceed 62″ (height × width × length) and which together do not exceed 124″. Penalties for excess baggage are high. In theory, you may also take only one piece of hand luggage onto the plane, though most airlines usually turn a blind eye to this rule.

It's an excellent idea to pack the bulk of your things in one large bag and put everything you need for overnight, or for two or three nights, in a smaller one, to obviate packing and repacking at brief stops.

Finally, remember to leave space for gifts. Most German shops will ship goods back to the States—essential for larger items and advisable for breakable items—but if you want to take gifts back with you, leave room for them!

Clothes. The German climate is comparable to that of New England, so take along the sort of clothes you would wear there, depending of course on the sort of vacation you plan to have. A light rain coat is essential, however.

Most hotels expect you to be reasonably smartly dressed for dinner but evening dress, for example, is not going to be expected anywhere but in a handful of the most expensive hotels and restaurants.

If you wear glasses, take along a prescription. Otherwise, there is no difficulty in getting medicines, but if you have to take a special preparation take along your own supply.

Don't forget your swim cap if you think you might swim in either indoor or outdoor pools. They're obligatory in Germany.

GERMAN CURRENCY. The unit of currency in Germany is the Deutschmark, written as DM. It is divided into 100 pfennigs. There are bills to the value of 1,000, 500, 100, 50, 20, and 10 DM, and coins to the value of 5, 2 and 1 DM and 50, 10, 5, 2 and 1 pfennigs.

At the time of writing (mid–1988), the mark stood at 1.83 to the U.S. dollar and 3.13 to the pound sterling.

Changing Money. All international airports and many larger rail stations in Germany have exchange offices operated by bona fide banks, all offering the official rate of exchange and most open outside normal banking hours (see below). Otherwise, outside banking hours, you can usually change money at tourist offices, some travel agents, most hotels and at any one of the growing number of private exchange kiosks *(Wechelstuben)* found in larger towns and cities. All, however, charge well above the official rate and should be used in emergencies only.

The best place to change money anywhere in Germany is at a bank. They are open 8.30 or 9–3 or 4 (5 or 6 on Thurs.)

If you think you are going to arrive in Germany outside banking hours, or know that there will not be an airport or rail station exchange office where you arrive, take along enough German money to get you through the first day or so. All banks in both the U.S. and U.K. can supply small quantities of Deutschmarks, though some may require a few days' notice.

COSTS IN GERMANY. Germany has an admirably high standard of living—among the highest in Europe—and can unquestionably be an expensive country to visit, particularly if you spend time in a large city like Munich. Similarly, the present disadvantageous exchange rate has certainly not helped. However, the vagaries of exchange rates being what they are, the situation could easily change, so it is essential to check them carefully both before and during your trip. You will also find that many items—gas, food, hotels and trains, to name but a few—are probably more expensive here than in the States. However, a number of crucial factors are on your side.

First, the country's low rate of inflation—itself an admirable testimony to the affluence and efficiency of the Germans—has helped keep costs well within manageable bounds, with the result that many of the staples of tourism have increased only slightly in price for many years and remain very competitive.

Second, naturally conscious of their high-price-tag reputation, the Germans have made significant efforts in offering a host of special deals. Hotels, restaurants, transport, sports—all have many excellent-value deals available of one sort or another. Both your travel agent and the German National Tourist Office should be able to help you. And once in Munich, you'll find that the local tourist office has a wealth of literature available, and a great deal of practical advice, on cost cutting.

Hotel and Restaurant Prices. The prices of hotels in Munich are high (see below for details) but not disproportionately so in comparison to other north European cities. Note, however, that there is no official grading system within Germany. Service charges and taxes are automatically included in all quoted room rates. Continental breakfast is usually, but not always, included—larger breakfasts are always extra—so check this before you book.

All restaurants, other than the least expensive, display their menus outside, and all prices on them will include tax and service, so shop around a bit before you decide where to eat. Note that all wine lists also include tax and service in the quoted prices. (See below for details of restaurant prices.)

We have divided all the hotels in our listings into four categories: Deluxe (L), Expensive (E), Moderate (M), and Inexpensive (I). These grades are determined solely by price.

Two people in a double room can expect to pay in DM:

Deluxe (L)	200 and up
Expensive (E)	160–200
Moderate (M)	100–160
Inexpensive (I)	60–100

In the more rural areas of Bavaria, these prices can often be as much as 50% less.

We have divided our restaurant listings in the same way. Approximate prices, per person and excluding drinks, in DM are:

Expensive (E)	65–95
Moderate (M)	45–65
Inexpensive (I)	25–45

These prices are for three-course meals. You will find that a single course naturally works out much less expensively. In addition, prices for lunch will be much less than those quoted here.

Both our hotel and restaurant lists give details of the credit cards accepted by each establishment. These are: AE for American Express, DC for Diner's Club, MC for MasterCard (incorporating Access and EuroCard) and V for Visa (incorporating Barclaycard).

Sample costs. Museum entrance DM. 3–8; cinema DM. 15; opera, anywhere from DM. 30–200; subway or bus DM. 3; one mile taxi ride DM 7; glass of whiskey DM. 8; bottle of beer DM. 1.20 (more in a restaurant); bottle of wine DM.8 (more in a restaurant); cup of coffee (in café) DM. 3; cigarettes DM. 3–4.

TAKING MONEY ABROAD. Traveler's checks are the safest and simplest way to take money abroad. The best-known are American Express, Bank of America, Cook's, and Barclay's, but practically all banks issue them and you will have no difficulty cashing them throughout Germany (see *Changing Money* above). It is, however, hard to say if it is more advantageous to take checks in dollars or marks; the former stand a chance of making or losing you a little if the exchange rate changes, the latter will of course retain their value throughout your time in Germany.

British visitors can also cash personal checks of up to £100 a day on production of a Uniform Eurocheque card and check book (available from all major banks in the U.K.); all banks in Germany displaying the Eurocheque symbol will accept these.

Credit Cards. All the major credit cards are generally, though by no means universally, accepted throughout Germany. In our hotel and restaurant recommendations we list which of the major cards—American Express, Diner's Club, MasterCard (incorporating Access and EuroCard), and Visa—are accepted by each establishment. But always be sure to check before reserving your room or ordering a meal that your particular piece of plastic is accepted. As a general rule, Visa is probably the most widely accepted, while practically all larger and more expensive establishments will take American Express. In the event of losing your credit card, immediately register the loss at one of the following offices: American Express (tel. 069–720016); Diners Club (tel. 069–26030); MasterCard/Access (tel. 069–79330); Visa (tel. 069–7562537).

PASSPORTS. Americans. All U.S. citizens need a valid passport to enter West Germany. Visas are not required. If you do not have a passport, apply in person at U.S. Passport Agency Offices, local county courthouses or selected Post Offices. If you have a passport not more than eight years old you may apply by mail; otherwise you will need:

—proof of citizenship, such as a birth certificate.

—two identical photographs, two inches square, in either black and white or color, on non-glossy paper and taken within the past six months.

—$35 for the passport itself plus a $7 processing fee if you are applying in person (no processing fee when applying by mail) for those 18 years and older, or if you are under 18, $20 for the passport plus a $7 processing fee if you are applying in person (again, no extra fee when applying by mail).

—proof of identity such as a driver's license, previous passport, any governmental ID card, or a copy of an income tax return.

Adult passports are valid for 10 years, others for five years; they are not renewable. Allow four to six weeks for your application to be processed, but in an emergency, Passport Agency offices can have a passport readied within 24–48 hours, and even the postal authorities can indicate "Rush" when necessary.

If you expect to travel extensively, request a 48- or 96-page passport rather than the usual 24-page one. There is no extra charge. When you receive your passport, write down its number, date and place of issue separately; if it is later lost or stolen, notify either the nearest American Consul or the Passport Office, Department of State, Washington DC 20524, as well as the local police.

Canadians. Canadian citizens apply in person to regional passport offices, post offices or by mail to Passport Office, Bureau of Passports, Complexe Guy Favreau, 200 Dorchester West, Montreal, P.Q. H2Z 1X4 (514–283–2152). A $25 fee, two photographs, a guarantor, and evidence of citizenship are required. Canadian passports are valid for five years and are non-renewable.

Britons. British subjects should apply for passports on special forms obtainable from main post offices or a travel agent. The application should be sent or taken to the Passport Office according to residential area (as indicated on the guidance form) or logged with them through a travel agent. It is best to apply for the passport 4–5 weeks before it is required, although in some cases it will be issued sooner. The regional Passport Offices are located in London, Liverpool, Peterborough, Glasgow and Newport. The application must be countersigned by your bank manager or by a solicitor, barrister, doctor, clergyman or justice of the peace who knows you personally. You will need two full-face photos. The fee is £15; passport valid for 10 years.

British Visitor's Passport. This simplified form of passport has advantages for the once-in-a-while tourist to most European countries (including West Germany). Valid for one year and not renewable, it costs £7.50. Application may be made at main post offices in England, Scotland and Wales, and in Northern Ireland at the Passport Office in Belfast. Birth certificate or medical card for identification and two passport photographs are required—no other formalities.

HEALTH AND INSURANCE. The different varieties of travel insurance cover everything from health and accident costs, to lost baggage and trip cancellation. Sometimes they can all be obtained with one blanket policy; other times they overlap with existing coverage you might have for health and/or home; still other times it is best to buy policies that are tailored to very specific needs. Insurance is available from many sources, however, and many travelers unwittingly end up with redundant coverage. Before purchasing separate travel insurance of any kind, be sure to check your regular policies carefully.

Generally, it is best to take care of your insurance needs before embarking on your trip. You'll pay more for less coverage—and have less chance to read the fine print—if you wait until the last minute and make your purchases from, say, an airport vending machine or insurance company counter. If you have a regular insurance agent, he or she is the person to consult first.

Flight insurance, which is often included in the price of the ticket when the fare is paid via American Express, Visa or certain other major credit cards, is also often included in package policies providing accident coverage as well. These policies are available from most tour operators and insurance companies. But while it is a good idea to have health and accident insurance when traveling, be careful not to spend money to duplicate coverage you may already have . . . or to neglect some eventuality which could end up costing a small fortune.

For example, basic Blue Cross-Blue Shield policies do cover health costs incurred while traveling. They will not, however, cover the cost of emergency transportation, which can often add up to several thousand dollars. Emergency transportation *is* covered, in part at least, by many major medical policies such as those underwritten by Prudential, Metropolitan and New York Life. Again, we can't urge you too strongly that in order to be sure you are getting the coverage you need, check any policy carefully before buying. And bear in mind also that most insurance issued specifically for travel will not cover pre-existing conditions, such as a heart condition.

Several organizations offer coverage designed to supplement existing health insurance and to help defray costs not covered by many standard policies, such as emergency transportation. Some of the more prominent are:

Carefree Travel Insurance, c/o ARM Coverage Inc., 120 Mineola Blvd., Box 310, Mineola, NY 11510 (516–294–0220), offers medical evacuation throughout Europe arranged by InterClaim. Carefree coverage is available from many travel agents.

International SOS Assistance Inc. has fees from $15 a person for seven days, to $195 for a year (800–523–8930).

IAMAT (International Association for Medical Assistance to Travelers), 417 Center St., Lewiston, NY 14092 (716–754–4883) in the U.S.; or 188 Nicklin Rd., Guelph, Ont. N1H 7L5 (519–836–0102).

Travel Assistance International, the American arm of Europ Assistance, offers a comprehensive program providing medical and personal emergency services and offering immediate, on-the-spot medical, personal and financial help. Trip protection ranges from $35 for an individual for up to eight days to $220 for an entire family for a year. Full details from travel agents or insurance brokers, or from *Europ Assistance Worldwide Services, Inc.,* 1333 F St., N.W., Washington, D.C. 20004 (800–821–2828). In the U.K., contact *Europ Assistance Ltd.,* 252 High St., Croydon, Surrey (01–680 1234).

The Association of British Insurers, Aldermary House, Queen St., London EC4N 1TT (01–248 4477), will give comprehensive advice on all aspects of vacation travel insurance from the U.K.

Baggage Loss. Another frequent inconvenience to travelers is the loss of baggage. It is possible, though often a complicated affair, to insure your luggage against loss through theft or negligence. Insurance companies are reluctant to sell such coverage alone, however, since it is often a losing proposition for them. Instead, this type of coverage is usually included as part of a package that also covers accidents or health. Should you lose your luggage or some other personal possession, it is essential to report it to the local police immediately. Without documentation of such a report, your insurance company might be very stingy. Also, before buying baggage insurance, check your homeowner's policy. Some such policies offer "off-premises theft" coverage, including the loss of luggage while traveling.

Cancellation Coverage. Trip cancellation coverage is especially important to travelers on APEX or charter flights. Should you be unable to continue your trip during your vacation, you may be stuck having to buy a new one-way fare home, plus paying for the charter you're not using. You can guard against this with "trip cancellation insurance." Most of these policies will also cover last minute cancellations.

STUDENT AND YOUTH TRAVEL. All student travelers should obtain an *International Student Identity Card,* which is generally needed to get student discounts, youth rail passes, and Intra-European Student Charter Flights. Apply to *Council On International Educational Exchange,* 205 East 42 St., New York, NY 10017 (212–661–1414); or 312 Sutter St., San Francisco, CA 94108. Canadian students should apply to the *Association of Student Councils,* 187 College St., Toronto, Ontario M5T 1P7 (416–979–2604). U.K. students should apply to the *National Union of Student Marketing,* 461 Holloway Rd., London N.7 (01–272 9445).

HINTS FOR HANDICAPPED TRAVELERS. Facilities for the handicapped in Germany are generally good if variable, though where are they not? The German National Tourist Office details facilities of those hotels with special amenities for handicapped visitors in their hotel listings. It also produces a leaflet—*Autobahn Service fuer Behinderte*—detailing all stopping places on the German autobahn network with facilities for the handicapped. Similarly, German Railways have introduced special jumbo-sized carriages in a number of Inter-city express trains to accommodate wheelchairs; details from German Railways. However, the principal source of information within Germany is the *BAG Hilfe fuer Behinderte e.V.* (German Disabled Association), Kirchfeldstrasse 149, 4000-Dusseldorf 1, Germany.

Otherwise, major sources of information are: *Access to the World: A Travel Guide for the Handicapped,* by Louise Weiss, an outstanding book covering all aspects of travel for anyone with health or medical problems; it features extensive listings and suggestions on everything from availability of special diets to wheelchair accessibility. Order from *Facts On File,* 460 Park Ave. South, New York, NY 10016 ($14.95). The *Moss Rehabilitation Hospital,* 12th St. and Tabor Rd., Philadelphia, PA 19141, gives information on facilities for the handicapped in many countries and also provides toll-free numbers of airlines with special lines for the hearing impaired; they can also provide listings of tour operators who arrange vacations for the handicapped. But for a complete list of tour operators, write to the *Society for the Advancement of Travel for the Handicapped,* 26 Court St., Brooklyn, NY 11242.

In the U.K., contact *Mobility International,* 228 Borough High St., London SE1 1JX; MENCAP, Mencap National Center, 123 Golden Lane, London EC1Y ORT; the *Across Trust,* Crown House, Morden, Surrey (they have an amazing series of "Jumbulances," huge articulated ambulances, staffed by volunteer doctors and nurses, that can whisk even the most seriously handicapped across Europe in comfort and safety). But the main source in Britain for all advice on handicapped travel is the *Royal Association for Disability and Rehabilitation* (RADAR), 25 Mortimer St., London W1N 7RJ.

LANGUAGE. The Germans are great linguists and you will find English spoken in all hotels, restaurants, airports and stations, museums and other places of interest. Similarly, the Munich tourist office will have at least one member of staff who speaks fluent English, though all of the staff will probably be similarly fluent. However, don't assume that everyone you deal with will automatically speak English. Away from Munich, English will definitely not be so widely spoken, and it is in any case only common courtesy to ask beforehand if the person you are dealing with speaks English. Needless to say, the Germans respond warmly to anyone who makes the effort to master a few words or phrases in German but the odds are that the reply will be in perfect English.

TIME. During the summer (dates vary every year, but generally this means from the end of March to the end of September), Germany is six hours ahead of Eastern Standard Time, seven hours ahead of Central Time, eight hours ahead of Mountain Time and nine hours ahead of Pacific Time. During the winter, Germany puts her clocks back one hour, but as all America does likewise, the time difference remains the same.

Similarly, Germany is one hour ahead of British Summer Time and, during the winter, one hour ahead of Greenwich Mean Time.

Staying in Munich

CUSTOMS ON ARRIVAL. There are three levels of duty-free allowance for people entering Germany. For those entering Germany from outside Europe the allowances are: 400 cigarettes or 100 cigars or 500 grams of tobacco; plus, 1 liter of spirits more than 22% proof or 2 liters of spirits less than 22% proof, plus 2 liters of wine; plus, a reasonable quantity of perfume (the Germans are uncharacteristically imprecise as to the definition of "reasonable"); plus, other goods to the value of DM 115.

Entering Germany from a country belonging to the EEC, the allowances are: 200 cigarettes (300 if not bought in a duty-free shop) or 75 cigars or 400 grams of tobacco; plus, one liter of spirits more than 22% proof (1.5 liters if not bought in a duty-free shop) or three liters of spirits less than 22% proof; plus, five liters of wine; plus 75 grams of perfume and one-third of a liter of toilet water; plus, other goods to the value of DM 780.

For those entering Germany from a European country not belonging to the EEC, the allowances are: 200 cigarettes or 50 cigars or 250 grams of tobacco; plus, 1 liter of spirits more than 22% proof or 2 liters less than 22% proof and 2 liters of wine; plus, a reasonable quantity of perfume; plus, other goods to the value of DM 115.

All tobacco and alcohol allowances are for those of 17 or over. All items intended for personal use may be imported and exported freely. There are no restrictions on the import and export of German currency.

TIPPING. The service charges on hotel bills suffice, except for bell hops and porters (DM 1 per bag or service). Whether you tip the hotel concierge depends on whether he or she has given you any special service.

Service charges are included in restaurant bills (listed as *Bedienung*), as well as tax (listed as *MWST*), but it is customary to round up the bill to the nearest mark or give about 5% to the waiter or waitress at the same time as paying the bill. You don't leave it on or under the plate as is customary in the U.S.

In taxis, round the fare up to the nearest full mark as a tip. More is not expected, except of course for special favors or if you have particularly cumbersome or heavy luggage.

MAIL. Post offices *(Postamt)* are identified by a yellow sign bearing a post-horn; mail-boxes are also yellow, with the same symbol. Postage stamps can be purchased from vending machines (make sure you have some small change handy) bearing the words *Postwertzeichen* or *Briefmarken* or at the appropriate counter at the post office. At the time of writing (mid-1988) mail costs are as follows, although increases for 1989 are scheduled: airmail letters to the U.S. and Canada cost DM 1.40; postcards cost 90 pfennigs. Airmail letters to the United Kingdom cost 80 pfennigs; postcards cost 60 pfennigs.

Telegrams. File your telegram at the post office. Charges to New York are DM 1.20 per word; to London 60 pfennigs a word.

TELEPHONES. As in most European countries the post office operates the telephone service. Local phone calls from pay stations (yellow kiosks) cost 30 pfennigs. Cheap rates on long distance calls within the Federal Republic operate between 6 P.M. and 8 A.M. and at weekends. Foreign calls can be made from call-boxes bearing the sign *Inlands und Auslandsgespräche*. But because you will probably need a large amount of small change, it is more convenient to inquire at a post office. Phone calls from hotels are considerably more expensive (often as much as four times the normal price).

Newly introduced in Germany are telephone kiosks which can *receive* calls. They are recognizable by their telephone numbers (Rufnummer) clearly visible on the outside of the doors, and a sign bearing a ringing telephone.

To call the operator dial 1188 for local directory information and 00118 for international directory inquiries.

OPENING AND CLOSING TIMES. Shops are generally open from 9.00 to 6 or 6.30 Monday to Friday, and closed on Saturday afternoons (larger department stores often remain open until 2.00 P.M.) and on Sundays. On the first Saturday of every month shops in large towns stay open all day. Longer hours may apply at important holiday resorts. At railway stations in larger cities travel provisions can be bought in the evenings and over weekends.

All shops and banks close over public holidays. For bank opening hours, see *German Currency*.

ELECTRICITY. In nearly all areas, the voltage is 220, AC current, 50 cycles. Better check before plugging in, however. Transformers to step down too-high voltage can be bought in special shops everywhere, along with adaptors for German sockets and plugs, which differ from the American and British varieties. It's always best to take along a battery-operated razor.

Leaving Munich

CUSTOMS ON RETURNING HOME. If you propose to take on your vacation any *foreign-made* articles, such as cameras, binoculars, expensive timepieces and the like, it is wise to put with your travel documents the receipt from the retailer or some other evidence that the item was bought in your home country. If you bought the article on a previous trip abroad and have already paid duty on it, carry with you the receipt for this. Otherwise, on returning home, you may be charged duty (for British residents, Value Added Tax as well). In other words, unless you can prove prior possession, foreign-made articles are dutiable *each time* they enter the U.S. The details below are correct as we go to press. It would be wise to check in case of change.

U.S. Residents. You may bring in $400 worth of foreign merchandise as gifts or for personal use without having to pay duty, provided you have been out of the country more than 48 hours and provided you have not claimed a similar exemption within the previous 30 days. Every member of the family is entitled to the same exemption, regardless of age, and the exemptions can be pooled.

The $400 figure is based on the fair retail value of the goods in the country where acquired. Included for travelers over the age of 21 are one liter of alcohol, 100 cigars (non-Cuban) and 200 cigarettes. Any amount in excess of those limits will be taxed at the port of entry, and may additionally be taxed in the traveler's home state. Only one bottle of perfume trademarked in the U.S. may be brought in.

Gifts valued at under $50 may be mailed to friends or relatives at home, but not more than one per day (of receipt) to any one addressee. These gifts must not include perfumes costing more than $5, tobacco or liquor.

If you are traveling with such foreign made articles as cameras, watches or binoculars that were purchased at home, it is best either to carry the receipt for them with you or to register them with U.S. Customs prior to departing.

Canadian Residents. In addition to personal effects, the following articles may be brought in duty free: a maximum of 50 cigars, 200 cigarettes, 2 pounds of tobacco and 40 ounces of liquor, provided these are declared in writing to customs on arrival and accompany the traveler in hand or checked-through baggage. These are included in the basic exemption of $300 a year. Personal gifts should be mailed as "Unsolicited Gift—Value Under $40." Canadian customs regulations are strictly enforced; you are recommended to check what your allowances are and to make sure you have kept receipts for whatever you have bought abroad. Canada Customs brochure *I Declare* has full details; to get a copy, contact Customs and Excise, 360 Coventry Rd., Ottawa, Ontario K1K 2C6, tel. 613–993–0534.

British Residents. There are two levels of duty-free allowance for people entering the U.K.; one, for goods bought outside the EEC or for goods bought in a duty-free shop within the EEC; two, for goods bought in an EEC country but not in a duty free shop.

In the first category you may import duty free: 200 cigarettes or 100 cigarillos or 50 cigars or 250 grams of tobacco (*Note* if you live outside Europe, these allowances are doubled); plus one liter of alcoholic drinks over 22% volume (38.8% proof) or two liters of alcoholic drinks not over 22% volume or fortified or sparkling wine; plus two liters of still table wine; plus 50 grams of perfume; plus nine fluid ounces of toilet water; plus other goods to the value of £32.

In the second category you may import duty free: 300 cigarettes or 150 cigarillos or 75 cigars or 400 grams of tobacco; plus 1½ liters of alcoholic drinks over 22% volume (38.8% proof) or three liters of alcoholic drinks not over 22% volume or fortified, sparkling or still table wine; plus 75 grams of perfume; plus 13 fluid ounces of toilet water; plus other goods to the value of £250. (*Note* though it is not classified as an alcoholic drink by EEC countries for Customs' purposes and is thus considered part of the "other goods" allowance, you may not import more than 50 liters of beer.)

In addition, no animals or pets of any kind may be brought into the U.K. The penalties for doing so are severe and are strictly enforced; there are *no* exceptions. Similarly, fresh meats, plants and vegetables, controlled drugs and firearms and ammunition may not be brought into the U.K. There are no restrictions on the import or export of British and foreign currencies.

MUNICH

City of Beer and Baroque

If there really is a capital of Germany, it's Munich (München), capital of the free state of Bavaria (Bayern) and the third largest city in the Federal Republic. Dating from 1158, beer capital of the world and cultural center of West Germany, it is an intellectual, entertaining and earthy meeting place which attracts the young much as does the West Coast in the U.S. or the Riviera in France. The city has about it an air of permissiveness which contrasts sharply with the puritanical uprightness of the Prussians in the north. The people of Munich are goodnatured and easygoing and possess an almost infinite capacity for fun and laughter. This bonhomie reaches its peak during Fasching, the carnival that runs from Epiphany on January 6 to Mardi Gras and which encompasses some 2,000 masked balls of every imaginable kind.

Real Fasching enthusiasts end these wild nights only the next morning with a *Weisswürst* breakfast (Munich white sausage) before going straight to work. It's not unusual to see costumed crowds walking the streets in the early morning, especially on Shrove Tuesday (Faschingsdienstag) when the shops close early and throngs of costumed revelers fill the city to ring out the carnival period in style.

Munich is a city bursting with atmosphere; it's exciting and easy to explore and is plentifully supplied with accommodations. Even though terribly ravaged by the war, its revival has been remarkable. With its operas and theaters, galleries and old buildings, parks and squares, splendid coun-

13

tryside within easy reach and wide variety of nightlife, Munich is too good for the vacationer to miss.

Exploring Munich

To explore the city, you should take your time. Munich's motto is *Gemütlichkeit*. It can't be translated exactly, but roughly speaking it means something like easygoing and relaxed. And that's exactly the approach you should adopt. Try sitting in one of the beer gardens, strolling through the pedestrian streets and generally watching the world go by, as the Münchners do. In between, you can take your sightseeing more seriously.

The heart of the city is the Karlsplatz, a square popularly known as Stachus. From here there is an area of some 100,000 square yards stretching between the Hauptbahnhof, the rail station in Schützenstrasse, and continuing through the Karlstor Gate, Marienplatz and Odeonsplatz. Now, it is virtually all one vast pedestrian zone, separated by a broad shopping avenue, the Sonnenstrasse, where it meets the Dachauerstrasse at Lenbachplatz. At the corner of Karlsplatz and Prielmayerstrasse is the grey Palace of Justice (Justizpalast), and on the other side there's the Sonnenstrasse, which leads down to Sendlingertor Platz. Here, there's another new pedestrian shopping zone running the length of the Sendlingerstrasse. The small, dazzlingly-decorated Baroque church of St. John Nepomuk is here. It's better known as the Asamkirche, after the two brothers Asam who built it with love (and their own money) in the 18th century. It's next door to the house where they used to live.

But our tour begins at the Karlstor, in front of which a graceful fountain plays. This is one of the old city gates. Beneath the Karlsplatz there's an underground shopping plaza, which stretches as far as the Hauptbahnhof. There are numerous escalator exits to all corners of the square and adjoining streets. Passing through the Karlstor, you enter the main thoroughfare of the old city, the bulk of which was sadly destroyed in the war. Today, it's a vast pedestrian mall, variously known as the Neuhauserstrasse and the Kaufingerstrasse. It reaches the center of the city at Marienplatz, but just before Marienplatz, on a small side square, is the Frauenkirche—the cathedral of Munich and the Parish Church of Our Lady—whose onion-shaped domes are the symbol of Munich. Built from 1468 in Bavarian Gothic style, it was largely destroyed in the war, but, like so many other important buildings in Munich, has been lovingly rebuilt. Indeed, the modern interior, immensely dignified in its simplicity, forms a striking contrast to the worn red-brick exterior. The interior is also remarkable for its great height, a characteristic exaggerated by the thin, white pillars that line the length of the nave. At the rear of the church is the elaborate Baroque tomb of the Emperor Ludwig of Bavaria, dating from the early-17th century. There are also an interesting series of photographs of the church before and after it was bombed, which make only too clear the near destruction of the building and its subsequent remarkable restoration.

Two other buildings in the Neuhauserstrasse are of interest: the small Bürgersaal Chapel, which has some lovely frescos and sculptures in its Rococo interior; and the Renaissance Michaelskirche, the Church of St. Michael. The latter is a magnificent building, spacious and handsome, and decorated throughout in plain white stucco. It was built originally for the Jesuits in the late-16th century and is closely modeled on the Gesù in

Rome. Like the Frauenkirche, it too was restored after bomb damage. Among much else of interest it contains the tomb of Napoleon's stepson, Eugène de Beauharnais, a suitably grave neo-Classical monument in the north transept, while in the crypt Ludwig II, doomed Dream King of Bavaria, lies buried. Next to the Michaelskirche is the former Augustine Church, now housing the hunting and fishing museum.

The Marienplatz

Continue along the Kaufingenstrasse to the Marienplatz, site of the city's market in the Middle Ages. On one side is the Gothic Neues Rathaus, the New Town Hall, built like so many of the city's more fanciful creations by Ludwig II towards the end of the 19th century. The central tower contains a superb Glockenspiel. Every day in summer at 11 and 5 two levels of performing figures—knights on horseback and folk dancers— revolve to the music of this giant musical box 90 meters (280 ft.) above the Marienplatz. The knights in fact represent a tournament held on the occasion of the marriage of Duke William V and Renate of Lorraine in 1567. There's a lift to the summit of the tower which, as well as giving fine views of the city, also gives the best external view of the Frauenkirche, otherwise obscured by the cluster of buildings surrounding it. A brief but telling inscription on the facade of the Town Hall states simply that the building was "Built in 1867–1874, Enlarged 1888–1908, Destroyed 1944–1945, Rebuilt 1952–1956."

In the center of the Marienplatz is a marble column, the Mariensäule, topped by a statue of the Madonna—hence the name of the square—that was built by the elector of Bavaria in 1638. It was put up to commemorate the sparing of the city by the occupying Swedish forces in the Thirty Years' War.

Across from the Town Hall is the Gothic Peterskirche, another landmark of the old city and dating originally from the 11th century. Its tower, over 90 meters (300 ft.) and offering an excellent view, is fondly called Der Alte Peter, Old Peter. Climb the tower if a white disc is posted on the north side of the platform; it means the view is clear all the way to the Alps. A red disc means visibility is limited to Munich.

Behind Peterskirche is the Tal, a street lined with furniture shops and also boasting the best umbrella shop in the city. It ends at the Isartor, built in 1337 and the one city gate that has remained largely as it was when originally built. However, before heading off down here, leave Marienplatz by its southeast corner and take a look at the Viktualienmarkt, the food market. Here, in the small beer garden, between the pretty stalls of fresh and inviting local produce, people meet and grumble about prices and politics or the day's events. The market women are as strong-armed and direct as ever and their regular customers much the same: self-confident, straight-forward, distrustful, good-humored, sly and ready to lend a hand. The famous Munich comedian, Karl Valentin, has his memorial fountain and statue on the Viktualienmarkt, standing with a bouquet of flowers in one hand; an anonymous tribute of love.

Another side trip from the Marienplatz also reveals one of the city's most famous and delightful treasures, the little Asamkirche, otherwise known as the church of St. John Nepomuk. Head south down Sendlinger-strasse, an excellent shopping street, for 200 or 300 yards. The church is

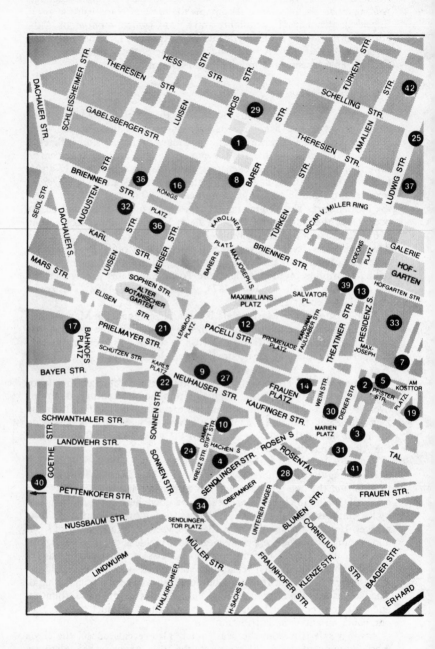

MUNICH

0 Miles ¼

0 Kilometers ¼

ENGLISCHER GARTEN

Points of Interest

1 Alte Pinakothek
2 Alter Hof
3 Altes Rathaus
4 Asamkirche
5 Bayerisches Hauptmünzamt (State Mint)
6 Bayerisches Nationalmuseum
7 Bayerisches Nationaltheater
8 Bayerisches Staatsarchiv
9 Bügersaal Kirche
10 Damenstiftskirche
11 Deutsches Museum
12 Dreifaltigkeitskirche
13 Feldherrnhalle and Preysing Palais
14 Frauenkirche
15 Gasteig Kulturzentrum
16 Glyptothek
17 Hauptbahnhof
18 Haus der Kunst
19 Hofbräuhaus
20 Isartor
21 Justizpalast
22 Karlstor
23 Kleine Komödie am Max II Denkmal
24 Kreuzkirche
25 Ludwigskirche
26 Maximilianeum
27 Michaelskirche
28 Münchner Stadtmuseum
29 Neue Pinakothek
30 Neues Rathaus
31 Peterskirche
32 Propyläen
33 Residenz
34 Sendlinger Tor
35 Siegestor
36 Staatliche Antikensammlungen
37 Staatsbibliothek
38 Stadtische Galerie
39 Theatinerkirche
40 Theresienwiese
41 Viktualienmarkt
42 Universität

on the right and, despite its small scale, its charming early-Rococo facade is easy to spot. It was built by the brothers Asam—Cosmos Damian and Egid Quirin—around 1730. Small though it is, it lacks nothing in grandeur of conception and execution, and is positively alive with movement, color, painting and statuary. To some extent, it may strike many as no more than a preposterously over-decorated jewel box, but repeated visits make clear an extraordinary depth of imagination, particularly in details such as the cunningly-lit bay over the altar. At the far end of Sendlingerstrasse is the Sendlingertor itself, much remodeled since the Middle Ages but still imposing.

Along the Isar

Returning to Marienplatz, head down to the river and the Isartor along Tal. As you leave the square, you'll go by the Altes Rathaus, or Old Town Hall, a 15th-century building whose lavish Renaissance interiors were entirely destroyed at the end of the war, as was the adjoining Rathaustor, or gate tower. The Isartor is decorated with a 19th-century fresco showing the victorious return of Ludwig of Bavaria in 1322 after his victory at Ampfing. The tower of the gate contains a curious museum, dedicated to Karl Valentin and bearing his name: the Valentin Museum. There's a handy and attractive coffee bar on the top floor. Continue down Zweibrückenstrasse and the river is ahead. The Isar is crossed here by the Ludwigsbrücke.

On the big island in the middle of the river is the colossal Deutsches Museum of Science and Technology. It was founded in 1903 by the engineer Oskar von Miller and for long was among the very finest science museums in the world. However, you may find that some of the exhibits are showing their age now somewhat.

Continuing downstream from the museum on the right bank of the river, you will pass the new Gasteig Kulturzentrum on your right, a recently completed mammoth, red-brick, multi-purpose cultural center conceived as a sort of Lincoln-Pompidou center. Its main function is the philharmonic hall, but there is also a library, conservatoire, theater playhouse and evening-class establishment. Further along the right bank you come to the circular Maximilianeum, built for Maximilian II in the mid-19th century and today the seat of the Bavarian Parliament. Cross back to the left bank of the river over the Maximiliansbrücke, which leads into Maximiliansstrasse, a broad avenue that heads back into the center of the city and is, together with the Theatinerstrasse, one of Munich's most elegant (and expensive) shopping streets.

Toward the Residenz

In the center of the Maximiliansstrasse is the large bronze monument to Emperor Maximilian, the Max II Denkmal, opposite which is the small comedy theater, Kleine Komödie am Max II Denkmal. Further on down the Maximiliansstrasse, past the Kammerspiele Playhouse on the left, the narrow Am Kosttor takes you into the tiny square called Platzl where you'll find the Hofbräuhaus. It was founded in 1589 by Duke Wilhelm V and is today a state brewery. This is the place where all your dreams (or nightmares) of throngs of jolly Germans at long tables clasping what seem to be buckets full of beer, shouting, singing and drinking—above all, drinking—as buxom wenches sway toward them with yet more foamy beer, will come true. Though be warned that you'll find more tourists in here than Germans. Still, the huge tap room is an absolute must, though don't be shocked by the bawdy atmosphere. It wouldn't be half as much fun if it wasn't noisy. You won't be able to drink anything other than beer—it comes by the liter—downstairs, but in the gallery above there's a quiet restaurant. Close by, via Pfisterstrasse, is the Alter Hof, the medieval residence of the Bavarian Dukes and the Emperor Ludwig.

Back on Maximiliansstrasse, you now enter Max-Joseph-Platz. Here, you are faced by the Residenz on one side and the National Theater with the Bavarian State Opera on the other. A large complex of buildings, the Residenz has been the home of the dukes, princes and kings of the House of Wittelsbach for over 650 years. Built on from the 16th to the 19th centuries, it was almost totally destroyed in the war. But enough of the rich furnishings were saved to enable a successful restoration to take place. The Residenz is divided into four sections: the Alte Residenz and central sections of the palace, which include the Cuvilliés Theater, the one-time court theater and a delightful specimen of Rococo architecture; the Königsbau, which houses the Schatzkammer or Treasury of the Wittelsbachs (containing, among its many treasures, a small Renaissance statue of St. George, studded with 2,291 diamonds, 209 pearls and 406 rubies); the Residence Museum itself, a vast complex brimming with paintings and tapestries; and the Festsaalbau, which includes the Herkules Saal concert hall, and, behind the palace, the Hofgarten, framed by arcades and full of flowers.

At the west end of the Hofgarten is Odeonsplatz, scene of the doomed putsch of 1923. Its southern end is dominated by the Feldernhalle, an open loggia built by Ludwig I in the mid-19th century and modeled on the early-Renaissance Loggia dei Lanzi in Florence. To one side of it is the Theatinerkirche, built at the end of the 16th century but with a facade added in the latter 18th century by Francois Cuvilliés. Its twin towers and high Baroque dome are a distinctive feature of the Munich skyline. Leading north away from Odeonsplatz, with a fine equestrian statue of Ludwig I marking the beginning, is Ludwigstrasse, an imposing and grandiose neo-Classical boulevard, with the State Library, the University and Ludwigskirche among its more notable buildings. Ludwigstrasse ends at the Siegestor, the Arch of Victory, also built by Ludwig I and copied from the Arch of Constantine in Rome. Beyond, is the district of Schwabing.

Schwabing and the Englischer Garten

What Greenwich Village is to Manhattan, Schwabing is to Munich. It is not a quaint old quarter, however, but a modern district and favored residential area. The main artery through Schwabing is the Leopoldstrasse, which in summer abounds with artists selling their work at open stalls (candlelit at night), cafés, ice cream parlors, and crowds of tourists.

Lying along the east side of Schwabing is the Englischer Garten. It's Munich's most famous park and the largest city-park in Europe. It was established by royal commission as long ago as 1790 by the American-Briton, Sir Benjamin Thompson, later Count Romford. The Garden covers a huge area and includes a Chinese pagoda (the Chinesicher Turm), the Monopteros (a small Greek temple with a fine view over the city), a boating lake, a lakeside café/restaurant with summer beer-garden, and endless walks. There is no better (or cheaper) way of experiencing a true Munich summer evening than to buy your own picnic supper *(Brotzeit)* from a butcher or supermarket and bear it off to the beer garden at the Chinese pagoda. After buying your mug of beer from the Ausschank, take a seat at one of the long wooden trestle tables and enjoy your supper. You will soon begin talking *Bayerisch,* the Bavarian dialect. You needn't feel self-conscious, for no German stands on formality before getting into conversation with a stranger here. Everyone greets everyone else with a jolly *Grüss Got* (God's greeting to you) and, given a liter of beer, the Bavarians are always keen to introduce any foreigner into the secrets of their language. This is the real Munich.

Munich's Major Museums

The city has a number of superb museums, of which several are of outstanding importance. Perhaps the two foremost are the Alte and Neue Pinakotheks (meaning old and new picture galleries). They are located opposite each other on the Barerstrasse just to the west of the Ludwigstrasse. The Alte Pinakothek, built between 1826 and 1836 (and badly damaged in the war, as is only too obvious from the exterior), houses a magnificent collection of Old Masters, with particular emphasis on North European works. The collection was begun by Duke Wilhelm IV (another of the myriad Wittelsbachs) in the 16th century and continued by his family in the succeeding centuries. A visit here should be a highlight of any trip to Munich. The Neue Pinakothek was founded shortly after the completion of the Alte Pinakothek, in 1846 to be exact, its purpose being to house modern—that is, 19th-century—works, carrying on, if you like, where the Alte Pinakothek left off. Though the collection contains a small number of 18th-century English paintings, it is accordingly rich in Impressionists and works of the Munich school. However, the originally 19th-century building that housed the collection was so severely damaged in the war that it eventually had to be demolished and the collection is now housed in a brand new and extremely lavish building on the site of its predecessor.

Until the new building was opened, the collection was temporarily housed in the Haus der Kunst in the Prinzregentstrasse, where today you will find the Staatsgalerie Moderner Kunst, a splendid collection of 20th-century works. In addition, important modern art exhibitions are held here, as well as annual antique and book fairs.

The Theresienwiese

Munich is probably most immediately associated in most people's minds with the Oktoberfest, the annual beer drinking festival that takes place every year around the end of September. It's an immensely popular event and attracts serious beer drinkers from all over the world, with Australians and Scots—deadly rivals in the beer drinking stakes—well to the fore. The city gets horribly crowded during the festival, however, so if you plan to visit then book well ahead.

The Oktoberfest dates from the celebrations held to mark the engagement of 1810 of Crown Prince Ludwig, later Ludwig I, to Princess Theresa, after whom the site of the festival is named. Today's celebrations have come a long way since then, however. Yet in spite of the very obvious commercialization, the crowds, the high prices and the frankly sordid atmosphere in most of the great beer tents, each of which holds several thousand people, most of them drunk, there is still something exhilarating about the festival, something that unquestionably captures the easy-going bonhomie of this very likeable city.

It all takes place at the Theresienwiese, a former horse-racing track to the southwest of the city center. The field itself is overlooked by a monumental statue of *Bavaria*—a sort of mini Statue of Liberty—some 35 meters or so (100 ft.) high. Like her cousin in New York, the bronze statue has a hollow head which you can climb up to, if you can manage the 130 steps. But don't go in the afternoon; the interior becomes positively furnace-like as the day heats up.

Palaces and Parks

Munich has a series of delightful palaces and castles surrounding it, the most famous of which is that at Nymphenburg in the northwest suburbs of the city, built as a summer residence by the rulers of Bavaria. The central and oldest part of the building dates from 1664, while the buildings and arcades that flank it were added over the next 100 years, the bulk of the work being undertaken in the reign of Max-Emmanuel between about 1680 and 1730. The gardens, a mixture of formal French parterres and English parkland, were landscaped over a similar period. The interiors are exceptional, especially the Banqueting Hall—a Rococo masterpiece in green and gold. But perhaps the greatest delight is the Hunting Lodge—the Amalienburg—in the grounds, the work of Cuvilliés, who was also responsible for the Residenz Theater in Munich itself. That the "hunting" the lodge was designed for was not necessarily always an outdoor pursuit, can be easily guessed by the decoration and atmosphere of courtly high life.

Also within easy reach of the city is Schlessheim, noted for the Neues Schloss, with frescoed hall and staircase and the beautiful Baroque Festival and Victory Halls, where concerts of Baroque music are given in the summer. The French Empire-style gardens contain a hunting lodge of their own, the Jagschloss, which today houses the largest collection of Meissen porcelain in Germany.

Nearby is Schloss Haimhausen, with a permanent exhibition of antiques, while, back in the suburbs at Obermenzing on the river Würm, there is Schloss Blutenburg, a moated castle and today home of the International Children's Book Library. Here too concerts are held in the summer in either the chapel or the Baroque hall.

Excursions from Munich

Taking advantage of the tentacle-like arms of the S-Bahn, stretching considerable distances into the countryside around Munich, it's easy to get out of the city and deep into the rolling hills of Upper Bavaria in as little as 30 minutes. Take a bicycle with you (they travel free on the S-Bahn at weekends) or hire one from any station once you get there, and you can get well off the beaten track. This is ideal country for cycling and walking.

The Funf-Seen-Land (literally, "Five Lakes Land") southwest of Munich is one of the most popular destinations; the lungs of the city. The lakes in question are the Starnbergersee, Ammersee, Wörthsee, Wesslingersee, and Pilsensee, all offering bathing, boating, walking and picnicking. There is also a peaceful cycle track from the city.

The largest is Starnbergersee. You can hire rowboats here, and there is also a steamer that makes a regular circuit of the lake. The town of Starnberg, rising from terraces from the lakeside, is itself of interest. It is primarily an elegant lakeside resort with a small yacht harbor, lakeside cafes, villas and hotels, and an expensive shopping center. However, there is also a 16th-century castle (it belonged originally to the Princes of Bavaria) and an 18th-century parish church, as well as an interesting Heimatmuseum (Local Museum). At the southern end of the lake is Seeshaupt, another popular little lakeside resort, dramatically framed by the snow-clad Alpine peaks behind it. Close by Seeshaupt is a small group of marshy lakes—the Ostersee lakes—that contain a wealth of animal and bird life.

Ammersee, though smaller than Starnbergersee, is perhaps more lovely still, being in mountainous country and further from the bustle of the city. There are a number of good beaches all round the lake, but the attractions here also include the Benedictine priory of Andechs on the Heiliger Berg (Holy Mountain). After climbing the 710 meters (2,333 ft.) to the summit, quench your thirst with the special dark beer brewed by the monks. At the southern end of the lake is the summer resort and market town of Diessen, with a fine Bavarian Rococo church and attractive craftsmen's quarter (the potteries and studios can be visited).

The Isar valley south of Munich is also an excellent region to visit, with plenty of good value accommodations for longer stays. From Munich, the first place you reach (some 10 km.—6 miles—from the city and easily accessible by S-Bahn or bus in about 20 minutes) is Grosshesselohe, famous principally for its magnificent iron railway bridge over the Isar. A marvel of engineering when it was built in 1857, sadly it has now been replaced by a new bridge. There is a good view along the valley from the bridge, but it's worth crossing also to get to Grünwald, opposite Grosshesselohe. Here you'll find Burg Grünwald, a fine 13th-century castle, renovated of late and today home to special exhibitions from the Munich Prehistoric Collection. Continuing down the Isar valley toward the Alps, some 16 km. (10 miles) from Grosshesselohe and Grünwald you reach Wolfrathausen, a picturesque old market town with the Alps towering impressively beyond it.

The most popular destination to the north of the city is Dachau, 18 km. (11 miles) from Munich and again easily reached by S-Bahn. The town is famous, or infamous, principally as the site of one of the Nazis' more notorious concentration camps (which can be visited). With the obvious exception of the camp, however, Dachau is actually rather a charming place. Its location is scenic and picturesque, while the origins of the town can be traced back as far as 800. 30 km. (19 miles) north of Dachau is Altömunster, with a convent dating from 730 and a fine 18th-century church. If you go by road, stop off at Indersdorf, halfway between Dachau and Altömunster, to visit the old monastery and fine 13th-century church.

Finally, if you feel like venturing a good bit further afield from Munich and penetrating into the Alps themselves, take one of the frequent excursion buses from the city (details from the tourist office) that go to the magnificent fairy-tale castles built by Ludwig II at Linderhof, Herrenchiemsee and, most famously, Neuschwanstein (see the next chapter). Buses also run to Berchtesgaden, site of Hitler's Alpine retreat—the Eagle's Nest— and to Garmisch Partenkirchen, Germany's premier winter sports resort and host to the 1936 and 1972 Winter Olympics.

(For further details of the German Alps, see the next chapter, *Along the Alps*).

PRACTICAL INFORMATION FOR MUNICH

TELEPHONES. The telephone code for Munich is 089. To call any number in this chapter, unless otherwise specified, this prefix must be used. Within the city, no prefix is required.

HOTELS. Munich is well supplied with hotels, but it is nonetheless advisable to book in advance, particularly during the Oktoberfest and the Fashion Weeks—*Mode Woche*—in March and October, and also on account of the many other trade fairs, exhibitions and international events which take place throughout the year.

The reservation service, *Zimmervermittlung,* of the tourist office will be glad to assist you, if you write to them in advance at *Fremdenverkehrsamt Müchen,* Zimmervermittlung Postfach, 8000 München 1. They do not accept telephone reservations. If you arrive in Munich without a reservation go to the accommodations service at Riem Airport or at the Hauptbahnhof (main station).

Munich hotels are among the highest priced in Germany, but tourist deflation in the past years has created panic among many, particularly the new American chain-hotels, who were among the first to join the special all-inclusive, out-of-season "Munich Weekend" package, which includes city and countryside tours, museum fees, etc.

These low-price arrangements include such packages as: "Munich Weekend Key," "Munich Christkindl Key" (valid from Nov. 28 to Dec. 24), "Munich's New Year's Eve Key" (valid from Dec. 25 to Jan. 6), "Munich Theater Key" (valid from Oct. 31 for one year), "Munich Summer Stop" (valid from June 11 to Aug. 30), and "Munich Easter Key" (valid from Holy Thursday for one week). (There are some exempted weekends when trade fares are held). In addition to the reduced hotel prices, they include breakfast, city sightseeing tour or an afternoon excursion to one of the Bavarian lakes, free ride to the top of the Olympic tower, shopping coupons, free admission to all museums and galleries as well as to Schloss Nymphenburg Palace and the Botanical Gardens. German Federal Railways *(Bundesbahn)* offer a considerable reduction on train fares in conjunction with these packages. The special arrangements offered by the City of Munich can be booked on all railroad stations or through a travel agency. Information from the tourist office *(Fremdenverkehrsamt),* tel. 23911.

Deluxe

Bayerischer Hof. Promenadeplatz 2–6 (21200). 700 beds, all rooms with bath or shower, some with large floor-level bath; studio rooms and suites also available. Sauna bath and heated rooftop swimming pool. Service is not always compatible with modern deluxe standards, though. Bayerischer Hof acquired the famous *Montgelas Palais* next door, had it restored and reopened as a hotel annex containing elegant period-furnished apartments and banquet and private dining rooms, some fashionable shops, and the rustic-style *Palais-Keller.* Restaurants include the *Grill* and *Trader Vic's* (pseudo-Polynesian), and the (loud) *Nightclub* with dancing. AE, DC, MC, V.

Grand Hotel Continental. Max-Joseph-Str. 5 (551570). 200 beds, all rooms with bath; private suites available. Near Maximilianplatz. Furnishings include antiques and art objects. Fine food in atmospheric *Conti Grill* and in rooftop restaurant. Cocktail lounge; terrace garden. AE, DC, MC, V.

Hilton. Tucherpark 7 (38450). 500 rooms, each with private bath and balcony, T.V. and other amenities. Between the Englischer Garten and the Isar. Swimming pool, sauna, shopping arcade, underground parking. Several restaurants: *Tivoli Grill* for "international" food, *Bayernstube* for Bavarian, *Isar-Café* for pastries; small beer garden overlooking little Eisbach river; rooftop *Marco Polo* with bar, for dining and dancing. AE, DC, MC, V.

Königshof. Karlsplatz 25 (551360). 120 rooms, all sound-proof, air-conditioned, most with bath. First-class food in restaurant overlooking Stachus (Karlsplatz). Underground parking. AE, DC, MC, V.

Romantik Hotel Insel-Muble. Von-Kahr-Str. 87 (81010). 37 rooms with bath. This former mill on the banks of the Wurm river, in Munich's leafy Untermenzing suburb, is one of the most appealing of what, to many, is the best hotel chain in the country. Impeccable service, atmospheric restaurant, and riverside beer-garden. AE, DC, MC, V.

Vier Jahreszeiten. Maximilianstr. 17 (230390). Palatial, it has served royalty and other important international figures, and is still Munich's leading hotel. Now owned by the Kempinski chain, it has a new wing at the back with rooftop pool and convention facilities. Several restaurants, with *Vier Jahreszeiten Bar* for dining and dancing, and the fine *Walterspiel,* which bears the name of the famous chef who used to own the place. AE, DC, MC, V.

Expensive

Ambassador. Mozartstr. 4 (530840). 100 beds, studio suites only, all with bath, radio, T.V. and kitchenette. In quiet spot near Theresienwiese. Good Italian restaurant *Alfredo.* AE, DC, MC.

Arabella. Arabellastr. 5 (92321). 400 beds on upper floors of super-modern 22-story apartment building in Arabella Park, Bogenhausen suburb. Restaurant and indoor pool with sauna on top floor with magnificent view. AE, DC, MC, V.

Deutscher Kaiser. Arnulfstr. 2 (558321). 300 beds, most rooms with bath (those without have inconvenient facilities). Near main station. Fine view from 15th-floor restaurant and café. Underground parking. AE, MC, V.

Eden-Hotel-Wolff. Arnulfstr. 4–8 (551150). 210 rooms with bath. Very comfortable hotel with a long tradition. Next to main station. Rustic *Zirbelstube* restaurant serves old-Munich specialties. No credit cards.

Excelsior. Schützenstr. 11 (551370). 180 beds, all rooms with bath and radio, top-floor terrace suites with T.V. On quiet pedestrian mall opposite main station. Game specialties in atmospheric *St. Hubertus* restaurant. AE, DC, MC, V.

Holiday Inn. Leopoldstr. 194 (340971). 400 rooms and series of suites, in three buildings connected by huge hotel hall. On outer edge of Schwabing, well-located for Nuremberg autobahn. Modern and comfortable; swimming pool; several restaurants and cocktail lounges; *Aquarius* nightclub; *Almstube* with zither player. AE, DC, MC, V.

Orbis. Karl Marx Ring 87 (63270). 185 rooms, pool, sauna, two restaurants and bar. In Perlach suburb, close to airport and with good public transport to city center. AE, DC, MC, V.

Palace. Trogerstr. 21 (4705091). 73 rooms and suites with bath. A modern hotel with old-fashioned elegance and decor. Four miles from the airport, 10-minute tram ride to downtown Munich. Roof garden, Jacuzzi, sauna, gym. No restaurant. AE, DC, MC, V.

Penta. Hochstr. 3 (4485555). 600 rooms, including some in the Deluxe range. On the Rosenheimer Berg, the hotel forms part of "Motorama" with car exhibitions and shopping center. Rooftop swimming pool. Cocktail lounge, self-service restaurant. *Münchner-Kindl-Stuben,* open to 2 A.M., offers Bavarian and international cuisine. AE, DC, MC, V.

Preysing. Preysingstr. 1 (481011). 60 rooms, all with bath, airconditioning, radio, T.V. Apartments available, also on monthly basis. Underground garage. One of Munich's best run and respected hotels. No restaurant in the hotel, but with first-class cellar-restaurant in same building. DC.

Prinzregent. Ismaningerstr. 42–44 (4702081). 70 rooms with bath. Excellently renovated Bavarian-style hotel centrally located off Prinzregentenstr.; comfortable and attractive. No restaurant, but good bar and breakfast room, plus sauna, pool, and garden. AE, DC, MC, V.

Residence. Artur-Kutscher-Platz 4 (399041). 300 beds. The latest in architecture, in quiet side-street in Schwabing. Swimming pool in basement. Restaurant *Die Kutsche.* AE, DC, MC, V.

Sheraton. Arabellastr. 6, Effnerplatz (924011). 650 rooms (1,300 beds). Arabella Park, Bogenhausen suburb. Top three floors, with outstanding view of the city, now devoted to business and convention guests. Several restaurants, including *Bayern Stube;* bar, nightclub. AE, DC, MC, V.

Teletap-Hotel-Drei-Löwen. Schillerstr. 8 (595521). 130 rooms, most with bath. 3 min. walk from station. Well-run, comfortable hotel, recently renovated. Private car-parking. *Strawberry* restaurant. AE, DC, MC, V.

Trustee Park Hotel. Parkstr. 31, near the Fair Grounds (5195421). 40 rooms with bath. Primarily a businessperson's hotel. Special family deals are often available. Restaurant, bar. AE, DC, MC, V.

Moderate

Ariston. Unsöldstr. 10 (222691). 100 beds, all rooms with bath or shower. Modern, garni. Quiet location, near Haus der Kunst. AE, DC, MC.

Arosa. Hotterstr. 2 (222691). 86 rooms with bath or shower. Central, garni, underground garage. AE, DC, MC, V.

Biederstein. Keferstr. 18 (395072). Small modern villa in Schwabing next to the Englischer Garten. Quiet, yet near Schwabing center. AE, V.

Braunauer Hof. Frauenstr. 40 (223613). 22 beds. Well-known Bavarian eating-place with a few rooms. Centrally located near Viktualien food market.

Bräupfanne. Oberföhringerstr. 107a (951095). 25 rooms, all with bath. In northeast suburb of Oberföhring, with bus service to city. Good value, and good restaurant. AE, DC, MC, V.

Central. Schwanthalerstr. 111 (510830). 50 rooms and 18 apartments. On Theresienhöhe in the Hacker-Pschorr-Zentrum. AE, DC, MC, V.

Daniel. Sonnenstr. 5 (554945). 80 rooms with bath. Modern, comfortable rooms with a good downtown location. No restaurant. AE, DC, MC, V.

Domus. St.-Anna-Str. 31 (221704). All rooms with bath and balcony. Near Haus der Kunst. Garni, underground garage. AE, DC, MC, V. Closed Christmas.

Edelweiss Park-Hotel. Menzingerstr. 103 (8111001). Small, modern, garni; in quiet residential area not far from Nymphenburg Gardens. AE, DC, MC, V.

Gästehaus Englischer Garten. Liebergesellstr. 8 (392034). 24 rooms, some next door and less comfortable. Renovated watermill with antique furnishings; central, yet idyllic location next to Englischer Garten. No credit cards.

Leopold. Leopold Str. 119 (367061). 120 beds, many single rooms. In Schwabing, garni, with old-fashioned Gasthaus in front, modern wing at the back. Parking. AE, DC, MC, V.

Hotel Pension am Markt. Heiliggeiststr. 6 (226844). 30 rooms, most with bath. Located in one of Munich's prettiest and quietest squares. No credit cards.

Metropol. Bayerstr. 43 (530764). 200 rooms, most with bath, all with radio. Opposite south exit of main station. Large underground garage. AE, DC, MC, V.

Moorbad-Wetterstein. Grünwalder Str. 16 (650051). 100 beds, all rooms with bath or shower. In suburb of Grünwald. Heated pool, mudpack and Kneipp cures. Garage.

Nymphenburg. Nymphenburger Str. 141 (181086). 80 beds, all with bath or shower. Half-way between Hauptbahnhof and Nymphenburg Palace. Restaurant. AE, DC, MC.

Platzl. Munzstr. 8 (293101). 200 beds, 100 baths. Opposite the Hofbräuhaus—rooms on this side are noisy. Indoor pool, own parking lot. Bavarian folklore shows presented nightly in large beer restaurant. AE, MC.

Reinbold. Adolf-Kolping-Str. 11 (597945). 74 rooms, small but well-appointed; airconditioned, with ice-box and drinks. Recent, near Hauptbahnhof and Stachus (Karlsplatz). AE, DC, MC, V.

Schweiz-Gebhardt. Goethestr. 26 (539585). Near Hauptbahnhof. Good restaurant. AE, DC, V.

Splendid. Maximilianstr. 54 (296606). 64 beds. Small, plush hotel, ideally located for sightseeing, entertainment, shopping. AE.

Inexpensive

Ariane. Pettenkoferstr. 44 (535529). 12 rooms, most with bath. Reserve well in advance for this small pension, with high standards of comfort and excellent central location. No credit cards.

Beck. Thierschstr. 36 (225768). 50 rooms, most with bath. In a handsome art nouveau building in Lehel, within easy walking distance of downtown. No credit cards.

Grobner. Herrnstr. 44 (293939). 30 rooms, some with bath. Friendly, family-run hotel with good central location. No credit cards.

Kriemhild. Gunterstr. 16 (170077). Pension. 40 rooms, half with bath. No restaurant. In western suburb, 30 minutes from downtown. Not far from Schloss Nymphenburg park. MC.

Lettl. Amalienstr. 53 (283026). Pension. In Schwabing, centrally-located and very good value. Rooms in old building not so good.

Monarchia. Senefeldstr. 3 (555281). 65 beds, most rooms with bath or shower. Quiet, with good restaurant.

Zur Mühle. Kirchplatz 5 (965042). 100 beds, all with bath or shower. In Ismaning suburb, about 20 minutes' drive from center; 5 minutes' from S-Bahn station. A newly reopened historic hostelry, this *Romantik Hotel* has a waterside terrace, beer garden, and restaurant with Bavarian specialties.

Camping

For full details write to either the Munich *Fremdenverkehrsamt* or the German Camping Club, *Deutsche Campingclub e.V.,* Mandlstr. 28, 8000 München 40 (tel. 334021). The *ADAC* (German Automobile Club) also issues maps showing Munich camping sites (tel. 76761). There are four main campsites in and around Munich, also equipped for caravans and camping buses.

Campingplatz am Langwieder See (tel. 8141566). North, at Langwieder See exit from Stuttgart autobahn. Open Apr.–15 Oct.

Camping Nordwest in Ludwigsfeld (tel. 1506936 or 1503790 after 9 P.M.). North, off Dachauer Str. Open May–15 Oct.

Camping Thalkirchen (tel. 7231707). In Isar Valley nature park, near Hellabrunn Zoo on Isar Canal. Open Mar.–Oct. Popular and crowded. Also winter camping.

Internationaler Wald-Campingplatz Obermenzing (tel. 8112235). Near beginning of Stuttgart autobahn. Very good. Open all year.

Youth Hostels

General information may be obtained from the *Jugend Informations-zentrum,* Paul-Heyse-Str. 22 (tel. 531655). There are three Youth Hostels *(Jugendherberge).* A YH card is needed, and the upper age limit is 27, as all over Bavaria. Hostels tend to get very full in summer, so reservations are advisable.

DJH Jugendherberge. Wendl-Dietrich-Str. 20 (131156). Nearest tram stop, Rotkreuzplatz. Fully modernized. Check-in times 6–9 A.M. and 12 A.M.–11.30 P.M.

DJH Jugendgästehaus Thalkirchen. Miesingstr. 4 (7236550). Near zoo, tram stop Boschetsriederstr. Check-in time 7 A.M.–11 P.M.

DJH Jugendherberge Burg Schwaneck. Burgweg 4–6 (7932381). 130 beds. In Pullach, about 12 km. (8 miles) south of city center. Renovated castle (1834) on hill above romantic Isar valley. Popular. Garden, sauna, tennis, bowling, bicycles for hire. Check-in time 5–11 P.M.

Youth Hotels

Christlicher Verein Junger Männer (YMCA and YWCA). Landwehrstr. 13 (555941). Very near main station; restaurant evenings only; age limit 27.

Haus International. Elisabethstr. 87 (185081). Good location near Schwabing, tram stop Nordbad; disco and swimming pool; no age limit.

Jugendheim Marienherberge. Goethestr. 9 (555891). Age limit 25, girls only.

HOW TO GET AROUND. From the airport. Munich's international airport—*Flughafen Riem*—is located about 10 km. (6 miles) from the city center. A bus leaves from outside the arrivals *(Ankunft)* building for the Hauptbahnhof, the main rail station in the center of Munich every half hour between 6 A.M. and 8 A.M., and every 15 minutes between 8 A.M. and 9 P.M.; thereafter, they run according to aircraft arrivals. A bus leaves the station for the airport every 15 minutes between 5 A.M. and 9 P.M. Either way, the 30-minute ride costs DM. 5.

A regular bus service, no. 37, goes from the airport to Riem S-Bahn station, where line S6 will take you directly to the Hauptbahnhof. Bus no. 37 also connects, at Steinhausen, with tram no. 19 to the city center.

A taxi from the airport to the main rail station will cost you about DM.25, luggage extra.

City transportation. In common with most large West German cities, Munich has an efficient, well-integrated system of buses, trams (streetcars), electric suburban railway (S-Bahn) and metro or subway (U-Bahn), which operates from about 5 A.M. to 1 A.M. Fares are uniform for the entire system and as long as you are traveling in the same direction, you can transfer from one system to another using the same ticket.

A single ticket *(Einzelfahrkarte)* for a ride in the inner, metropolitan, area costs DM.2.40, or DM.1.86 for a short journey of a few blocks.

Strip tickets *(Mehrfahrtenkarten)* can save you money. A strip of 7 (red) tickets for short journeys in the inner zone and for children costs DM.5; 8 (blue) for longer rides DM.6.50; 13 (blue) DM.12 (including the outer area). You must cancel your ticket—minimum of 2 sections for each journey in the inner area—in one of the blue machines marked with a yellow "E" *(Entwerterautomaten),* found on platforms and inside buses and trams. Failure to do this *before* starting your journey may cost a DM.40 fine.

The best deal for you may be the *24-Stunden-Ticket,* valid on all forms of transport for 24 hours. It costs DM.6.50 (children 4-14 years, DM.2) for the inner area (blue zone), and DM.12 (children DM.4) for the suburban and *S-Bahn* network (blue and green zones) as well.

All tickets can be obtained from the blue dispensers at U- and S-Bahn stations, some bus and tram stops, kiosks with the sign *"Mehrfahrtenkarten"* and a white "K" on a green background, bus and tram drivers displaying the same sign, or from tourist offices.

Note that if you already hold a Youth Pass, EurailPass, Inter-Rail Card, or DB Tourist Card, you can travel free on the S-Bahn network.

By taxi. Usually Mercedes and always cream-colored, taxis are easily hailed in the street or at any one of the numerous cab ranks or telephone 2161 (there's an extra charge for the drive to the pick-up point). Rates start at DM.2.90 for the first mile. There are additional charges of 50 pf. for every piece of luggage. Figure on paying DM.7–DM.10 for a short trip within the city. However, especially in view of the excellent public transport in the city, save taxis for emergencies; charges quickly mount up.

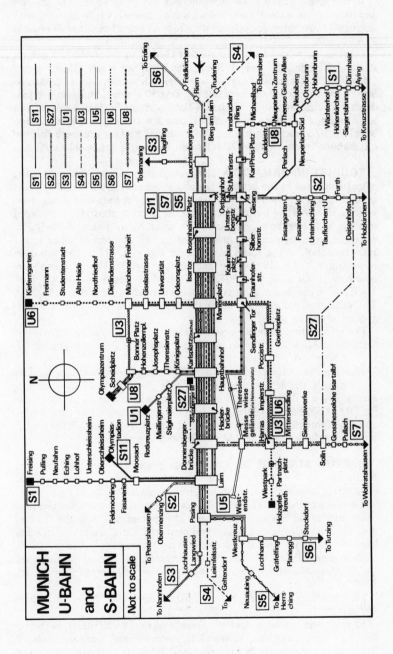

By bicycle. Cycling is an excellent way of seeing Munich as the city and its environs are well endowed with cycle tracks. A map of them, with suggested tours, may be obtained free from all branches of the *Bayerische Vereinsbank.*

Bicycles can be hired at the Englischer Garten, at the corner of Königinstr. and Veterinärstr. (tel. 397016), for DM.5 an hour, DM.15 a day (May–Oct., Sat. and Sun. in good weather). Lothar Borucki, Hans-Sachs-Str. 7 (tel. 266506) hires them out for DM.50 a week, and also has tandems. Bicycles can also be hired at S-Bahn stations for DM.5 a day if you have used public transport to reach the station (show your ticket), otherwise DM.10. For cycling further afield you may find the brochure *Fahrrad am Bahnhof* useful—from *DB* (German Railways) ticket offices.

TOURIST INFORMATION. The *Fremdenverkehrsamt* (central tourist office) is located in the heart of the city at Sendlingerstr. 1 (23911), just around the corner from Marienplatz. This office can help with room reservations; if you arrive out of hours, call the number above for a recorded message detailing hotel vacancies. It's open Mon.–Thurs. 8.30–3, Fri. 8.30–2. Longer opening hours are kept by the city tourist office at the Hauptbahnhof, at the south entrance on Bayerstr. (2391256). It's open Mon.–Sat. 8.30 A.M.–10 P.M., Sun. and holidays 1–9.30. There are also tourist offices at Riem Airport (907256), open Mon.–Sat. 9 A.M.–10 P.M., Sun. 11–7; and in the Rathaus (city hall) on Marienplatz (open Mon.–Fri. 9–5). The municipal information office (Stadtbüro) is in the Stachus underground shopping area.

For information on regions outside Munich, contact the *Fremdenverkehrsverband München-Oberbayern* (Upper Bavarian Regional Tourist Office) at Sonnenstr. 10, near the Karlsplatz (597347).

The Tourist Office produces an official program of events in the city every month, the *Monatsprogramm,* which gives details of all upcoming events. It is available at most hotels, newsstands, and at all tourist offices for DM. 1.30. English tourist information on museums, galleries, castles, and city sights can be obtained around the clock by dialing 239162 (museums and galleries) and 239172 (castles and city sights).

USEFUL ADDRESSES. Consulates. *American Consulate General,* Königinstr. 5–7 (23011). *British Consulate General,* Amalienstr. 62 (394015). *Canadian Consulate,* Maximiliansplatz. 9 (558531).

Currency exchange. There is a 24-hour automatic money changing machine outside the Stadtsparkasse bank at Sparkassenstr. 2 in the Tal area near the Viktualienmarkt, which will convert US dollars, Austrian schillings, Swiss francs, and Italian lire into deutschmarks.

Emergency. *Police,* tel. 110. *Fire department,* tel. 112. *Ambulance,* tel. 19222. *Medical emergencies,* tel. 558661. *Pharmacy emergency service,* tel. 594475.

Lost property. *City lost property office,* Ruppertstr. 19 tel. 233; *main rail station,* tel. 1286664; *post office,* tel. 139552.

Pharmacists. *Ludwigs Apotheke,* Neuhauserstr. 8 (2603021), in the pedestrian zone near the Marienplatz; international pharmacy. *Inter-Apotheke,* at the corner of Luisenstr. and Elisenstr. 5 (main rail station, north exit), tel. 595444, stocks American and British products. Open Mon.–Fri. 8–5.30, Sat. 8–1.

Post offices. *Main post office,* Bahnhofplatz 1, at main rail station; open 24 hours; also money exchange; public telex facilities, daily 7 A.M.–11 P.M. There are also post offices inside the main rail station and at Riem airport.

Travel agents. *American Express,* Promenadeplatz 6 (21990). *Amtliches Bayerisches Reisebüro* (Official Bavarian Travel Office), Promenadeplatz 12; Karlsplatz; Sendlingerstr. 70–71; Arabella Park; etc.; central tel. no. 12040. *Cooks,* Lenbachplatz 3.

TOURS. Organized by the *Munich Sightseeing Tours Company,* the blue buses for sightseeing tours (in German and English) leave all year round from the rail station square, Bahnhofplatz, near Hauptbahnhof (no student reductions). They include:

Short tour (1 hour), daily at 10, 11.30, and 2.30, DM.13. With trip to Olympia Turm (2½ hours), daily at 10 and 2.30, DM.23.

Long tour with visits to Frauenkirche, the Neues Rathaus and Alte Pinakothek (2½ hours), daily (except Mon.) at 10, DM.23. With visits to Schloss Nymphenburg and Amalienburg (2½ hours), daily (except Mon.) at 2.30, DM.23.

"Munich by Night" with visits to three nightspots (approx. 5 hours), Wed.–Sat. at 7.30, including dinner, DM.100.

Further details of all these tours, and many others, are available from the tourist office (tel. 23911) or the tour operator (tel. 1204-248).

EXCURSIONS. Bus excursions to the Alps, into Austria, to the royal palaces and castles of Bavaria, or along the Romantic Road can be booked from the Tourist Office or from the following travel agents: *ABR* (Official Bavarian Travel Office) at the main rail station (tel. 591315 or 59041), *Reiseburo Autobus Oberbayern,* Lenbachplatz 1. (558061), or *"Isaria" Reisen,* Neuhauserstr. 47 (237230). All tours leave from Elisenstr., in front of the Botanischer Garten.

The Upper Bavarian Regional Tourist Office—*Fremdenverkehrsverband München-Oberbayern,* Sonnenstr. 10 (near Karlsplatz), (597347)—provides information and brochures for excursions, roundtrips and accommodation outside Munich.

The S-Bahn can take you quickly to some of the most beautiful places in the countryside around Munich, for example line S6 will take you in half an hour to the lakeside of Starnberger See, and the S4 goes to the depths of the Ebersberger Forest. You can also take a bicycle with you on S-Bahn trains.

SPORTS. The Olympia Park, built for the 1972 Olympics, is the largest sports and recreation center in Europe. For general information about clubs, organizations, events, etc. contact the *Haus des Sports,* Brienner Str. 50 (520151), or the *Städtischen Sportamt,* Neuhauserstr. 26 (2336224).

Golf. There are courses at Strasslach (near Grünwald), (08170450), with 18 holes, and at Thalkirchen, with nine holes, tel. 7231304. You must already be a member of a golf club in your own country to play at either. Green fee is DM.57. Visitors are not admitted at weekends.

Mini-golf courses can be found all over town. Information from the *Bayerischer Bahnengolfverband,* Thomas v. Kempen Weg 12 (754812).

Ice-skating. There are ice rinks at the *Eissportstadion* in the Olympia Park, Spiridon-Louis-Ring 3, and an outdoor rink next to it; *Prinzregenten*

Stadium, Prinzregentenstr. 80; *Eisbahn-West,* Agnes-Bernauer Str. 241; and outdoor skating in winter on the lake in the Englischer Garten and on the Nymphenburg Canal—watch out for danger signs *(Gefahr)* warning of thin ice. Information from *Bayerischer Eissportverband,* Brienner Str. 52 (521336).

Mountain-walking and climbing. Information from the *Deutsche Alpeinverein,* Praterinsel (293086), and from the sports stores *Sport Scheck* (21660) and *Sport Schuster* (237070).

Rowing boats. These can be hired on the Olympiasee lake in the Olympia Park, daily, 10–7 on the southern bank; also on the Kleinhesseloher See in the Englischer Garten, or Hinterbrühler See near the zoo in Thalkirchen.

Sailing and windsurfing. There is sailing and windsurfing on Ammersee and Starnbergersee. Windsurfers should pay attention to restricted areas at bathing beaches. Information on sailing from the *Bayerischer Segler-Verband,* Augustenstr. 46 (5244); on windsurfing from the *Verband der Deutschen Windsurfing Schulen,* Weilheim (0881 5267).

Swimming. In the Isar at Maria-Einsiedel if you are hardy; the river flows from the Alps and the water is frigid. Warmer natural swimming from the beaches of the lakes near Munich, for example Ammersee and Starnbergersee.

Pools: *Cosima Bad* with man-made waves, corner of Englschalkingerstr. and Cosimastr. in Bogenhausen; *Dantebad,* Dantestr. 6, outdoors, heated in cold months; *Florian's Mühle,* Floriansmühlerstr. in Freimann suburb; *Michaelibad,* Heinrich-Wieland-Str. 24; *Olympia-Schwimmhalle,* Olympic grounds; *Volksbad,* Rosenheimerstr. 1.

Nude bathing: on certain days of the week at the city's pools; *Freizeitparadies Isartal;* Feringasee lake in Unterföhring.

Tennis. Indoor and outdoor courts at: Münchner Str. 15 in München-Unterföhring; corner of Drygalski-Allee and Kistlerhofstr. in München-Fürstenried; *Rothof Sportanlage,* Denningerstr., behind the Arabella and Sheraton hotels. In addition there are about 200 outdoor courts all over Munich. Courts can also be booked from *Sport Scheck,* tel. 21660, who have installations all over town.

Prices vary from DM.18–25 an hour, depending on the time of day. Full details from the *Bayerischer Tennis Verband,* Brienner Str. 50 (524420).

PARKS AND GARDENS. Botanischer Garten (Botanical Garden). Menzinger Str. 63, Nymphenburg suburb. Impressive collections of orchids, cacti, cyads, Alpine plants and rhododendrons; 14,000 other varieties. Open air sections open daily 9–5. Hothouses, 9–12 and 1–4.

Englischer Garten (English Garden). One of the largest city parks in Europe, stretching from Prinzregentenstr. northwards for miles along the left bank of the Isar. The brainchild of British-American Benjamin Thompson. Boating lake, four large beer gardens, charming Greek temple—the Monopteros—on top of little hill with fine views of old Munich, plus the famed Chinese pagoda.

Hirschgarten. Large recreation ground in Nymphenburg with wild deer enclosure, playgrounds, beer garden. S-Bahn to Laim.

Hofgarten (Palace Park). Off Odeonsplatz, in city center. Formal garden in French style, with arcades, fountains and small temple. Only a few minutes' walk from main stores.

Luitpold Park. Karl Theodor Str. Schwabing's city park.

Olympia Park. Constructed for 1972 Olympic Games, now one of Europe's largest sports and recreational centers as well as a thriving "village." 275-meter (900-ft.) Olympia-Turm (Olympic Tower) with T.V. mast, observation platform and revolving restaurant (quite expensive). Easily reached by U-Bahn or bus.

Tierpark Hellabrunn (Zoo). South of center in Isar valley. 4,000 animals living in 170 beautiful acres. The only zoo in the world that arranges the animals according to their geographical origins. Bus from Marienplatz.

West Park. Site of 1983 International Horticultural Exhibition (IGA '83). Some 710,000 sq. meters formed to resemble the Lower Alpine landscape of Upper Bavaria, with undulating hills, man-made lakes and valleys, and regional and international flora. Restaurants, cafés, beer-gardens, children's playgrounds, openair theater, concert arena. Admission free. U-Bahn lines U3 and U6 to West Park or Reuland Str.

HISTORIC BUILDINGS AND SITES. Admission to many of the following is free. Admission fees and opening times can be checked with the Tourist Office. For information in English telephone 239175.

Alter Hof. Entrance in Burgstr. First of the Wittelsbach castles, originally forming the northeast corner of the city. Built about 1255 by Ludwig the Stern. Emperor Ludwig the Bavarian also lived here, thus making the castle the first permanent imperial residence. Today the building houses the Munich finance authorities.

Altes Rathaus (Old Town Hall). Burgstr. near Tal. Built 1474 by Jörg Ganghofer who also built the Frauenkirche. The Ballroom was considered one of the most beautiful Gothic halls in Germany. Interior wholly destroyed during World War II, but the exterior was rebuilt according to original plans.

Bayerisches Hauptmünzamt (Bavarian State Mint). Pfisterstr. 4. Built by Wilhelm Egkl in 1563–67, originally for ducal stables and art collection. Classical facade added 1809. Inner courtyard divided into three stories, each with own architectural style.

Maximilianeum. On bank of Isar. Seat of Bavarian State Parliament and Senate, built 1857. Terrace in front is open to visitors, view over city and parks.

Neues Rathaus (New Town Hall). Marienplatz. Completed 1909. Glockenspiel, the largest in Germany, is famous for its clockwork figures of the Munich *Schäffler* (coopers) which dance daily at 11 A.M. In the evening at 9 P.M. the *Münchner Kindl* (little monk) is put to bed by nightwatchmen.

Residenz. Max Joseph Platz 3. Built 16th–19th centuries. Home of generations of the Bavarian House of Wittelsbach, of dukes, princes and kings. Magnificent interior—completely reconstructed after severe World War II bomb damage—forms the *Residenz Museum.*

Schloss Blutenberg. Moated castle on River Würm at Obermenzing, west Munich. Former hunting lodge of Duke Albrecht III who married a barber's daughter from Straubing, Agnes Bernauer. International Children's Book Library. Summer concerts in chapel or Barocksaal hall, or outdoors in monastery gardens a mile south.

Schloss Nymphenburg. About eight km. (five miles) northwest of city center. The building of Nymphenburg Palace was begun in 1664 and went on for 100 years. Beautiful park with pavilions, including *Amalienburg,* a hunting lodge designed by Cuvilliés. The *Marstallmuseum* is a carriage museum which contains Ludwig II's luxurious sleighs; on the first floor is the new Bäumler Collection of Nymphenburg porcelain. Botanical gardens, laid out 1909–14 adjoin the park. The famous porcelain factory is also in the palace grounds.

Schloss Schleissheim. About 19 km. (12 miles) north of Munich, the new palace (Neues Schloss) of Schleissheim contains a renowned Baroque art gallery and a magnificent ballroom famous for its concerts of Baroque music (June–Sept.). 18th-century French style gardens. *Lustheim,* a little garden palace, houses Germany's largest collection of Meissen porcelain.

Viktualienmarkt. Behind Peterskirche. Munich's popular daily food market, complete with beer garden and numerous snack stalls.

CHURCHES. Asamkirche (Church of St. John of Nepomuk, or of the Asam brothers). Sendlingerstr. Designed and built next door to their home by the Asam brothers, 1733, it shows remarkable harmony. A seminal early-Rococo masterpiece.

Burgsaal Kirche. Neuhauserstr. 47. Built 1710 by Viscardi; virtually destroyed in World War II. Ignaz Günther's *Schutzengelgruppe* (guardian angel group) sculpture is worth seeing. In crypt is grave of Rupert Mayer, Munich Jesuit priest persecuted by Nazis for helping Jews.

Frauenkirche (Cathedral and Parish Church of Our Lady). Frauenplatz. Built 1468–88 in late-Gothic style by Jörg Ganghofer, it suffered severe damage in 1944 but has now been largely restored. Original tomb of Emperor Ludwig the Bavarian was undamaged. Its twin towers with onion domes have become Munich's symbol. Take the elevator up the south tower for magnificent view.

Ludwigskirche. Ludwigstr. 22. 19th-century building, with second largest church fresco in the world, painted 1836–40 by Peter Cornelius. Byzantine and early-Renaissance elements of the building are unusual for Munich.

Michaelskirche. Neuhauserstr. 52. In pedestrian zone. The most important Renaissance church in Germany, built 1583–97; badly damaged in World War II and rebuilt. In crypt is tomb of Ludwig II; Eugène de Beauharnais, Napoleon's stepson, is also buried here.

Peterskirche. Just off Marienplatz. Munich's oldest parish church (a fourth St. Peter's was consecrated on the original site in 1368) and a well-known landmark. Climb its tower for a good view of the city.

Theatinerkirche (Church of the Theatines). Odeonsplatz. Former court church of the Bavarian Electors. Begun 1651; facade, however, is by Cuvilliés, 1768. Former monastery buildings on south side.

MUSEUMS AND GALLERIES. Opening times vary, so it's best to check with the Tourist Office or their *Monatsprogramm.* For information in English, call 239174. Most museums and galleries are open Tues. to Sat., 9.30 or 10–4.30; Sun. 10–1; closed Mon. Some open one or two evenings a week, 7–9. Admission charges are usually DM.2–5, with reductions and sometimes free entry for students; all museums are free on Sundays and holidays. There are also numerous temporary art exhibitions held in banks, offices, stores and hotels.

Alte Pinakothek. Barerstr. 27. One of Europe's great picture galleries. European paintings from the 14th to the 18th centuries. Among the chief treasures of this museum are works by Van der Weyden, Memling, Hieronymus Bosch, Holbein, Dürer (including one of the most famous self-portraits), Grünewald, Breughel, a rich group by Rubens, Van Dyck, Frans Hals, Rembrandt, Poussin, Chardin, Boucher, El Greco, Velasquez, Giotto, Botticelli, Leonardo da Vinci, Titian, Raphael, Tintoretto. Not to be missed by any remotely interested in painting.

Antikensammlungen (Museum of Antiquities). Königsplatz 1. Greek, Roman and Etruscan art.

Bayerisches Nationalmuseum (National Museum of Bavaria). Prinzregentenstr. 3. Remarkable collection of medieval art and sculpture, miniature art, arts and crafts, folk art, applied art, etc. Largest collection of early German sculpture in the country, the best tapestries in Germany, a fine group of woodcarvings by Tilman Riemenschneider, 16th-century armor and the unique Krippenschau, Christmas crib collection.

Bayerisches Staatsbibliothek (Bavarian State Library). Ludwigstr. 23. Over 3 million volumes, including 16,000 incunabula and medieval texts such as the Bible of Emperor Otto III, with its Reichenau illuminations and its ivory binding inset with gems.

BMW Museum. Lerchenauer Str. 36. Opposite Olympia Park. Vintage cars and motorcycles displayed using dazzling audio-visual techniques.

Deutsches Jagd- und Fischerei Museum (German Museum of Hunting and Fishing). Neuhauserstr. 53. In former Augustinian church. Trophies, weapons, dioramas.

Deutsches Museum (German Museum of Science and Technology). Museum Island. First-rate scientific museum, with 16th-century alchemists' workshops, excellent mining and historical railroad sections, planetarium, vast aerospace halls. Open Mon., too.

Glyptothek. Königsplatz 3. Ancient Egyptian, Greek and Roman sculpture.

Haus der Kunst. Prinzregentenstr. 1. Antique fairs, art and book exhibitions. Houses *Staatsgalerie für Moderne Kunst* with art and sculpture of the 19th and 20th centuries.

Münchner Stadtmuseum (City Historical Museum). St.-Jakobs-Platz 1. The history of Munich. Also musical instruments, photographs, puppets, fairground exhibits, and more.

Museum für Völkerkunde (Museum of Ethnology). Maximilianstr. 42. Fine collections from the Far East and South America.

Neue Pinakothek. Corner of Barerstr. and Theresienstr. Some of the best of 18th and 19th century art. French Impressionists, German Romantics, plus Goya, Turner, Manet; housed in magnificent new building.

Prähistorische Staatssammlung (State Prehistoric Collection). Lerchenfeldstr. 2. Prehistoric finds from all over Bavaria.

Paleontologische und Geologische Staatssammlung (State Collection of Paleontology and Geology). Richard Wagner Str. 10. Fossils, ancient life forms, 10-million-year-old mammoth.

Residenzmuseum. Max-Joseph-Platz 3. State rooms and princely suites in Renaissance, Rococo and neo-Classical styles. Porcelain and silver. *Schatzkammer* (treasury) with gold and jeweled masterpieces going back ten centuries. Rococo *Altes Residenztheater* (Cuvilliés-Theater). The State

Collection of Egyptian Art *(Staatliche Sammlung Agyptischer Kunst)* is now here, entrance in Hofgartenstr.

Schackgalerie. Prinzregentenstr. 9. Late 19th-century German painting—Böckling, Feuerbach, Schwind.

Staatliche Graphische Sammlung (State Collection of the Graphic Arts). Meiserstr. 10. Drawings and prints from the late Gothic period to the present.

Städtische Galerie im Lenbachhaus (Municipal Gallery). Luisenstr. 33. Works by Lenbach; the *Blaue Reiter* (Blue Rider) school (Kandinsky, Marc, Macke); Paul Klee.

Theatermuseum. Galeriestr. 4a. In the Hofgarten Arcade. 40,000 volume library, portraits of actors, designs for stage sets.

Valentin-Museum. In the tower gate of Isartor. Museum of curiosities and nonsense dedicated to the German comedian.

Villa Stuck. Prinzregentenstr. 60. Restored villa of Franz von Stuck with original frescos, paintings, graphics and documents from the early 1900s.

THEATERS. Munich has scores of theaters and variety show haunts, though most productions will be largely impenetrable if your German is shaky. But we nonetheless list all the better-known theaters, as well as some of the smaller and more progressive spots, as a visit should prove the city's reputation for cultural excitement.

Prices for most are reasonable, but all opera productions—and Munich is one of the great European centers for opera—are very expensive. Moreover, tickets for performances at the Bavarian National Theater (the State Opera House) are well nigh impossible to obtain. However, you could try one of the following agencies: *ABR-Theaterkasse,* am Stachus; *Bauer,* Landschaftstr. 1 (in Rathaus building); *Max Hieber,* Kaufingerstr. 23; *Radio-RIM,* Theatinerstr. 17; and in some bookshops. Most theaters are closed in July and August.

Bayerisches Nationaltheater (State Opera House). Max-Joseph-Platz. Home of the Bavarian State Opera Company. Rebuilt and reopened 1963 following severe bomb damage, and interiors again refurbished in 1987; the auditorium is magnificent with stuccoed ceiling and 180-light chandelier suspended from the dome. Huge underground parking lot with direct access to theater. Tickets from the Opera ticket office, Maximilianstr. 11; open Mon. to Fri. 10–1 and 4–6; Sat., Sun. and holidays 10–1.

Bayerisches Staatsschauspiel/Neues Residenztheater (Bavarian State Theater/New Residence Theater). Max-Joseph-Platz. (2185413). Mainly classical theater. Box office open Mon.–Fri. 10–1 and 3.30–5.30, Sat. 10–12.30; also one hour before performance.

Cuvilliés-Theater/Altes Residenztheater (Old Residence Theater). Max-Joseph-Platz. (221316). Breathtakingly-beautiful Rococo theater designed by court architect Francois Cuvilliés. Molière, Baroque period operas, Richard Strauss. Box office open Mon.–Fri. 10–1 and 3.30–5.30, Sat. 10–12.30; also one hour before performance.

Deutsches Theater. Schwanthaler Str. 13. (593427). Musicals and spectacular shows with international stars. Vast auditorium. Box office open Mon.–Fri. 12–6, Sat. 10–1.30.

Intimes Theater. Künstlerhaus, Lenbachplatz 8. Mainly comedies.

Kammerspiele im Schauspielhaus. Maximilianstr. 26. (23721328). Classical and contemporary plays. Box office open Mon.–Fri. 10–6, weekends and holidays 10–1.

Kleine Komödie. Bayerischer Hof Hotel, Promenade Platz 6 (292810) and at Max II Denkmal, top end of Maximilianstr. (221859). Two small theaters performing popular comedies. Box office, Bayerischen Hoff, open Mon.–Sat. 11–8, Sun. and holidays 3–8. Box office Max II Denkmal, open Mon. 11–7, Tues.–Sat. 11–8, Sun. and holidays 3–8.

Marienkäfer (Ladybird). Georgen, corner Schraudolphstr. 8. Music, poetry, contemporary theater.

Marionettentheater. Blumenstr. 29a. (265712). Puppet theater. Box office open Tues.–Sun. 10–12.

Platzl. Munzstr. 8–9 (23703355). On the tiny square of the same name. Shows with typical Bavarian humor, yodeling and *Schuhplattler.* Shows Sun.–Fri.

Puppentheater. Künstlerhaus, Lenbachplatz 8. Puppet theater.

Scala Theater am Wedekindplatz. Drugstore, Feilitzschstr. 12. Small cozy cabaret theater with bar, for guest appearances and one-man shows.

Schwabinger Brettl. Walter Novak, Occamstr. 11. Modern interpretations of prose and poetry, with musical interludes.

Theater in der Brienner Strasse. Brienner Str. 50. Mainly drama.

Theater "Die Kleine Freiheit" ("Small Freedom"). Maximilianstr. 31. (221123). One of Munich's boulevard theaters, showing Broadway type plays. Box office open Mon.–Sat. from 11, Sun. from 2.

Theater am Gärtnerplatz. Gärtnerplatz 3. Light opera and operettas.

Theater der Jugend. Franz Joseph Str. 47, at Elizabethplatz in Schwabing. (23721365). For children and youngsters. Box office open Tues.–Sat. 1.30–5.30.

Theater am Marstall. Marstallplatz. Mainly drama.

Theater 44. Hohenzollernstr. 20. Avant-garde, experimental theater.

CONCERTS. Munich has several big concert halls, as well as a number of churches in which choral concerts are performed. The four main orchestras are the Munich Philharmonic, the Bavarian State Orchestra, the Bavarian Radio Orchestra and the Symphony Orchestra Kurt Graunke. Choral societies include the famous Bach Choir, the Münchner Motettenchor and the Musica Viva, the latter for contemporary music.

Full details of forthcoming concerts can be obtained from *Vorschau* or *Monatsprogramm* and tickets can be bought from the following: *Otto Bauer, Musikalienhandlung,* in the Rathaus (221757); *Buchhandlung Lehmkuhl,* Leopoldstr. 45 (398042); *Residenz Bücherstube,* Residenzstr. 1 (220868); *Radio-RIM,* Theatinerstr. 17 (44170253); *Hieber Max* Liebefrauenstr. 1 (226571).

Concert Halls

Alabamahalle. Schleissheimerstr. 418. One-time factory. To the north of the city; presents mainly avant-garde works.

Amerika Haus. Karolinerplatz 3.

Bayerischer Rundfunk. Rundfunkplatz 1. (558080). Concert Hall of Bavarian Radio. Box office open Mon.–Fri. 9–12 and 1–5.

Cuvilliés-Theater. Residenz, Max-Joseph-Platz.

Galerie im Lenbachhaus. Luisenstr. 33. (521041). Soloists and chamber music groups.

Gasteig Kulturzentrum. Corner of Rosenheimerstr. and Am Gasteig. (4181614). Open since 1984 and now the city's major concert hall, home of the Munich Philharmonic. A multi-purpose cultural center. Box office open Mon.–Fri. 10.30–2 and 3–6, Sat. 10.30–2.

Herkules Saal in der Residenz. (224641). The big concert hall inside the Residenz (Max-Joseph-Platz). Box office opens one hour before performances.

Hochschule für Musik. Arcisstr. 12. (559101). For soloists and chamber music.

Kongress Saal, Deutsches Museum. Museumsinsel 1 (298430 or 221790). On its island in the middle of the Isar. The second most important concert hall in Munich, and the largest. Box office opens one hour before performances.

Festsaal, Künstlerhaus. Lenbachplatz 8. For recitals and chamber music.

Olympiahalle, (30613577). Pop concerts. Box office open Mon.–Thurs. 8–5, Fri. 8–2.

Schauspielhaus. Maximilianstr. 26.

Sophiensaal. Sophienstr. 6. With a fine organ.

Church Music

The best church music is provided by the choirs of *Michaelskirche* (St. Michael's), Neuhauserstr.; *Matthäuskirche* (St. Matthew's), Sendlinger Tor Platz; and the *Dom Chor* (Cathedral Choir) which sometimes sings in the *Frauenkirche* and sometimes in the *Dreifaltigkeitskirche* (Holy Trinity) in Pacellistr.

Summer Concerts

One of the summer delights of Munich are the many concerts held in palaces and castles in and around the city. Tickets can usually be bought from large travel agents. Among the regular venues are:

Schloss Amerang. Near Wasserburg. Medieval castle about 50 km. (30 miles) southeast of Munich. Concerts of Baroque music and folklore take place in courtyard (covered in bad weather) from late June to mid-August.

Schloss Blutenberg. Moated castle, west of Munich. Concerts in castle or in monastery garden at Würminsel near Marienplatz in Pasing about 1½ km. (one mile) south of the castle. The Schloss Blutenberg organization also arranges concerts of Renaissance music in the French Gardens of Schloss Schwaneck at Pullach on the Isar 16 km. (ten miles) south of Munich. Advance booking: *Theatergemeinde,* Goethestr. 24.

Benediktbeuern. Near Bad Tölz. 1,200-year-old monastery. Concerts of Baroque music or by Tölzer Knabenchor (boys' choir), June–end Aug., in Barocksaal, Basilika (famous double-towered church), or outdoors in cloister courtyard. Tickets for Basilika concerts from *Theaterkasse,* ABR, Stachus-Karlsplatz, Munich, tel. 59815.

Brunnenhof, Residenz. Residenzstr. End of June through Sept. Concerts in courtyard or Herkulessaal in bad weather. Concert Organization, tel. 6091198.

Schloss Herrenchiemsee. Island of Herrenchiemsee. Chamber music in palace ballrooms, 17 May–27 Sept., Sat. at 7.30 and 8.30. Ferryboats from Prien on Chiemsee to the island, last one leaves island 9.50. Bus excursions from Munich offered by American Express and Autobus Bayern, Lenbachplatz 1.

Schloss Nymphenburg. Nymphenburg, West Munich. Summer Music Festival 22 June–13 July in the Steinerner Saal of the palace.

Schloss Schleissheim. Schleissheim, 19 km. (12 miles) north of Munich. Concerts held, June–Sept., in Grosser Barocksaal. International Music Weeks, 1–29 June. Concert Organizer, tel. 6091198.

SHOPPING. Munich has some fascinating shopping streets and pedestrian zones. The main ones are: pedestrian mall from Karlsplatz (Stachus) to Marienplatz; Wein and Theatinerstr., and Diener and Residenzstr.; the pedestrian zone from the Hauptbahnhof, the main station, to Karlsplatz. Other fine shopping streets are Briennerstr., Maximilianstr., the Maxburg block at Pacellistr. and the small streets near the Hofbräuhaus and the pedestrian zone in Sendlingerstr. The largest department stores are *Kaufhof, Karstadt, Hertie,* and *Beck* (of Fifth Avenue fame) at the corner of Diener Str. between the old and new city halls.

Antiques. The expensive and select dealers are to be found around the Viktualienmarkt, in *Antic Haus* at Neuturmstr. 1 near the Hofbräuhaus (50 dealers on three floors), and in side streets in Schwabing— Schellingstr., Amalienstr. and Türkenstr. *Boheme* at Türkenstr. 79 is a tavern selling antiques. *Schloss Haimhausen* out at Schleissheim is a palace full of antiques.

Less expensive are the shops in the Haimhauserstr., Siegestr. and Ursulastr., and *Antiquarius* in the courtyard at Leopoldstr. 61. The antique fleamarket in the Dachauer Str. is fun, with a huge range of items.

Beer steins and pewter. *Ludwig Mory* in the Rathaus am Marienplatz sells particularly beautiful and varied pewter articles and a large selection of beer mugs. *Franz Mayer'sche Hofkunstanstalt,* Seidelstr. 20, has handpainted glass mugs. *Wallach,* Residenzstr. 3 for original beer steins. *Sebastian Weseley,* Rindermarkt 1, for beer steins, glass, wood-carvings and local handicrafts.

Clocks. *Andreas Huber,* Weinstr. 8; *Hauser,* Marienplatz 28, Neuhauserstr. 19.

Chocolates and candy. *Elly Seidl,* Am Kosttor, in street opposite opera house, manufacturer of fine confectionery for over 60 years; *Bonbonniere,* Westenriedstr.

Dirndls and folk dresses. *Dirndl Eck* on Platzl near Hofbräuhaus; *Dirndlstube,* Karlsplatz 8; *Haslinger,* Rosental 10, at the Viktualienmarkt; *Leder-Moser,* Herzogspitalstr. 7 (entrance at Karlstor on Stachus), for leatherwear; *Loden-Frey,* Maffeistr. 7–9, famous for Bavarian fashions; *Wallach,* Residenzstr. 3, for fine and elegant folk costumes and hand-printed cottons. Handicrafts. *Bayerischer Kunstgewerbeverein* (Bavarian Association of Artisans), Pacellistr. 7, for handicrafts with a modern touch; *Weinberger,* Herzogspitalstr. 7 (near the Karlstor).

For typical Bavarian woodcarvings, try: *Karl Storr,* Kaufingerstr. 25; *A. Kaiser,* Rindermarkt 1 (next to the Peterskirche).

For wax candles, try: *Koron,* Mazaristr. 1 (near the Frauenkirche); *Wachszieher am Dom,* Sporerstr. 2 (also near the Frauenkirche).

Porcelain. *Nymphenburger Porzellanmanufaktur,* Nördliches Schloss-rondell 8, Nymphenburg. In grounds of Schloss Nymphenburg, eight km. (five miles) northwest of city center is the famous porcelain factory. Exhibition and sales rooms open Mon. to Fri., 8–12 and 1–5.

RESTAURANTS. Munich has ten times more places to eat than there are days in the year, with specialty restaurants from all parts of the globe, French, Italian and Chinese topping the bill. You will find everything from the only 3-star restaurant in Germany through exotic and elegant gourmet temples, regional specialty eating houses, wholesome family taverns and the cheap, quick snack-bars *(Imbiss)* on the corner.

Among the best known Munich specialties are *Leberkäs,* a meat loaf made from pork and beef, and *Weisswurst,* a small, white, nonsmoked sausage made from veal and various other ingredients; both are eaten warm, with sweet Munich mustard, and as a snack rather than a main meal course and call for copious drafts of beer; tradition has it that the Weiss-wurst should be eaten only between midnight and noon. Delicious *Bra-thendl* (chicken from spit) and *Steckerlfisch* (fish grilled on sticks) are served primarily during the Oktoberfest and are intended to work up your beer appetite. Other typical Munich dishes include *Kalbshaxe* (veal shank), *Schweinshaxe* (pork shank), and various types of *Geselchtes* (smoked pork), accompanied by the Bavarian type of *Knödel* (potato or bread dumplings). *Radi* (white or red radishes) are another beloved bite to go with beer.

Although there are numerous restaurants with first-class wine cellars and taverns specializing in wine from certain regions, such as Pfalz or Franken, the "national" drink of Munich is, of course, beer. In the most typical beer halls the minimum you can order is a *Mass,* a "measure" which in this case means a 1-liter mug (a bit over a U.S. quart); elsewhere *ein grosses* (½ liter) or even *ein kleines* (¼ liter) can be had. You order *helles* (light) if you like the regular or *dunkles* (dark) if you prefer a somewhat heavier, sweeter type. You will meet the product of several dozen breweries, but the great names among them have remained the same for several centuries: Löwenbräu, Paulaner-Salvator-Thomasbräu, Hackerbräu, Spatenbräu, Augustinerbräu, and Pschorr Bräu. Weihenstephan beer produced in nearby Freising since 1040 is the oldest brew in Germany. Among the several seasonal types of beer, all of them stronger than the "regular", are: *Wiesenbier,* brewed for Oktoberfest which takes place on the Wiesen (meadows) hence the name; various kinds of *Starkbier* (strong beer) produced during the Lent season, with Latin names, the best known of which is *Salvator; Maibock,* brewed and drunk in May. If none of these should be available and you wish for a strong beer, ask for *Bock* (light or dark). If you prefer wheat beer, order a *Weissbier.*

The following lists of restaurants are only a small selection of Munich's countless eating and drinking establishments. All hotels with restaurants already listed (see *Hotels* above) are not given here unless they are of outstanding quality. Good-value, plain eating can be found in most of the large department stores—*Kaufhof, Karstadt* and *Hertie*—while at the Viktualienmarkt there are *Imbiss-Buden* (snack-bars) serving a variety of tasty snacks.

Lunch is normally served from noon until about 2.30, dinner from 6 P.M. In all cases, you should check opening times and *Ruhetage,* closing days each week.

Expensive

Aubergine. Maximilians Platz 5 (598171). Munich's finest and most expensive restaurant, serving highest quality *nouvelle cuisine.* Small, quiet and elegant. Advanced booking essential. Reservations from 12–1.30 and 6.30–9.30. Allow four hours for your meal. Closed Sun., Mon., Christmas and New Year's, and the first three weeks of Aug. MC

Austern Keller. Stollbergstr. 11 (298787). Large, vaulted cellar-restaurant near opera; for lovers of oysters and scallops (fresh fish flown in daily from the Riviera). Popular, sometimes noisy, reserve well in advance. Closed Mon. and Christmas. AE, DC, MC, V.

Bogenhausener Hof. Ismaninger Str. (985586). Munich's newest elite spot with cuisine to match. Small and very popular—reservations essential.

Boettner's. Theatinerstr. 2 (221210). The oldest of Munich's classy restaurants provides a quiet, gracious contrast to the bustle of the city center outside. Seafood dominates the menu. Reservations essential. AE, DC, MC, V. Closed Sat. for dinner, Sun., and holidays.

Bouillabaisse. Falkenturmstr. 10 (297909). Wide variety of fish specialties as well as fine all-round menu. Cozy, on two floors with wine-cellar tavern. Open to midnight; meeting place for performers from the ballet and opera. Must reserve. Closed Sun., Mon. lunch, and Aug. AE, DC, MC, V.

La Cave. Maximilianstr. 25 (223029). Elegant, exclusive restaurant and bar, open to 2 A.M. Mostly French cuisine, crawfish a specialty. AE, DC, MC.

Chesa Rüegg. Wurzerstr. 18 (297114). Fine Swiss cuisine in chalet-style building near the National Theater. Special theatergoers menu starting at 6 P.M. with cocktails, and continuing after the performance. Swiss wines. AE, DC, V.

Csarda Piroschka. Prinzregentenstr. 1 (295425). In Haus der Kunst. Hungarian food; served to the accompaniment of authentic gypsy orchestras from Budapest. AE, DC, MC.

Dallmayr. Dienerstr. 14 (213500). On first floor of huge, world-famous delicatessen shop. Delicious selections in small rooms. AE, DC.

Le Gourmet. Ligsalzstr. 46 (503597). Next to Messegelände. Particularly comfortable, with antique furnishings. Reservations advised. Closed Sun. and first week in Jan. AE, DC, MC.

Halali. Schonfeldstr. 22, between Königinstr. and Ludwigstr. (285909). Small and pretty hunting-lodge style restaurant numbering among the top Munich addresses for fine Bavarian specialties with international flair. Book well in advance.

Hax'nbauer Stuben. Twin, rustic-style establishment: the larger one at Sparkassenstr. (Münzstr. 2, tel. 221975); the smaller, more exclusive one, with mountain hut interiors, around the corner (at Münzstr. 5, tel. 295309). *Schweinshaxen* and *Kalbshaxen* from the open fire; other Bavarian delicacies. MC, V.

Ile de France. Rosenheimer Str. 32 (4481366). In the Motorama building near the Penta Hotel. Fine, good-value cuisine and first-class service.

Käferschänke. Corner of Prinzregentenstr. and Schumannstr. (41681). Another delicatessen paradise, with large store downstairs, and cellar where they serve everything from truffles to quails' eggs and vintage champagne. Reservations advised. Closed Sat. and holidays. AE, DC, MC.

Königshof. Karlsplatz 25 (558412). Reputedly the best hotel-restaurant in Munich; on first floor with view across the bustling Karlsplatz. International cuisine and excellent service. AE, MC, V.

Maximilian Stube. Maximilianstr. 27 (229044). International cuisine, but accent on Italian. Evening dining to zither accompaniment. AE, DC, MC, V.

La Mer. Schraudolphstr. 24 (2722439). Exclusive fish restaurant of almost exaggerated elegance. Fine conventional cuisine. AE, DC, MC.

Mifune. Ismaningerstr. 136 (987572). In Bogenhausen suburb. Munich's premier Japanese restaurant—traditional style and decor. AE, DC, MC.

La Piazetta. Oskar von Miller Ring 3 (282990). Large dining restaurant-rosticceria, serving fine food, with one of the longest Italian wine lists in town. Adjoining it is a sophisticated coffee bar open to 6 A.M. with music, snacks, beer garden.

Preysing Keller. Innere Wiener Str. 6 (481015). Elegant, rustic restaurant in vaulted 16th/17th-century cellar. Fine reputation and excellent service. International menu; large impressive wine cellar (German, French, Austrian wines). Reservations essential. Closed Sun., Christmas, and New Year's. No credit cards.

Sabitzer. Reitmoorstr. 21 (298584). Elegant and pricey little place in fashionable old-town quarter of Lehel. *Nouvelle cuisine* with emphasis on exquisite sauces. Menus devised by chef-patron (four courses at lunch, seven at dinner). Wine is expensive; service efficient and discreet. Reservations essential. Closed Sat., Sun., July, and Aug. AE, DC, MC.

Tai Tung. Prinzregentenstr. 60 (471100). In beautiful old Villa Stuck. Munich's oldest (and finest) Chinese restaurant. Good service and friendly atmosphere in stately surroundings. DC, MC.

Tantris. Johann-Fichte-Str. 7 (362061). At northern end of Schwabing in modern building in side street. Pop-art decor but perfect service in one of the best restaurants in Germany, with the largest selection of French food in town (introduced *nouvelle cuisine* to Munich). Reservations essential. Closed Sat. lunch, Sun., Mon., first week in Jan., and 3 weeks in Aug. AE, DC, MC.

El Toula. Sparkassenstr. 5 (292869). Franco-Italian cuisine in elegant surroundings. Personal service and very good wine list. AE, DC, MC, V.

Walliser Stuben. Leopoldstr. 33 (348000). Features Swiss food and wines. AE, DC, MC, V.

Weinhaus Schwarzwälder. Hartmannstr. 8 (227216). Traditional old Munich establishment, still boasting the largest wine list in town. Interesting for its old interiors, otherwise rather over-priced. DC, V.

Zum Bürgerhaus. Pettenkofer Str. 1 (597909). Munich's second-oldest eating establishment in attractively restored Biedermeier house with appropriate decor. French cuisine and Bavarian specialties. Popular, so book. DC, MC.

Moderate

Asia. Einsteinstr. 133 (472124). Good-value Chinese restaurant with lower-priced lunchtime menus. Enormous portions; crowded in evening. DC, MC, V.

Bier Museum. Burgstr. 12 (224315). Between the Alte Hof and Marienplatz. Good-value old Munich restaurant dating from 1252. Wholesome local dishes with a touch of haute cuisine. Oldest vaulted cellar in Munich. AE, MC.

Bistro Terrine. Amalienpassage, corner Türkenstr. (entrance Türkenstr. 84), (281780). Typical French bistro-style restaurant. Reservations advised. Closed Sun. AE, MC.

Braunauer Hof. Frauenstr. 40 (223613). Favorite hotel-restaurant for visitors and locals alike. Building full of local atmosphere. Jovial chefpatron; traditional Bavarian specialties, plus international dishes. Open 11.30–2.30 and 6–10.

La Coquille. Römerstr. 15 (390539). Small, cozy cellar-restaurant in quiet Schwabing street. Specializes in small, delicate suppers for late-night homegoers. Open until midnight. DC, MC.

Datscha. Kaiserstr. 3 (341218). Food from Caucasus, Turkestan and Russian in wooded-hut interiors. Colorful courtyard in summer with open grill. Fiercely moustachioed waiters add to exotic atmosphere. AE, DC, V.

Don Quijote. Biedersteiner Str. 6 (342318). Quaint cellar with corner tables serving Spanish food. Menus from shrimp with garlic to Steak Torero; good Spanish wines. AE, DC, MC, V.

Goldene Stadt. Oberanger 44 (264382). Authentic Bohemian specialties. Reservations advised. Closed Sun. AE, DC, MC.

Hamburger Fischstrbe. Isartorplatz 8 (225420). This no-frills fish restaurant features north German seafood at terrific prices. Reservations advised. AE, DC, MC, V.

Hannen Stube. Prannerstr. 2 (220774). Behind Bayerischer Hof hotel. In addition to Bavarian and international specialties.

Hundskugel. Hotterstr. 18 (264272). Munich's oldest tavern, dating from about 1640. Wholesome, good-value home cooking. DC.

Kasak. Friedrichstr. 1 (391771). The best Greek food in town. Reservations advised. AE, DC, MC, V.

Kay's Bistro. Utzschneiderstr. 1 (260584). The bizarre decor changes weekly, the menu is similarly varied. This is the place for a chic and fun night out. Reservations essential. No credit cards.

K.U.K. Monarchie. Reichenbachstr. 22 (2015671). Near the Gärtner Platz Theater. Evening restaurant with specialties from the far reaches of what was once the Austrian Empire. DC.

Mykonos. Rathausplatz 1 (6414052). In Grünwald. Old-established and much frequented Greek restaurant. DC, MC.

Nürnberger Bratwurstglöckl. Frauenplatz 9 (220385). Nürnberg sausages and charcoal grilled meats in colorful interiors. Reservations advised. No credit cards.

Oma's Kuche. Leopoldstr. 194 (340971). In Holiday Inn hotel. Recent, but full of nostalgia with decor and menu as in grandmother's day. Open all week until 11 P.M.

Ratskeller. Marienplatz 8 (220313). In cellar of Rathaus. A series of more or less modern rooms, some small and inviting, some uncomfortably barn-like, replacing the old, tradition-filled Ratskeller. The food, however, remains good—emphasis on Bavarian specialties—and is served until midnight. Reservations advised. AE, MC, V.

Straubinger Hof. Blumenstr. 5 (2608444). Authentic Munich-Bavarian menu. Good-value, quick service; shady garden; popular so must reserve.

Torggelstuben. Platzl (292022). Antique furnishings on upper floor; rustic and wine decor on ground floor and in cellar wine tavern. Outstanding food; mostly wine drinking in cellar.

Zum Bögner. Tal 72 (226750). Halfway between Rathaus and Isartor gate. Old Munich restaurant. AE, DC, MC, V.

Zum Spöckmeier. Rosenstr. 9 (268088). Famous old Munich restaurant in a new building, with sidewalk tables on the pedestrian mall in summer.

Inexpensive

Berni's Nudelbrett. Peter's Platz 8 (264469). Near pedestrian zone and Rindermarkt. Set meals at various prices. Lots of pasta and pizza.

Bratwurst Glöckl Am Dom. Frauenplatz 9 (220385). Dark, smokey atmospheric old Munich grill-sausage restaurant near the Cathedral. Very traditional.

Gebo's. Frauenstr. 18 (224309). Café-restaurant serving breakfast (English-style if required), snacks and gourmet meals at reasonable prices.

'Grüner Hof. Bayerstr. 35 (595571). Opposite south exit of main rail station, the Hauptbahnhof.

Hundskugel. Hotterstr. 18 (264272). Munich's oldest tavern, dating back to 1640, serves simple Bavarian fare at its best. Try the Spanferkel (roast suckling pig). Reservations advised. No credit cards.

Kanzleirat. Oettingenstr. 36 (220084). Between Englischer Garten and Prinzregenten Str. Balkan specialties, with friendly service and generous portions.

Max-Emanuel-Brauerei. Adalbertstr. 33 (2715158). One of the oldest genuine Bavarian eating houses, with small stage and beer garden. Reservations advised. DC, MC.

Il Mulino. Görresstr. 1 (5233335). Italian spot in Schwabing, with cozy interior; pretty full but you'll probably find a place. Garden.

Murr-Imbiss. Snack bar in all Vincenz-Murr butcher's shops. Good for small, hot meals such as *Leberkäs,* grilled chicken *(Halbes Hendl),* thick soups.

Scheck-Alm. Sendlingerstr. Next door to sports shop of same name. Alpine decor with typical Bavarian snacks as well as more expensive dishes. Breakfast buffet-bar. Ideal lunch spot for shoppers and sightseers.

Wurstküchl. Amalienstr. 87 (281577). World's oldest sausage bar. DC, MC.

In addition there are **McDonald's** at Martin-Luther-Str. 26, Leopoldstr. 17, Augustenstr. 53, Schwanthalerstr. 8 and in many other places in town. **Wienerwald** restaurants can be found at many locations, including Leopoldstr. 44, Ungererstr. 56, Fraunhoferstr. 39 and Odeonsplatz 6. **Wendy's** are at Leopoldstr. 60, Tegernseer Landstr. 44a, Zweibrückenstr. 1 (near Marienplatz), Arnulfstr. 12 (near main station).

Traditional Beer Halls

These establishments, mostly owned by large breweries, are enormous in size. Similarly gargantuan are the mugs of beer, the portions of food, and the waitresses serving them. The liveliest activity is concentrated in the large main hall (in summer usually in a vast garden) where a brass band plays merry folk tunes, although a series of restaurant rooms is often attached to the place. Usually dancing on weekends. Prices are inexpensive to moderate.

Augustiner-Keller. Arnulfstr. 52 (594393). Has Munich's largest and perhaps most attractive beer garden.

Hofbräuhaus. Platzl 9 (221676). The most famous beer hall in the world. Rowdy *Schwemme* (watering place) on the ground floor; first-class restaurant for Bavarian specialties one flight up; large hall with brass band and dancing further up; courtyard garden in summer. Touristy but atmospheric nonetheless.

Löwenbräukeller. Stiglmaierplatz (526021). Similar to the *Hofbräuhaus* with indoor and outdoor sections.

Mathäser Bierstadt (Beer City). Bayerstr. 5 (592896). Near Hauptbahnhof. Don't be put off by exterior. Also owned by Lowenbräu and probably the largest beer hall in the world. Cellar-restaurant features *Weissbier.*

Pschorr-Keller. Theresienhöhe (501088). Near Messegelände (exhibitions grounds). Beer-hall/restaurant which has lost some of its original flavor. Shady beer garden seats 3,500. DC, MC. *Hackerkeller* nearby is similar.

Salvator-Keller. Hochstr. 77 (483274). At the Nockherberg, home of the famous *Starkbier* (strong beer), which is on draft during its lively beer festival Mar./Apr. This beer really knocks you out, so stick to small quantities. Garden.

Beer Restaurants/Cellars

These are usually sponsored, if not owned, by large breweries. They are intended, however, primarily for eating and serve mainly Bavarian fare and the sponsor's beer, although some wine can be had in most of them. Prices range from moderate to inexpensive. Most of them are vast establishments, often occupying several floors.

Augustiner Grossgaststätten. Neuhauserstr. 16 (2604106). Historic beer restaurant.

Franziskaner und Fuchsenstuben. Perusastr. 5 (645548). Not far from Rathaus; an establishment with great tradition, dating back to the early-15th century. *Weisswürst* breakfast, *Leberkäs* for lunch, international and Bavarian specialties in the evening.

Haxnbauer. Munzstr. 2 (221922). The most sophisticated of the beer restaurants, with a greater emphasis on the food. Reservations advised. MC, V.

Schneider's Weisses Bräuhaus. Tal 10 (299875). Favorite haunt of locals, typically Munich.

Spatenhaus. Residenzstr. 12 (227841). Famous for good food and old-fashioned atmosphere. MC.

Welser Küche im Feldherrnkeller. Residenzstr. 27 (296565). Dine as in the Middle Ages. Ten-course banquet with dark beer, Bavarian humor and tradition. Book well in advance. AE, DC, MC.

Zum Pschorr-Bräu. Neuhauserstr. 11 (2603001). Large establishment in pedestrian zone. DC, MC.

Wine Taverns

Munich has a series of genuine wine taverns where the accent is on drinking rather than on eating. In addition to the long lists of bottled wines they usually offer some two dozen types of open wine, sold by the ¼-liter glass, prices ranging according to quality. Long tables call for making acquaintances with your drinking neighbors. Prices are moderate to inexpensive.

Altdeutsche Weinstube. Tattenbachstr. 6 (225268). In Lehel section. Extensive list of German wines, and a good selection of foods to accompany them. Open Fri. until 1 A.M., Sat. until 3. Music.

Bacchus Keller. Innere Wiener Str. 18 (595151). Round the corner from the Gasteig Cultural Center. Open all week. Own garage. International wines.

Hahnhof. Five establishments in Munich, the most popular of which is at Leopoldstr. 32 in Schwabing. Sells wines from its own vineyards in the Pfalz. AE, DC, MC.

Neuner. Herzogspitalerstr. 8 (2603954). Old wine tavern with good food. AE.

Pfälzer Weinprobierstube. Residenzstr. 1 (225628). Highly atmospheric and warren-like; in Residenz. Also specializes in Pfalz wines. No reservations. No credit cards.

St. Georg. Prinzregentenplatz 13 (473038). One of the few wine taverns open until the early hours of the morning.

Weinhaus Neumer. Herzogspitalstr. 8 (2603954). Munich's oldest wine tavern serves good food as well as superior wines. Reservations advised. Closed Sun. AE, DC, MC.

Weinkrüger. Maximilianstr. 21 (229295). Favorite meeting place for opera and theatergoers. Also in Feilitzschstr. 25 in Schwabing, recent, but in old tavern tradition. Wines from all over Germany.

Weinstadl. Burgstr. 5 (221047). Very atmospheric, in what is probably the oldest house in Munich (last rebuilt in 1551).

CAFÉS. Two chains offering good-value coffee and pastries are *Eduscho* and *Tschibo*. Their stand-up coffee shops are cheaper than the cafes with waitress service. Two branches on Rosental, right by the Viktualienmarkt, another in Leopoldstr.

Café Extrablatt. Corner Georgenstr. and Leopoldstr. in Schwabing. New 1982, owned by Munich's most prominent society columnist; the clientele is very much "in." American-style breakfast served until midnight; excellent coffee; good range of beer, wine and light meals in '20s atmosphere. Prices Moderate.

Café Glockenspiel. Marienplatz 28 (top floor). Difficult to find (entrance in the passage next to *Schuh Klein* shoeshop) but offers fine pastries and excellent view of Rathaus and Glockenspiel.

Café Hag. Residenzstr. 26. Munich's oldest pastry shop.

Café Höflinger. Elisabethstr. 19 and Schleissheimerstr. 87. Famous breakfast meeting place for early risers.

Café Luitpold. Brienner Str. 11. Also has grill room and sidewalk tables as well as the ubiquitous pastries. Elegant and pricey, but worth visiting.

Café Wintergarten. Elisabethplatz. Intimate, art-nouveau style; piano. Also a sort of bistro serving snacks outside in summer.

NIGHTLIFE. As you will have realised by now, one of the cheapest forms of entertainment in Munich is an evening in a beer hall (listed above). However, Munich's nightlife has variety, amusement and not a little class—as long as you don't let yourself be talked into visiting one of the clip-joints of the Goethe-, Schwanthaler-, Schiller- and Josephsspitalstr. area or near the *Platzl* variety hall. Some taxi drivers get a pay-off for every guest they deliver to these dubious nightclubs. So choose your nightspot for yourself and keep to the city center and the well-known streets of Schwabing.

Bars, clubs and discos are in general, as everywhere else, expensive, although you can spend an evening in a regular bar without breaking the bank. Keep off spirits and stick to glasses of wine or beer. A Scotch can cost DM.10–12 or more, and a bottle of wine *(Flaschenwein)* from the wine list at least three times as much as in a supermarket. *Offene Wein* or wine in a carafe is cheaper.

If you really don't fancy exploring the night scene alone join one of the conducted "Munich by Night" coach tours, which take in three typical nightspots. These trips leave every Friday and Saturday at 7.30 P.M. from the corner of Prielmayerstr. near the station, and cost about DM.100, including evening meal. Call *Munich Sightseeing Tours* on 5904314 for more information and reservations.

Most bars and clubs are open only until 1 A.M. at the latest. A few are open until 3 A.M., a very few the whole night long. Here is a small selection.

Alter Simpl. Türkenstr. 57. Once a literary café, still frequented by Schwabing arty crowd. Nightly show.

Aquarius. *Holiday Inn* hotel, Leopoldstr. 194, Schwabing. New. Formerly *Yellow Submarine,* still an underwater nightclub built into a steel tank, but now without the 40 sharks.

Bayerischer Hof Nightclub. In the luxury hotel, Promenadeplatz 2–6. Expensive, frequented by the haute monde for dancing to live bands.

Eve's Cabaret. Maximiliansplatz 5. International program of first-class strippers, dancers and good music. Show begins 11 P.M., best after midnight. AE, MC.

Harry's New York Bar. Falkenturmstr. 9. Copy of typical American bar. Good international beers, realistic prices, piano music in cellar. AE.

Intermezzo. Maximiliansplatz 16. Excellent nightspot for cabaret and striptease. Elegant surroundings. 10 P.M.–4 A.M. MC.

Kay's Bistro. Utzschneiderstr. 1 (2603584). *The* meeting place for media personalities, the chic and the blue-bloods. Very expensive.

Lola Montez. Am Platzl 1. (Near Hofbräuhaus.) Non-stop show, primarily striptease. AE, MC.

Maxim. Färbergraben 33 (corner Altheimer Eck). Large bar. Plushy niches for intimate conversation, attractive hostesses, variety show mixed with strip. 9 P.M.–4 A.M. AE, MC.

P-1 Club. Prinzregentenstr., in the Haus der Kunst. The original Munich jet set still meets here, with a smattering of the aristocracy. 9 P.M.–3 A.M. AE, MC.

Rigan Club. Apianstr. 7(3087171). Best show begins at midnight.

St. James' Club. Briennerstr. 10. Cozy bar with somewhat British atmosphere. Very popular with Munich's trendies. Large selection of cocktails in plush surroundings.

Other luxury hotel have nightclubs and dancing, such as **Marco Polo** and **Bavaria** in the *Hilton,* **Vibraphon** in the *Sheraton,* and the **Bayerischer Hof Nightclub** in the hotel of the same name.

Discos

Black-out. Herrnstr. 30. Relatively new disco for the young.

Charly M. Maximiliansplatz 5. Frequented by the high-society of Munich disco freaks. Pricey; selected admission. AE, DC.

Crash. Lindwurmstr. 88 (773272). Well-established disco for youngsters, lively and loud. Admission charge entitles you to a drink.

East Side. Rosenheimer Str. 30. In Motorama building, near *Penta Hotel.* Chic nightclub/disco for up to 600 visitors. Get there early to ensure a seat. Ties obligatory (for men). AE, DC, MC.

Namenlos. Oscar von Miller Ring 25. Perhaps the most popular of all. Crowded dance floor; males outnumber females. AE, DC, MC.

Sugar Shack. Herzogspitalstr. 6. The latest in disco-lighting; very hi-tech and glamorous. Selected admission.

Why Not. Brienner Str. 12. Disco open to anyone and everyone.

Jazz and Rock

Star performances by big names take place mainly in the Circus Krone building, the Olympia Halle and the Alabamahalle. Open-air pop concerts are put on in summer in the Theatron of the Olympic Park, and the Olympic show-jumping arena in Riem.

The following are just a few of the nightspots on the jazz and rock scene which have live bands to listen to or dance to, soloists, or just a good pianist.

Allotria. Türkenstr. 33 (287342). Jazz.

Alte Burg. Bismarckstr. 21 (331452). Open 7 P.M., music from 9 P.M. Jazz.

Arena. Occamstr. 8 (344974). Jazz and rock.

Doktor Flotte. Occamstr. 8. Jazz.

Domicile. Leopoldstr. 19 (399451). One of Munich's best known jazz and rock spots. Regularly changing program of live bands. Open from 9 P.M. Best nights Fri. and Sat.

Fregatte. Sonnenstr. 17. Live bands of international fame. Mixed and slightly older crowd. Reasonable prices. Open to 4 A.M.

Jenny's Place. Georgenstr. 50. Run by a vivacious English performer with a great voice and a warm welcome for U.S. and British visitors. Jazz.

Kaffée Giesing (6934873). Very popular, crowded and "in." Jazz, rock and cabaret.

Kleines Rondell. Luisenstr. 25 (554653). Jazz.

Oklahoma. Schäftlarnstr. 156 (7234327). Out of town, towards Hellabrunn Zoo. Country and Western music with live bands. Changing program.

Schwabinger Podium. Wagnerstr. 1 (399482). Renowned jazz club. Open from 8 P.M.

Waldwirtschaft Grosshesselohe. Georg Kalb Str. 3 (795088). Down by the Isar in Grosshesselohe, summer only. Gasthof in the forest with live Dixieland jazz bands.

ALONG THE ALPS

From Bodensee to Berchtesgaden

The German Alps of Upper Bavaria, or Oberbayern, run the length of the country's southern border, a matter of some 250 km. (155 miles) in all, from Lake Constance, or Bodensee as the Germans know it, in the west to Berchtesgaden on the Austrian border in the east. The area in all comprises nine different regions, and as well as the purely Alpine area stretches northwards to Munich to include the Alpine lowlands around the valleys of the rivers Iller, Lech, Isar and Inn.

In many ways, the multitude of Germany's little Alpine villages, a *Gasthof* seemingly on every corner, zither music and brass bands resounding in every inn, and the low houses strewn in summer with flowers, correspond more nearly than any other single attraction in Bavaria to most people's idea of Germany's largest state. But the Alps also contain winter-sports resorts of unimpeachable sophistication—with prices to match—a clutch of exquisite Rococo churches, such tourist meccas as Lake Constance (Bodensee) and Berchtesgaden, and, perhaps most spectacular of all the man-made delights, Ludwig II's idiosyncratic and extravagant palaces and castles. However, it is the mountains that remain the principal attraction, rearing to 3,050 meters (10,000 ft.) in places and providing excellent vacation areas for lovers of mountain scenery, folklore and, of course, winter sports.

Bodensee

Our exploration of the Alps begins at Bodensee, at the extreme west of the Alpine region on the Swiss-German border in the state of Baden-Württemberg. The lake, through which the Rhine flows, is shaped like some weird crustacean from whose main body—Bodensee itself—two arms project: the Überlingersee in the north, the Untersee in the south. Scattered around its perimeter are wine villages and medieval towns. The largest town on the lake is Konstanz, lying in the fork formed where the lake splits.

To the west of Konstanz in the heart of the Untersee is the little island of Reichenau. It is believed that the island was the site of one of the earliest cultures in the whole of Germany. A Benedictine abbey was founded here in 724, which at the peak of its power boasted no fewer than 1,600 monks and was the seat of one of the country's most famous schools of medieval painting. The abbey was secularized in 1799, but the three churches at Mittelzell, Oberzell and Niederzell provide potent testimonials of its resplendent past.

Konstanz itself lies directly on the Swiss border, where the lake narrows before passing into the Untersee. Unlike most other larger south German cities, Konstanz escaped the devastations of the war almost entirely, not least as a result of its proximity to neutral Switzerland, and the center of the old town is chock full of delightful old buildings. The main sights include the 14th-century Rathaus, or Town Hall, originally the seat of the linen weavers' fair and later named after the Council of Konstanz (1414–18), because the conclave which elected Pope Martin V was held in this building in November 1417; the imposing cathedral, whose construction was started in the 11th century and completed in the 16th, but has additions in many different styles from many different periods up to the mid-19th century; the hotel Insel, once a Dominican Monastery and a hotel since 1875, still preserving the original magnificent cloisters— Count Ferdinand von Zeppelin, the inventor of "Zeppelins", was born here and a memorial to him stands at the boat landing stage nearby; the Renaissance City Hall; Rheintor and Schnetztor tower gates and Pulverturm, "the powder tower," since it was once used as a depot for gunpowder; St. Stephan's Church at the square of Obermarkt surrounded by patrician houses.

Just to the north of Konstanz is the little island of Mainau, located at the southern end of the Überlingersee. It's known as "the little island of flowers," and from spring to fall a staff of 300 ensure that Mainau is thickly carpeted with thousands of flowers: tuilips, narcissi and hyacinths in April and May; irises and lilies in July; dahlias in September; and a great variety of roses from June to the end of September. In addition, there are hothouses of orchids, palms, lemon and orange trees, and rare and old trees in its arboretum. The Baroque palace on the island used to be the summer residence of the Grand Dukes of Baden, and was inherited shortly after World War II by Prince Wilhelm of Sweden from his mother, Queen Victoria of Sweden, a sister of the Grand Duke of Baden. Today it is inhabited by Count Lennart Bernadotte, uncle of Carl Gustav of Sweden, and his family.

Located at the mid-point of the northern shore of the Überlingersee is Überlingen, with its close-set old houses hugging the lakeside. Once an imperial free town, it has preserved many of its towers, defense walls and old patrician homes, such as the Reichlin-Meldegg House, built in 1462, and now containing the local museum. The five-nave Gothic cathedral has a famous Renaissance altar and the Rathaus, also Gothic, is known for its Pfennig Tower and the woodcarved grand hall from 1492. Überlingen, which is also well known for Kneipp (cold water) cures, is referred to locally as the German Nice, in reference to its mild climate, which, of course, it shares with all the lakeside resorts.

A few miles inland from Überlingen in the hills back from the lake is Heiligenberg, boasting a castle containing magnificent works of art, and in which the Renaissance Knights' Hall is particularly striking.

Continuing along the lake shore, you could hardly make a mistake stopping anywhere at random: Birnau, with its Rococo church on the high shore; Unteruhldingen, where there are reconstructions of the homes of the ancient lake dwellers (this is another point from which you can go to Heiligenberg); peaceful Meersburg, a marvelous old town with Germany's oldest inhabited castle (Altes Burg), one of whose towers dates from the 7th century, a wine-growing center boasting several colorful old taverns, and a particularly favored summertime lake resort. The 18th-century former Prince Bishops Baroque Palace is well worth a visit, especially during the international concert season (Jun. to Sept.) when concerts are held in its splendid Hall of Mirrors (Spiegelsaal). A panoramic path along the heights between Meersburg and Hagnau offers another magnificent view of the entire lake and the Austrian and Swiss Alps. From Meersburg, ferryboats cross to Konstanz day and night, thus considerably shortening the journey around the lake if you are in a hurry.

From Meersburg, the next stop along the lake is Friedrichshafen. This is a place that has helped make aeronautic history. It was the birthplace of the Zeppelins, named after Count Zeppelin, their inventor. Their hangars and the plants which built them were here, and it was from here that they started out on their transatlantic flights in the days before disaster ended their career. It was here, too, that the Dornier flying boats were built, and their powers tested over the convenient, wide, calm, landing surface provided by the lake before they took off on their flights to America. It is rather quieter today, the chief traffic being provided by ferryboats, for this is the point from which they leave for the crossing to Romanshorn, in Switzerland.

You will find the lake more attractive if you stop at smaller places than this, the smaller the better. Beyond Friedrichshafen is the charming town of Langenargen with its Montfort Castle; the town clustered along the lake is a favored vacation spot. A little further is another small place, Nonnenhorn. You will enjoy the town square with its chapel and the lakeside walks among the fruit trees and vineyards.

The other little settlements along the lake are equally entrancing—Wasserburg, with its splendid church rising from the peninsula on which it stands, and Bad Schachen, a lakeside spa in a lovely setting.

Lindau is in the lake rather than on it—it's built on an island. It doesn't look quite credible from the shore, floating on the water as if moored by the two narrow bridges which hold it to the land like hawsers, with its towers rising here and there from its trees and houses. It doesn't look quite credible when you get there, either, with its narrow, twisting streets lined with fine old buildings. You should be warned that a lot of people have discovered how attractive Lindau is, and the place gets packed out.

At the lakeward end of the island you can sit and gaze out through the twin pillars of its little harbor (they are not identical twins; one is a lighthouse, the other a statue of a lion) towards the mountains beyond the lake. On a clear day you will be able to see the peaks known as The Three Sisters in neighboring Liechtenstein, the tiny independent principality lying between Switzerland and Austria.

In addition to the pretty little harbor, the main sights in Lindau include the beautifully-frescoed Altes Rathaus (the Old Town Hall), built in 1422 and the scene of the 1492 Imperial Diet held under the Emperor Maximilian; the Cavazzan House, one of the finest burgher houses in the Lake Constance area and home today of a folklore museum and Lindau's notable art collection; the Stadtmuseum, or City Museum; the two principal city churches (one Catholic and one Evangelical) on the same square; the Diebsturm (Thief's Tower) with a section of the old town walls; the nearby Romanesque Peter's Church, reputed to be the oldest on the lake, with frescos by Hans Holbein the Elder (today the church is a war memorial chapel); the many narrow streets lined with romantic old houses.

The Allgäu

Lindau lies just within the Allgäu—or the Westallgäu as it here is, to be more exact—which in all comprises three separate districts, the Westallgäu, Oberallgäu and Ostallgäu, and stretches between Lindau and Füssen, 80 km. (50 miles) to the east. Although a distinct geographical region in itself, the Allgäu nonetheless forms part of Bavarian Swabia—Bayerish Schwaben—one of the local government districts of Bavaria proper.

From Lindau or Friedrichshafen, the principal areas of interest north of Lake Constance are Ravensburg, whose impressive gates and towers date from the time when it was the Swabian stronghold of the Guelphs, and, a few miles north, Weingarten, site of the second largest Baroque church in Germany. It was designed by Moosbrugger and consecrated in 1742; the ceiling frescos are partly the work of the celebrated Cosmas Damian Asam. As is characteristic of many of southern Germany's finest Baroque and Rococo churches, the plain exterior gives little indication of the richness within. Alternatively, head for Wangen, 20 km. (14 miles) northeast of Lindau, for a look at its centuries-old gates and fine medieval streets.

Heading east from Lake Constance soon brings you into the Oberallgäu, known chiefly for its winter sports resorts, though you will also find that many of the towns and villages farther to the north make excellent bases for trips into the mountains. This is true of charming Sonthofen, in the upper Iller Valley, reached from Lindau via the scenic German Alpine Road through two more winter sports centers: Oberstaufen, known especially for its unique Schroth cures based on dieting, and Immenstadt with a 17th-century castle and a Baroque parish church. But Oberstdorf, a little to the south, is the best known winter sports center and Alpine summer resort in the region, lying in a broad valley ringed by lofty peaks. A three-mile-long (5 km.) new cable-car leads up to the 2,250-meter (7,380-ft.) Nebelhorn and its gigantic ski jump. Seven smaller valleys lead up into the

Alpine stillness. Especially recommended is the walk along the Heilbron-nerweg, reaching the Kempter refuge at 1,830 meters (6,000 ft.).

From Oberstdorf it is also possible to explore Kleinwalsertal (Small Walser Valley—the Great Walser Valley being on the other side of the mountain barrier in Vorarlberg)—a mountain fastness of incomparable beauty and site of the villages of Riezlern, Hirschegg and Mittelberg. There is a bus from Oberstdorf rail station that runs the length of the 19-km. (12 mile) valley. Oddly enough, the valley itself is actually in Austria, but being inaccessible to Austria other than by twisting footpaths has been integrated economically with Germany for many years now. Take your passport with you if you intend to explore the area, or you may have diffi-culties crossing the border. A final curiosity provided by this little section of the Oberallgäu is found in Unterbalderschwang, 14 km. (9 miles) north-west of Oberstdorf, site of Germany's oldest tree, a double-trunked yew reputed to be 4,000 years old.

Due north again of Oberstdorf some 32 km. (20 miles) is the capital of the Allgäu, Kempten. It's also the home of the famous Allgäuer cheese, first-cousin to Emmentaler and Gruyère. Appropriately, the south Ger-man Cheese Exchange (Käsebörse) is located here, while in the numerous *Käskuchä* or cheese dairies you can watch master cheese-makers at work, churning out 70-kilo cheeses by hand. For culture vultures, Kempten's major attractions are the Allgäu Folklore Museum (Allgäu Heimat Muse-um) in the Corn House, or Kornhaus, which, in addition to a collection of ancient coins, charts the city's history from its Roman foundation—the Romans called the town Cambodunum—through the Middle Ages and the Renaissance. The building itself is one of the finest of its kind in the Allgäu and together with the Basilica of St. Laurence—the first significant Baroque church in south Germany, completed in 1666—and the Residenz give the Kornshausplatz, in which they stand, a charmingly romantic as-pect. Also of note is the Rathaus, the City Hall, built in 1382 but with a Renaissance staircase and Baroque towers.

Heading north again from Kempten to Memmingen, 14 km. (20 miles) away, you come to Ottobeuren, site of the largest Baroque church in Ger-many. It is the church of the Benedictine Abbey here, founded originally under Charlemagne in 764, though the present Abbey buildings date from the early-18th century. The massive church itself was largely the work of Johann Michael Fischer and in the grandeur of its conception and execu-tion is generally considered to represent the climax of German ecclesiasti-cal Baroque architecture. Its highlights include the magnificently detailed and carved choir stalls and the world-famous organ. But simply to wander around its lustrous and brilliantly decorated interior is a highlight in itself.

A few miles farther north again is Memmingen, which, once a free impe-rial city, has preserved five towers and part of its walls. Its Rathaus square and several narrow streets are lined with gabled, arcaded or half-timbered houses, while the Church of St. Martin contains fine Gothic choir stalls. Similarly, the Frauenkirche boasts frescos from the same period. East of Memmingen and Ottobeuren, among forests and meadows, lies Bad Wör-ishofen, the principal cold water health resort in Germany, where Father Sebastian Kneipp invented and started the famous cold water treatments in the last century. The Kneipp Museum is in the Dominican Convent and a monument to him stands in the town which, once a little village, has become an important spa with up-to-date installations and all modern amenities.

The remaining attractions of the Allgäu lie in the Ostallgäu, southeast of Kempten and Memmingen. Coming from Kempten, you cross into the Ostallgäu at Nesselwang, a health resort and popular winter sports center. It lies at the foot of the 1,400-meter (4,600 ft.) Alpspitze, the summit of which is served by a chair lift. 5 km. (3½ miles) farther southeast is Pfronten, the largest vacation resort in the Ostallgäu and famous as a regular venue for the annual World Cup ski competition. A cable car will take you up to the 1,870-meter (4,500 ft.) Breitenberg, while a chair lift goes all the way to the summit of the 1,600-meter (5,250 ft.) Hochalp, from where a series of excellent walks, offering sensational views, are available. Perhaps the most romantic sight in the area, however, is provided by the ruined castle at Falkenstein, 1,030 meters (3,380 ft.) above sea level, and the highest castle ruin in the country. Ludwig II had plans to rebuild the castle, but sadly even he baulked at the immense practical difficulties involved.

From Pfronten, it's no more than 10 km. or so (6 miles) to Füssen, the road skirting along the northern edge of the Weissensee Lake, lying at the end—or beginning—of the Romantic Road, which runs between here and Würzburg in Franconia. Füssen-Bad Faulenbach, to give the town its full name, spa and winter sports resort, is an old mountain town that owes its location to the fact that it was originally the site of a fort guarding a pass through the Alps; but its position might just as easily have been chosen with the idea of giving it perfect scenic surroundings. From a majestic wall of mountains behind the town, the river Lech comes tumbling down to the green plains cradled within the encircling heights, and flows by the ancient stone buildings of the town. Lakes dot the country about Füssen— the Alpsee, the Schwansee, the Bannwaldsee, the Hopfensee, the Weissensee and the lake-river formed by the broadening of the Lech, the Forggensee. The best of the many fine views of Füssen is from a point where the Lech rolls over a long low fall. Beyond it rise the ancient walls of the castle, the churches, and the medieval buildings of the town; beyond them rise the Alps. Wander through the town, and you will find that all the streets are picturesque; but what you should particularly not fail to visit are the castle (Hohes Schloss), once the summer residence of the Prince Bishops of Augsburg; the St. Mangkirche, which has a much admired Romanesque crypt; and Hiebeler's *Totentanz* (The Dance of Death) in St. Anne's Chapel.

The town also makes an excellent base from which to visit the two neighboring castles of Hohenschwangau and Neuschwanstein, and which, no more than a mile apart, can easily be visited together. Hohenschwangau, built between 1832 and 1836 in a Romantic and somewhat fanciful Gothic style by Maximilian II, was the childhood home of Ludwig II and in large part provided Ludwig with the inspiration to build his own fairy-tale castle, Neuschwanstein, perched on its pinnacle of rock. In almost every respect Neuschwanstein, constructed from 1870 onwards, surpasses Hohenschwangau, being larger, more flamboyant, more dramatic and much more expensive to build. But at the same time it is wholly lacking in any of the domesticity that makes Hohenschwangau a real castle (Ludwig in fact scarcely lived here at all), and has instead a melancholy and strangely unloved quality. Nonetheless, it has enormously lavish interiors and superb views; concerts are held here at the beginning of September.

From the obsessive 19th-century splendor of Hohenschwangau and Neuschwanstein, head north to Steingaden and Rottenbuch, 21 km. (13 miles) and 30 km. (18 miles) respectively north of Füssen for three architectural experiences of a very different kind. Steingaden is the site of an impressive and somewhat incongruous Abbey church, founded originally in the 12th century and retaining its heavy Romanesque exterior but with an 18th-century interior. The Abbey church at Rottenbuch has a similar juxtaposition of contrasting architectural styles. Parts of the interior were remodeled in the 18th century, but significant sections of the original 15th-century Gothic interior were left intact. The third building here, however, presents no such difficulties. This is the little Wieskirche, located mid-way between Steingaden and Rottenbuch. Built by Dominikus Zimmermann between 1746 and 1754, it represents, in tandem with the pilgrimage church at Vierzehnheiligen in North Bavaria, the culminating point of German Rococo ecclesiastical architecture. As at Vierzehnheiligen, the simple interior gives no hint of the glittering treasures within. A complex oval plan is animated by a series of brilliantly colored stuccos, statues and gilt, while an enormous ceiling fresco completes the decoration. The choir and organ loft are especially beautiful.

The final halt in this exploration of the Allgäu is Schongau, situated on the river Lech and fond of calling itself "The Town in Front of the Mountains," not unreasonably perhaps as this is the first point, were you coming from the other direction, where you would see the dramatic backdrop of the Alps looming over the horizon. Schongau today is a quiet rural center, but during the middle ages was a lively staging post on the busy trade route between Augsburg, to the north, and Italy. Its little town center is accordingly crammed with old city walls, towers and historic buildings. In addition, there is a fine church, the Pfarrkirche Mariä Himmelfahrt, or Parish Church of the Blessed Virgin Mary of the Assumption, to give it its full name.

Landsberg and Augsburg

At this point a detour is in order, to Landsberg and, north again, to the ancient city of Augsburg, both on the Romantic Road. Neither are Alpine towns, but both, lying in that part of Bavarian-Swabia just to the north of the Alpine lowlands, have played important roles in the history of Bavaria and the Alpine regions, their folklore and culture.

Landsberg, straddling the river Lech, is perhaps *the* place to visit to see the Rococo wonders of Dominikus Zimmermann, burgomaster of Landsberg (aside, that is, from the Weiskirche). Among the highlights are St. Johann's Church (Johannskirche), dating from 1740–54, and the Ursulinenkirche. More famously, he also built the facade of the Altes Rathaus, the Old Town Hall, the interior of which dates from 1699. Among the town's other attractions are the Bayertor, or Bavarian Tower, one of the most beautiful late-Gothic city gates in Germany, dating from 1425, and the 14th-century Schöner Turm, or Beautiful Tower, by the Town Hall. There's also a City Museum, the Stadtmuseum, in the Mutterturm on the banks of the Lech. Every fifth year the Rüthen Festival in the middle of

July, during which 1,500 children parade in historical costumes, draws hordes of visitors to the town.

From Landsberg, the road crosses the Lechfeld, where the German Emperor Otto the Great inflicted a crushing defeat upon the Magyars in 995, stopping forever their predatory incursions into Germany and contributing to their pacification and final settlement in what is today Hungary. The road then takes you through the Red Gate (Rotes Tor), providing a spectacular introduction to a spectacular city, the greatest city on the Romantic Road, gateway to the Allgäu and the Alps, and the oldest town in Bavaria—Augsburg. This impressive complex of tower, bridge, ramparts, and moat, against whose massive background open-air opera is staged in summer, gives you a foretaste of the architectural riches of a city that also has been accumulating them for 2,000 years. 1985 saw the 2,000th anniversary of the city.

Though in Bavaria, Augsburg is in many other ways more Swabian than Bavarian: the architecture, dialect, and food are all distinctly different from those in the rest of the State. Perhaps this difference is appropriate, given the immensely distinguished history to which the city can lay claim. Founded originally by the Romans, Augsburg grew to prominence in the early Middle Ages, a status it retained at least until the 18th century. By the 10th century, for example, it had become an international center of trade, while in the 15th and 16th centuries it could lay claim to being the richest town in the whole of Europe, whose leading lights were the two families Fugger and Welser—a Welser was subsequently to *own* Venezuela! The Fuggers, comparable to though if anything wealthier than the Medicis in Florence, were perhaps the dominant family, financing wars and pulling the strings that determined the fate of the Holy Roman Empire.

Among other famous sons of the town were both Holbeins and Leopold Mozart, father of the composer (the famous 18th-century piano maker, Stein, was also a native of the city). Elias Holl, the architect who built the Rotes Tor, is buried here. Bertolt Brecht was born in this city in 1898 and his birthplace still exists. The Würzburg Theater presents many of his works.

Augsburg is known also by an important date in German history. In 1555 the Augsburger Religionsfriede (Religious Peace of Augsburg) was ratified in the form of a treaty between the Catholic and Lutheran princes of the Holy Roman Empire, which provided that any member state of the empire might set up either creed as its official religion. Those who refused to conform were guaranteed the right to dispose of their estates and emigrate.

Augsburg is the seat of the oldest social settlement in the world, the Fuggerei, built in 1519 to house indigent but deserving families at a nominal rent and still doing so. The present rent is the same as at the time of its foundation, the equivalent of one Rhenish Florin of those times, or, in today's terms, one mark and 71 pfennigs a year. Augsburg is also important industrially, it has been the biggest textile center in southern Germany for 500 years, it is the birthplace of Rudolf Diesel, inventor of the Diesel engine, and in addition to the Diesel plant, important factories here include those of the Messerschmitt airplane makers and the National Cash Register Company.

A complete list of the sights of Augsburg would fill an entire book. Among the most important are the cathedral, begun in 995, which boasts

the oldest stained glass in the world (11th century) and altar paintings
by Hans Holbein the Elder; an early 11th-century bronze door, and a series
of tombs in the cloister (from the 13th to the 18th century); St. Ulrich,
which not only has two towers but is two churches—for as a Protestant
and Catholic church, it embodied in stone the spirit of the Religious Peace
of Augsburg, achieved in 1555; the Maximilianstrasse, considered the finest Renaissance street in Germany; the Perlach tower and the Rathaus
beside it, one of the most impressive creations of German Renaissance
buildings, by Elias Holl; and in the Schaezler Palais, where the municipal
art collections are displayed, is the Festive Hall, opened in 1770 to receive
Marie Antoinette, then on her way to Paris from Vienna to become the
bride of Louis XVI. In summer candle-lit concerts are held in the Rococo
hall.

For contemporary outdoor recreational needs Augsburg has constructed the Rosenaustadion, a thoroughly up-to-date athletic stadium, seating
45,000 spectators and located near the Wertach River, and the world's
first canoe-slalom stadium (24,000 spectators), on the Lech River, site of
this event in the 1972 Olympics. Also in the southern outskirts of the city
in the pleasant Siebentisch woods are the new botanical garden (on the
site of the 1985 State Horticultural Show and retaining the original Japanese gardens) plus a fine zoo.

Ammergauer Alps and Werdenfelser Land

Continuing eastward again along the Alps, brings us to the next two
regions of Germany's Alps—the Ammergauer Alps and Werdenfelser
Land. They contain perhaps the two best-known towns in the entire Bavarian Alps: Oberammergau and Garmisch-Partenkirchen.

Coming from Munich, if you first wish to visit Oberammergau and the
Garmisch area and prefer not to use the autobahn, travel through Starnberg on the Starnberger Lake and continue through the old market town
of Murnau, located at Staffel Lake with its wooded islets, to either Oberammergau or Garmisch. A scenically more rewarding route to Oberammergau (you must have a car) is from Starnberg through Weilheim to
Schongau on the Romantic Road; then through Rottenbuch with its Rococo decorated monastery church and over Echelsbacher Brücke, a single-
span bridge above the Ammer River.

Oberammergau is, of course, famous mainly for its Passion Play, performed every ten years in years ending with zero. The next performance
is scheduled for 1990, though in 1984 a celebratory 350th-anniversary performance was staged. Even if there is no play the year when you are visiting, you can see the theater in which it is given and the bearded actors
carrying on their everyday occupations—many of them carving wood, for
Oberammergau is a great woodcarving center, with a school that teaches
the craft. The play, which was first given in 1634 in fulfillment of a vow
to present it every decade if the Black Plague were ended, requires over
1,000 performers. As they are all natives of Oberammergau, whose population is only 5,000, it is evident that it is very much the focal point of life
in the town.

Play year or not, Oberammergau is a rewarding place to visit, with its
attractive old houses and its pleasant parish church lying peacefully
among broad grassy fields, from which the great rocks of the Alps rise

abruptly. From it you can take the bus trip into the Graswangtal Valley, to visit Schloss Linderhof, one of Ludwig II's most fanciful castles. In front is an artificial pond with a gilded statue of Flora and a 31-meter (105-ft.) fountain. The castle itself was built in Rococo style and has a number of ornate suites. In the park King Ludwig II also had constructed an artificial blue grotto in imitation of the one at Capri and a Moorish Kiosk with enameled bronze peacocks.

Oberammergau is also an ideal starting-off point for hiking tours in the surrounding mountains. There are a variety of marked footpaths to choose from, and every year on 24 August anyone can take part in an organized Mountain Hiking Day (Gebirgswandertag) called "In King Ludwig's Footsteps" in memory of the "Dream King" of Bavaria. The day ends with a spectacular sight when, at dusk, huge bonfires are set ablaze on the surrounding mountainsides.

Proceeding from Oberammergau or Linderhof to Garmisch the road passes through Ettal, known mainly for its beautiful Benedictine Abbey founded in 1330. Its church was built first in Gothic style and was changed in the early 18th century into a Baroque structure with a large dome whose ceiling was painted by Johann Jakob Zeiller.

An alternative route from Munich to Garmisch-Partenkirchen is southward via Wolfratshausen, the railroad then making straight for Bichl, while the road makes a slight loop to the east to pass near Bad Heilbrunn. From this minor spa, or from Bichl via Bad Heilbrunn, it is a short side trip to a major one, Bad Tölz, delightfully located on the Isar against a background of high mountains. It is an old place (the Romans had a settlement here in the 5th century, named Tollusium) and it remains conscious of tradition. This is local costume country and if you happen to be on hand on November 6, you can take in the Leonhardi Ride, in honor of the patron saint of horses.

Continuing south from Bichl, road and rail alike pass through Benediktbeuern, where there is a 1,200-year-old monastery, whose double-towered church bears the familiar onion domes of this region. At Kochel there is a lovely lake, the railroad ends and train travelers must take to the bus. The road continues through Walchensee, where there is another delightful example of the beautiful lakes that characterize this region, with the mountains rising steeply straight from the water; Wallgau, a pleasant little village of 900 inhabitants, nestled in a small valley cupped by mountains, and Krün, somewhat larger but in a situation much the same, to Garmisch-Partenkirchen.

Garmisch-Partenkirchen

This town is among the world's top winter sports centers, and the largest in Germany. Before World War I, there was only a village here; it took ten hours to reach the peak of the Zugspitz, where, in those days, it was assumed only eccentrics would want to go. Now thousands reach its top every year in minutes by the cable car from the nearby Eibsee.

Garmisch-Partenkirchen lies on comparatively flat ground in the valley of the River Loisach, from which mountains spring to terrifying heights on every side. The giants of the group are the Wank to the east, 1,780 meters (5,840 ft.); the Hausberg and Kreuzeck to the south, 1719 meters (5,640 ft.); nearby the Alpspitze, 2,219 meters (7,285 ft.) and to the southwest, on the Austrian border, Germany's highest mountain, the majestic Zugspitze, 2,963 meters (9,717 ft.). These great peaks, plus Garmisch's famed sunny climate, which made it a health resort before skiing seized upon it, and the fact that snow can be depended upon here from the latter part of November until the middle of May, are the natural factors which account for the popularity of this resort. Man-made attractions have completed its assets.

The Olympic Ski Stadium and Olympic Ice Stadium were built for the winter Olympic Games held here in 1936. The Olympic Ski Stadium has two ski jumps and a slalom course. There is room for 100,000 people, although "only" 30,000 of them can be accommodated in the grandstands. The Olympic Ice Stadium provides nearly an acre of ice surface and its grandstands can take 12,000 spectators. Another rink, with stands for 6,000 persons, is next to the first one.

There are any number of breathtaking excursions from Garmisch. There is a beautiful four-mile walk to Grainau, offering superb views. There are two gorges well worth visiting, the Partnachklamm and the Höllentalklamm. The lovely little Riessersee is a lake on the outskirts of Garmisch, while further away is the Eibsee, with the tremendous rock wall of the Zugspitze rising above it. The Wank is reached from Partenkirchen by small cable cars; the Kreuzeck, Graseck, Eckbauer and Hausberg are also reached by cable car. But for the Zugspitze, the Number One excursion from Garmisch, you have your choice between a Bavarian mountain railway and cable car and a Tyrolean cable car (from Obermoos which can be reached by train and bus from Garmisch), since the Zugspitze marks the Germany/Austria border.

For the full variety of the marvelous scenery, the best idea is to go by one route and return by the other. On the Bayrische Zugspitzbahn you pass the dark-blue Eibsee, framed by deep-green pine forests, and reach Schneefernerhaus through a long tunnel. At this point a broad skiing area spreads out, the highest in Germany, the Zugspitzplatt; if your object is not skiing, but the view, a cable car will take you still higher, to the Summit Station, anchored by cables to the lofty pinnacle on which it stands, from which you can see all the way to the central Alps of Switzerland. You can also reach the peak of Zugspitze directly from Eibsee by cable car.

Garmisch, together with Partenkirchen, however, is not only a sports center and a point of departure for trips and excursions. It is a very attractive town in its own right, with balconies and painted façades on its Alpine-style houses, and with the Baroque parish church and 15th-century Church of St. Martin. Garmisch is also a health resort with a lovely Kurpark staging outdoor summer concerts.

Some 16 km. (10 miles) southeast of Garmisch, in the valley of the Isar, is Mittenwald, one of the most beautiful Alpine towns, with the rugged rocky face of Karwendel rising almost vertically above it. Many colorful houses line the streets, some with magnificent façade paintings, such as the Neunerhaus at Obermarkt. The Baroque church with frescoed tower was originally built in Gothic style. In front of it stands the monument to the violin-maker Mathias Klotz, who in the 17th century introduced his craft to the town, and set Mittenwald on the path to world fame in this field. The Geigenbau- und Heimatmuseum (Museum of Violin-Making and Regional Life) in Ballenhausgasse has good displays illustrating the history of violin-making here. A two-stage lift (first stage chair and second stage gondola) takes you to the 1,390 meter (4,560 ft.) Kranzberg with a magnificent view of the Karwendel and Wetterstein mountain ranges and a cable car takes you close to the top (to about 2,240 meters 7,350 ft.) of Karwendel.

In the vicinity of Mittenwald are several small blue-green lakes such as Lautersee, Ferchensee and Barmsee. A few miles north of Mittenwald are the villages of Krün and Wallgau which you have passed earlier on one of the routes to Garmisch. Another very scenic and less frequented road follows the Isar Valley (toll road for a while) from Wallgau through Fall and the unpretentious climatic resort of Lenggries, completing the round-trip back once again at Bad Tolz.

Between the Loisach, Isar and Inn

East of Bad Tolz and the Isar Valley, in a ring of high mountains lies Tegernsee, one of the most beautiful Bavarian lakes, dotted with sails in summer and spinning ice skaters in winter; its tree-lined shores garland it with flowers in the spring while in the fall they provide a magnificent contrast between the red and golden leaves and the already snow-capped peaks in the background. All the localities on the lake are summer and winter resorts; the most important are Gmund in the north; Tegernsee with the former Benedictine monastery (now ducal castle and parish church), which was founded in 747, on the eastern shore; Bad Wiessee with chloride, iodine, and sulfuric springs and a large spa establishment on the western shore including a modern covered promenade connected with the music pavilion; Rottach-Egern with Walberg Mountain, reached by cable car, at the southern end. Farther south is the idyllic village of Kreuth from where the road continues through Wildbad Kreuth, a tiny spa, and Glashütte to Austria.

Continuing eastward from Tegernsee we come to another lovely lake, the Schliersee, whose main community bears the same name, and less than 11 km. (7 miles) south, high up along a twisty mountain road, is yet another blue gem of the Bavarian Alps, the tiny Spitzingsee, a favorite winter sport and summer hiking resort. About 16 km. (10 miles) southeast of Schliersee is the village of Bayrischzell with a sharply-pointed church spire, another important skiing center and summer resort. Above Bayrischzell to the north is Wendelstein Mountain (1,838 meters, 6,029 ft.) which can be reached via a new cable car. There's also a cogwheel railway that runs up the north side and is the oldest of its kind in Germany. At the top there's a little church, designed in 1888–90 by Max Kleiber, no mean mountaineer himself—he carried the cross for the roof up the mountain on his back—where extravagant alpine weddings take place. And on the very summit stands the tiny St. Wendelin chapel dating from 1718.

The Inn River comes rushing from Austria and flows north under the high bridge of the Munich—Salzburg autobahn, reaching Rosenheim a few miles beyond it. Rosenheim, which has been a market town since 1328, is a busy industrial city. The Old Town has several picturesque old facades, onion-shaped steeples, and arcaded streets, and is separated from the New Town by the 14th-century Mittertor (Middle Gate). About 11 km. (7 miles) west of the city is Bad Aibling with peat and mud baths, one of the nicest Kurparks in Bavaria with a modern concert hall, music pavilion and remodeled Kurhaus, and the oldest and largest flea-market in Bavaria. About 8 km. (5 miles) east of the city is the quiet lake of Simsee, the summer playground for the inhabitants and visitors of Rosenheim. Following the Inn due north of Rosenheim you reach Wasserburg am Inn, a picturesque medieval town, whose riverside waterfronts have given rise to its second name of Kleine Venedig (Little Venice).

Chiemgau

Traveling east from Rosenheim you enter the Chiemgau region of Bavaria and in Prien you find yourself on the shores of the largest lake in Bavaria, the Chiemsee, sometimes called the Bavarian Sea, whose greatest attractions are the two islands, Frauenchiemsee, with a 1,200-year-old convent and minster church, and Herrenchiemsee, where one of the fantastic castles built by Ludwig II stands. On Saturday nights (in summer) the great ballroom is lighted by thousands of candles, with classical chamber groups performing.

In addition to Prien and its lake section of Stock, from where the lake boats take you to Herreninsel and Fraueninsel, a cluster of small and unspoiled towns is strung around Chiemsee. Not much more than 8 km. (5 miles) from the eastern shore of the lake is Traunstein, a market town with a long history, which is presently known primarily as a health resort offering brine and mud baths and cold water Kneipp cures. South from the Chiemsee is the very popular Alpine resort of Reit im Winkl, close to the Austrian border. If you are coming from Prien, there is no direct railway connection, but postal buses leave five times daily for this tranquil vacation spot. As a winter sports center, it has the reputation of receiving the heaviest snowfalls in Bavaria.

From Reit im Winkl proceed on the very scenic section of the German Alpine Road to the pleasant town of Ruhpolding, surrounded by high mountains—there is a cable car on Rauschberg—its houses hugging a small hill crowned by a church.

The Berchtesgadener Land

Continuing south on the Alpine Road, you come to the Berchtesgadener Land, the biggest tourist attraction in the whole of the eastern Bavarian Alps, with its giant rugged mountains and exquisite Alpine lakes.

Striking deep into the heart of the region, you come first to the little village of Ramsau, an excellent base for mountain climbing, the principal peak here being the Hochkalter, towering over the village. A few miles to the east is Hintersee, a small lake surrounded by steep slopes, while south again is the tumultuous torrent that pours down through the Wimbach Gorge, originating in the snowfields separating the Hochkalter from the even higher and wilder peak of the Watzmann at 2,714 meters (6,900 ft.).

The center of the Berchtesgadener Land is of course Berchtesgaden itself, an ancient market town and long the site of an Augustinian Abbey, secularized in the early-19th century. The pretty little town is extremely popular—as a winter sports resort it is second only to Garmisch—and frequently extremely crowded, especially in summer.

The main sight in the town is the Königliche Schloss Berchtesgaden, the Royal Castle, originally the Abbey but taken over by the Wittelsbachs, rulers of Bavaria, in 1810. It is now a museum, many of whose treasures were originally collected by Prince Rupert of Bavaria, who died here in 1955. The 13th-century cloisters and Gothic dormitory plus a number of fine Renaissance rooms provide the principal exhibition spaces for the Prince's collections, which are particularly rich in 15th- and 16th-century German wood-carvings. The adjoining Abbey church, built in the 12th century but with many later additions, is also very beautiful. Berchtesgaden is a wood-carving center, and the Heimatmuseum, the Local Museum, in Schroffenbergallee, has a good collection of carvings from the area.

However, perhaps the most famous sight in Berchtesgaden is the Salzbergwerg, the Salt Mines, source of the town's prosperity since the early-16th century. A visit here is a unique experience. You will be provided with protective clothing—trousers, apron and cap—and a leather "seat" on which you then slide down a 500-meter (1,640-ft.) chute into a labyrinth of tunnels and galleries, their walls shimmering with salt crystals. A boat trip across an underground lake and short film-show, outlining the development of the mines, end the trip. The mines are open all year, but for limited periods only from October to May.

There are a number of excellent excursions from the town, of which perhaps the best is to Königsee, a beautiful fjord-like lake set between almost vertical mountain-walls in the middle of the Berchtesgaden National Park, a nature and wildlife reserve. Electric boats, the only sort allowed on the lake, take you from the little town of Königsee at the head of the lake to the 18th-century chapel of St. Bartholomä, whose clover-leaf shaped dome is the symbol of Berchtesgaden.

Another excellent trip is from Berchtesgaden to Kehlstein, reached by post bus via Obersalzburg—site of Hitler's luxurious mountain retreat—some three miles out of town. From here special buses run up the private road, the highest in the country and built by Hitler in 1937–39, to the Eagle's Nest, some 1,834 meters (6,017 ft.) high and today an inn and restaurant. (It's worth pointing out that despite its name and dramatic location, this was not the site of Hitler's Alpine stronghold). The view from the top, and from the road too, is sensational. An alternative trip is along the Rossfeld Höhenringstrasse, again reached via Obersalzburg, the second-highest road in the country.

The final halt in this exploration of the Berchtesgaden Land is the fashionable spa of Bad Reichenhall, source of the most powerful saline springs in Europe, a few miles north of Berchtesgaden. The town is best-known as a luxurious health resort, and boasts many excellent hotels, practically all of which specialize in health treatments, and in all has the rather discreet atmosphere of many of Germany's more expensive spas, an effect encouraged by the well-tended parks, Botanic garden, casino and concert hall. However, it is also a popular winter-sports resort, and summer and winter a cable runs up to Predigstuhl, from where there is a splendid view of the rocky giants of Berchtesgaden Land. The town also has an interesting Romanesque Cathedral, St. Zeno's, much of which was remodeled in the 16th and 17th centuries. In addition, there is a remarkable Salt Works, the Alte Saline—like Berchtesgaden, Bad Reichenhall was an important salt-producing center—which Ludwig I built in 1834 in an extraordinary medieval manner, the whole as lavish as it is unlikely.

PRACTICAL INFORMATION FOR THE ALPS

TELEPHONES. We have given telephone codes for all the towns and villages in the hotel and restaurant lists that follow. These codes need only be used when calling from outside the town or village concerned.

HOTELS AND RESTAURANTS. With very few exceptions, all hotels and *Gasthäuser* in the Bavarian Alps and lower alpine regions are in local, traditionally styled, low-roofed alpine chalets with wooden balconies and a multi-colored mass of flowers in summer. Standards are generally high. Breakfasts in smaller establishments are simple.

Upper Bavaria offers everything from super-luxurious hotels to the simplest *Gasthof* out in the country, not forgetting the large choice of farmhouse and self-catering accommodations. Garmisch-Partenkirchen and Berchtesgaden head the field in this region, which is bountifully supplied with accommodations in all categories and special spring, fall and, particularly, winter seven-day packages. Although prices are higher here than in other mountain areas, there are still many lesser-known resorts (Inzell, Kreuth) and inexpensive hotels and pensions everywhere, plus a number of beautifully situated mountain hotels. A few of the resort hotels may close for a short period in the fall.

Accommodations in the Allgäu tend to be about ten to 20 percent less than in the Bavarian Alps proper, and the further away from the mountains you are the cheaper it is. Outside the main tourist centres it is even possible to find bed and breakfast for as little as DM.10. There are also special package arrangements, particularly in such places as Balderschwang, Fischen, Kleinwalsertal, Oberstaufen and Scheidegg, as well as in the better-known tourist centers. You can write to any of the regional tourist offices (see below) and ask for their brochure of *Pauschalangebote* (special arrangements), which include stays from between three days and two weeks often combined with sporting activities.

Amerang (Inn Valley). *Gasthof Palm* (M), Wasserburgerstr. 10 (08075–207). With annexe, 30 beds, most rooms with bath. Terrace, swimming pool, and restaurant. *Pension Steinbauer* (M), Forellenweg 8 (08075–211). With quietly located annexe. 100 beds. Indoor pool (closed in summer) as well as an outdoor one. Cycles for hire.

Aschau (Chiemgau). *Pension Alpenblick* (M), Spitzensteinstr. 13, in Sachrang section (08052–360). 23 rooms with bath. Very quiet and picturesque location; indoor pool. *Edeltraud* (M), Narzissenweg 15, in Aschau (08052–552). 15 rooms with bath. Lovely mountain view. *Gasthof Weissbräu* (I), Frasdorferstr. 7 in Aschau (08052–1424). Good-value traditional quest-house, located near the swimming pool.

Augsburg (Bavarian Swabia). *Steigenberger Drei-Mohren* (L), Maximilianstr 40 (0821–510031). 110 rooms with bath, and operating since 1723. One of Germany's historic hotels; former guests include Russian czars and German emperors, as well as Mozart and Goethe. Fine restaurant, terrace cafe, and dance bar. *Fuggerkeller* wine cellar is located in same building (Maximilianstr. 38), serving first-class Franconian wines. AE, DC, MC, V. *Alpenhof* (E), Donauwörther Str. 233, in the northwest suburbs (0821–413051). 136 rooms with bath or shower. Indoor pool, sauna, fitness room, games room, casino, restaurant. A Ringhotel. AE, DC, MC, V.

Dom Hotel (M), Frauentorstr. 8 (0821–153031). 43 rooms with bath or shower. Very quiet location in the old town near the station. Breakfast only. MC, V. *Holiday Inn* (M), Wittelsbacherpark (0821–577087). 185 rooms with bath. Europe's tallest (35-story) hotel tower. Indoor pool, sauna, solarium. Grill specialties in the top floor Panorama restaurant. AE, DC, MC, V. *Riegele* (M), Viktoriastr. 4, near station (0821–39039). 57 beds. Smaller hotel, good restaurant. AE, V. *Gästehaus Iris* (I), Gartenstr. 4 (0821–510981). 10 rooms, most with shower or bath. Centrally but quietly located near the Dominican Monastery. Breakfast only. AE, DC, MC. *Post* (I), Fuggerstr. 5/7, at Königsplatz (0821–36044). 45 rooms, most with bath or shower. Terrace restaurant. Closed Christmas and New Year's. AE, DC, MC, V.

Restaurants. *Berteles Weinstuben* (E), Philippine-Welser-Str. 4 (0821–3119). Definitely superior tavern. DC, MC. *Die Ecke* (E), Elias-Holl-Platz (0821–510600). Old Augsburg atmosphere for gourmets and wine connoisseurs. Reservations advisable. DC, MC. *Welser Küche* (E), in the old Patrician Stiermann house Maximilianstr. 83 (0821–33930). A rare dining experience: you can enjoy original recipes in 16th-century style (Mon. to Sat. at 8 P.M.; Sun. 7 P.M.), prior telephone arrangements are a must. AE, DC, MC. *Fischertor* (M), Pfärrle 16 (0821–518662). In the narrow side streets of the old town, serving fine Swabian regional specialties. MC, V. *Fuggerei-Stube* (M), Jakoberstr. 26 (0821–30870). Specialty restaurant in the world-famous Fuggerei. Popular among the locals. AE, DC, MC. *Ratskeller* (M), in the Rathaus with *Elias-Holl-Stube* and *Badische Weinstube* (0821–517848). AE, DC, MC. *Zeughausstuben* (I), Zeugplatz (0821–511685). In the historic armory building. Very atmospheric specialty restaurant; beer garden in summer. MC.

Bad Reichenhall (Berchtesgadener Land). *Kurhotel Luisenbad* (E), Ludwigstr. 33 (08651–5011). Traditional and old-established cure-hotel. 84 beds, all rooms with bath, indoor pool, sauna, fitness center, cosmetic studio. Elegant *Luisenbad* restaurant, rustic *Holzstubin* tavern. *Steigenberger's Axelmannstein* (E), Salzburgerstr. 4 (08651–4001). 167 rooms, most with bath. Luxurious hotel in the famous Steigenberger chain. Excellent *Parkrestaurant* with terrace, cocktail bar, own thermal bath. Located in large park with swimming pool; also indoor pool and tennis courts. AE, DC, MC, V. *Bavaria* (M), Am Münster 3 (08651–5016). 173 spacious studio-apartments. Located in a fine private park, quiet, but still only a short walk from the pedestrian zone. Indoor pool, sauna, health facilities, two restaurants. *Bayersicher Hof* (M), Bahnhofsplatz 14 (08651–5084). 64 rooms with bath or shower. On the main station square. Pool on roof terrace, health facilities, café with afternoon music, nightclub and three restaurants. Closed Jan. 5–Feb. 20. AE, DC, MC, V.

Alpenhotel "Fuchs" (M) Nonn 50 (08651-61048). In the Nonn section, above the town, surrounded by forest and meadow. 36 rooms, most with own bath. First-class restaurant. Tennis courts five minutes away. Hotel has its own ski-training slope for novices. Closed Nov. 1–Dec. 22. AE, DC, MC, V. *Tiroler Hof* (M), Tirolerstr. 12 (08651–2055). A Ring Hotel located in the pedestrian zone. 45 rooms with bath or shower. Indoor pool, garden and garages. Colorful, wood-beamed restaurant dating back to 1634. AE, DC, MC, V. *Schlossberghof* (M), Schlossberg 5, in the Marzoll section (08651–3002). 100-bed hotel with apartments, near the ancient Schloss Marzoll castle. Good value. Indoor pool, large restaurant, beer garden and coffee terrace. *Carola* (I), Friedrich-Ebbert-Allee 6 (08651–2629). 20 rooms, 15 with shower. Quietly located two to three minutes from the Kurpark. No restaurant. Closed Nov. 1–Feb. 20. No credit cards.

Bad Tölz (Isar Valley). *Jodquellenhof* (E), on the left bank of the Isar at Ludwigstr. 13–15 (08041–5091). 78 rooms and 3 suites with bath. Three pools, one with thermal iodine water, open March through October. Restaurant with special dietary menu. AE, DC, MC, V. *Hiedl* (M), Ludwigstr. 9 (08041–9774). 28 beds. Cozy, rustic-style hotel-pension with particularly good cooking in its *Bürgerstuben* restaurant. *Kolberbräu* (M), Marktstr. 29 (08041–9158). In the same family since 1600; good restaurant. MC. *Gästehaus Bergblick* (I), Benedikt-Erhard-Str. 6 (08041–3622). 16 rooms, half with bath or shower. Quiet; no restaurant.

Restaurants. *Altes Fährhaus* (M), An der Isarlust 1 (08041–6030). Directly on the banks of the Isar; former ferry boat station. Serves typical Upper Bavarian specialties with a touch of gastronomic élan. *Schwaighofer* (M), Marktstr. 17 (08041–2762). Located in the town center.

Bad Wiessee (Tegernsee). *Kurhotel Lederer am See* (E), Bodenschneidstr. 9 (08022–8291). 190 beds, 90 baths, 3 apartments. Lovely location on lake with own beach and tennis courts. Comfortable restaurant and tavern. DC. *Kurhotel Rex* (E), Münchner Str. 25 (08022–82091). 56 rooms and 2 suites with bath or shower. Park. Closed Nov. 1–Apr. 15. No credit cards. *Terrassenhof* (E), Adrian-Stoop Str. 50 (08022–82761). 86 rooms, all with bath. Pool, café, wine tavern and summer dancing. *Kurheim Wilhelmy* (M), Freihausstr. 15 (08022–81191). In pleasant location, 28 rooms. *Resi von der Post* (M), Zilcherstr. 14 (08022–82788). 30 rooms. Quiet and comfortable, some apartments. *Wiesseer Hof, der Kirchenwirt* (M), Sanktjohanserstr. 46 (08022–82061). Belongs to the Ring hotel group. Rustic restaurant. AE, DC, MC, V. *Haus Börner* (I), Seestr. 24 (08022–8558). 14 rooms, some with bath. Small hotel, but particularly comfortable and with excellent service; no restaurant. Quiet, and pleasant view. *Berggasthof Sonnenbichl* (M) (08022–81365). On the slopes above the town at Sonnenbichlweg 1. Has own ski lift and some rooms.

Restaurant. *Freihaus Brenner* (M), Freihaushohe 4 (08022–82004). Rustic restaurant in an old farm house high above the town. A real local tip; its popularity makes reservations essential in summer—in winter it's often cut off from the town. Hearty Bavarian specialties mixed with international cuisine at more than reasonable prices. MC.

Café-Restaurant: *Bauer in der Au* (M) (08022–81171). At almost 900 meters (3,000 ft) on the mountainside—accessible by foot only on well-marked hiking trails from Weissach—with a 200 year-old covered courtyard. Serves some of the best cakes around. Open until 7.00 P.M.

Balderschwang (Allgäu). *Pension Lässer* (M), Wäldle 8 (08328–1018). 26 rooms, half-board terms only. Fine view. Sauna, solarium and sports room. *Luisenhof* (M) (08328–1054). 42 beds.

Bayrischzell (Schliersee). *Meindelei* (E), Michl.-Meindl-Str. 13 (08023–318). Romantik Hotel located on the south slopes of the Wendelstein in a quiet position. 15 rooms, all with bath. Furnished with old Bavarian peasant furniture and antiques. Restaurant with open fireplace and ceramic tile oven. Small indoor pool. MC, V. *Alpenrose* (M), Schlierseestr. 6 (08023–620). 50 beds, all rooms with bath or shower. Well-known restaurant serving Bavarian specialties, as well as international menu. Some holiday apartments available. *Schönbrunn* (M), Sudelfeldstr. 23 (08023–726). On the road up to Sudelfeld, located in own large park near the Kneipp Center. Fine restaurant and café. MC. *Berghotel Sudelfeld* (I), Unteres Sudelfeld (08023–607). 71 rooms. On the mountain at Sudelfeld, right next to the ski slopes. *Feuriger Tatzelwurm* (I) (08034–8695). Alpine Gasthof. Located at the end of the "Alpine Road," at the famous Tatzelwurm waterfalls. Cozy atmosphere, good restaurant. MC.

Berchtesgaden. In **Markt Berchtesgaden**: *Geiger* (E), Stanggass (08652–5055). 40 rooms, 8 apartments and 3 suites with bath. In quiet location on outskirts; indoor and outdoor pools, fitness room, trout specialties in restaurant, antique furnishings. Closed Nov. AE, DC, V.

Bavaria (M), Sunklergässchen 11 (08652–2620). Most rooms with shower. Cozy atmosphere. Centrally located near the main station, but still with a splendid panoramic view of the Watzmann summit and surrounding mountains. *Grassl* (M), Maximilianstr. 15 (08652–4071). Large rooms but street front can be noisy; breakfast only. AE, DC, MC, V. *Krone* (M), Am Rad 5 (08652–2881). Small and quiet, on the outskirts. *Vier Jahreszeiten* (M), Maximilianstr. 20 (08652–5026). 62 rooms and 3 apartments with bath or shower. Centrally-located; has belonged to the same family since 1876. Indoor pool, sauna, solarium, fitness room. *Hubertusstuben* restaurant serving game specialties. AE, DC, MC, V. *Watzmann* (M), Franziskanerplatz 2 (08652–2055). 37 rooms, half with shower. Very comfortable inn just opposite the church; good value restaurant, own butchery, heated garden-terrace. Closed Nov. 1–Dec. 22. AE, MC, V.

Café Waldluft (I), Bergwekstr. 37 (08652–2328). 55 beds, most with own shower. Peacefully located on the edge of a forest and at the foot of the Obersalzberg peak. Ten minutes from the center. Restaurant and terrace café. *Weiherbach* (I), Weiherbach Weg 6–8 (08652–2333). 22 rooms, most with shower. Ten minutes' walk from the center, five minutes' from the skilift; rustic building, quiet. Closed Nov. 3–Dec. 20. No credit cards.

Restaurants. *Gasthof Neuhaus* (M), Marktplatz 1. AE. *Gasthof Bier-Adam* (I), Marktplatz 22 (08652–2390). Quality Bavarian fare served with style. Closed Wed. in winter. AE, DC, MC, V.

In **Königssee**: *Restaurant-Pension Lichtenfels* (M), Alte Konigseer Str. 15 (08652–4035). Conveniently located between town center and Konigsee with good public transport. Good restaurant. **In Oberau**: *Alpenhotel Denninglehen* (M) (08652–5085) located on the mountainside at about 3,000 ft. Alpine styled building with all modern facilities of a luxury hotel. Restaurant and beauty farm. Reservations advised. Closed Dec. 1–20. No credit cards. In **Obersalzburg**: *Zum Türken* (I), Hintereck 2

(08652–2428). 17 rooms, half with bath or shower. Small mountain hotel in quiet location. Closed Nov. 1–Dec. 20. AE, DC, MC, V. In **Ramsau:** *Alpenhof* (I), Am See 27 (08657–253). Near Hintersee Lake; well-located for walking, angling or pony rides; pleasant terrace garden.

Restaurants. *Haslinger am Luitpoldpark* (M), Kälbersteinerstr. 2 (08652–2605). *Kurhaus* (M), Maximilianstr. 9 (08652–4364). With splendid view from terrace.

Bergen (Chiemsee). *Säulner Hof* (M), ten minutes from the lakeside near the Hochfelln cable car station Saulnerweg 1 (08662–8655). 15 rooms with bath or shower. Very comfortable hotel-restaurant in local style, with excellent food: a combination of regional and *haute cuisine* at reasonable prices. Ideal for both winter and summer vacations. Closed Nov. V.

Bischofswiesen (Berchtesgadener Land). *Brennerbascht* (M), Hauptstr. 46 (08652–7021). 54 beds, some apartments, all with own bath or shower; rustic-style terrace, sunbathing lawn. *Bauernstube* restaurant serving Bavarian and international dishes from own hunting and fishing grounds. *Gästehaus Elvira* (I), Reitweg 25 (08652–2631). 18 beds. Small pension, on a quiet southern slope only 2 km. (1.2 miles) from Berchtesgaden itself. Heated indoor pool.

Chiemsee (Chiemgau). In **Chieming:** *Gasthof Unterwirt* (I), Hauptstr. 32 (08664–551). 20 rooms, 8 with bath. Good restaurant with local specialties, particularly *renke* and trout. Garden. Closed Oct. 21–Nov. 25. No credit cards.

Restaurant. *Gasthof zur Post* (M), Laimgruber Str. 5 (08664–447). Has *Zwergclause restaurant* for late dining.

In **Gstadt:** *Pension Jägerhof* (I), Breitbrunner Str. 5 (08054–242). 30 rooms, 11 with bath or shower. Particularly comfortable hotel-pension. Terrace, sauna, solarium and sports room. Closed Nov.–Mar. AE, DC, MC, V.

In **Ising:** *Hotel Gutsgasthof Zum Goldenen Pflug* (E), Kirchberg 3 (08667–421). All rooms with bath; plus seven apartments. Typically Bavarian rustic hotel with attractively furnished rooms in various period styles, beautifully-located in fields and meadowland. Six different restaurants with Bavarian and Austrian specialties as well as an international menu. Riding school, large stables, own bathing beach on Chiemsee lake, 20 minutes' walk away. Sailing, surfing and golf-course nearby. AE.

In **Prien:** *Sport und Golfhotel* (E), Erlenweg 16 (08051–1001). 40 rooms with rustic furnishings, all with own bath; two apartments. Modern Bavarian-style building; indoor pool, pleasant garden, good restaurant serving game specialties, also a café. A few minutes from a nine-hole golf course. MC. *Gästehaus Drexler-König Ludwig Stuben* (M), Seestr. 95 (08051–4802). 17 rooms, about half with own bath or shower. Right next to the Chiemsee ferry quay. Beer garden and cafe. *Reinhart* (M), Seestr. 117 (08051–1045). 28 rooms, most with own bath or shower. Quietly-located with panoramic view over the lake. Terrace, cafe and restaurant. AE, MC, V. *Gaststätte-Lindenhof* (I), Rathausstr. 24. 17 beds. Simple Gasthof in the town center. Good wholesome food and shady beer garden. *Pension Bartlhof* (I), Seestr. 100 (08051–2807). On the lake.

In **Rimsting:** *Seehof* (M), Schafwaschen 4 (08051–1697). Right on the lakeside with its own mooring jetty and beach; large lakeside café terrace.

In **Seebruck:** *Landgasthaus-Hotel Lambachhof* (M), Lambach 10 (08667–427). 56 beds, most with own bath or shower. Large local-style hotel, outside the town center on the lakeside road at picturesque Maler-winkel. Shady garden surrounded by meadowland. Rustic restaurant with excellent local specialties, including lamb from own farm. *Post* (M), Ludwig-Thomas-Str. 8 (08667–216). 100 beds. On the lake with its own beach. Garden restaurant, bar.

Restaurant. *Malerwinkel,* Lambach 23 (08667–488). Very popular excursion destination. Large hotel-restaurant directly on the lake with a lovely view across to Fraueninsel. Good food, but crowded with poor service in high season.

In **Seeon:** *Pension-Restaurant Gruber Alm* (I), in the Roitham section, Almweg 18 (08624–696). 50 beds. Sauna, solarium. Home-made bread and wine.

Ettal (Ammergauer Alps). *Benediktenhof* (M), Zieglerstr. 1, a little out of town on the way to Oberammergau (08822–4637). 17 rooms, each furnished with Bavarian Baroque or rustic furniture, most with own bath; also one apartment. An original farmstead with plenty of wooden beams and painted walls, over 500 years old. The hotel restaurant (with terrace and café) serves excellent local and international cuisine. *Hotel Ludwig der Bayer* (M), Kaiser Ludwig Platz 10 (08822–6601). 66 rooms, most with own bath, two apartments. Indoor pool, sauna, game rooms, garden, restaurant. Closed Nov. 9–Dec. 20. No credit cards. *Hotel-Gasthof Zur Post,* Kaiser Ludwig Platz 18 (08822–596). Has annexe (M). 18 rooms, 4 apartments, most with bath or shower. Terrace and café. Two good-value restaurants, *Post Stüberl* and the *Gästehaus Restaurant* in the annex at Hauptstr. 15. Closed Nov. 10–Dec. 20. AE, DC, MC, V.

Fischen (Allgäu). *Kur-und-Sport Hotel Sonnenbichl* (E), Sagestr. 19 (08326–1851). In nearby Langenwang. Most rooms with bath or shower. Small indoor pool, tennis. Particularly comfortable with fine view. *Gästehaus Burgmühle* (M), Auf der Insel 4 (08326–7352). All rooms with bath or shower. Garni. *Haus Rosenstock* (M), Berger Weg 14 (08326–1895). All rooms with balcony. *Kur-und-Sporthotel Tanneck* (M), next to the ski lift, a bit outside town and higher up, Maderhalmer Weg 20 (08326–1888). 180 beds, all with bath or shower; apartments. Excellent restaurant and small indoor pool and sauna. *Pension Haus Alpenblick* (I), Maderhalmer-weg 10 (08326–337). At about 900 meters (3,000 ft.). Café with homemade pastries.

Fraueninsel (island in Chiemsee). *Hotel Linde* (M) (08054–316). Pleasant garden and restaurant.

Restaurants. *Inselwirt* (M) (08054–630). Also with a garden and well-known for its good food, particularly excellent fish from the lake. *Kloster Café* (I), near the *Inselwirt* and next door to the convent (08054–653). Here you can taste the famous Chiemsee *Klosterlikör,* a liqueur made by the nuns of the 1,200 year-old convent. Full restaurant service as well as café. All these only open in summer.

Friedrichshafen (Bodensee). *Buchhorner Hof* (M), a Ring Hotel, Friedrichstr. 33 (07541–2050). 65 rooms, about half with bath; 2 apartments, 2 suites. Sauna, solarium. A good restaurant with the accent on local fish and game. Closed Dec. 20–Jan. 10. AE, DC, MC, V. In nearby Schnetzenhausen, *Hotel City-Krone* (M), Schanzstr. 7 (07541–22086). For good value comfort. Large, quiet rooms; good location. Indoor pool and restaurant. Closed Dec. 12–Jan. 20. AE, DC, MC, V.

Füssen (Allgäu). *Hirsch* (E), Schulhausstr. 2–4 (08362–6055). Near Augsburger-Tor-Platz. 47 rooms, about half with bath. Authentic rustic furnishings, tavern, restaurant. Closed Nov. 15–Dec. 20. AE, DC, V. *Alpenkurhotel Filser* (M), Säulingerstr. 3 (08362–2068). Hotel and sanatorium. Quiet location with Kneipp water cures. *Kurhotel Wiedemann* (M), in the Bad Faulenbach suburb, Am Anger 3 (08362–37231). Quiet and pleasant, also with Kneipp cures. *Sonne* (M), Reichenstr. 37 (08362–6061). 32 rooms with bath or shower. Cheerful, modern hotel with traditional furnishings, café, disco/nightclub. No restaurant. AE, DC, MC, V. *Sailer's Kur-und-Ferienhotel* (M), Bildhauer Sturm Str. 14 (08362–7089). 40 beds, all rooms with own bath. Indoor pool, sauna, solarium. Located in one of the prettiest parts of town at the foot of the Galgenbichl heights. "Cure hotel" with all the best health facilities. *Seegasthof Weissensee* (M), on the shores of Lake Weissensee (08362–7095). 40 beds, all rooms with bath and lakeview. On its own bathing beach. Good local fish specialties in restaurant.

Restaurants. *Alpen-Schlossle* (M), Alatseestr. 28 (08362–4017). Rustic restaurant on a mountain site. Reservations advised. Closed Tues. and Nov.–mid-Dec. No credit cards. *Pulvertum* (M), in the Kurhaus, Schwedenweg 1 (08362–6078). Fine view from the terrace. MC. *Gasthaus zum Schwanen* (I), Brotmarkt 4 (08362–6174). Good regional cooking with no frills at low prices. Closed Sun. evening, Mon., and Nov. No credit cards.

Garmisch-Partenkirchen (Werdenfelser Land). *Clausing's Posthotel* (E), Marienplatz 12 (08821–58071). 31 rooms, most with bath or shower. A Romantik Hotel. A Baroque chalet with a long tradition and outstanding Bavarian cuisine. Dancing in the evening. AE, DC, MC. *Dorint Sporthotel* (E), Mittenwalder Str. 59 (08821–7060). New 1985. 480 beds, including some apartments; pleasant harmony of elegance and rustic charm. Wide variety of sports facilities and ski school run by German champions Rosie Mittermaier and Christian Neureuther. *Grand-Hotel Sonnenbichl* (E), Burgstr. 97 (08821–7020). 100 rooms, all with own bathroom; some suites available. Opposite the Garmisch golf course in beautifully wooded area. Excellent cuisine, either in the elegant gourmet restaurant or Bavarian specialties in the cozy *Zirbelstube*. Tennis, skating and fishing, as well as golf, nearby. DC, V. *Holiday Inn* (E), Mittenwalderstr. 2 (08821–7561). 117 rooms, all with bath. In Partenkirchen; the resort's largest hotel. *Kurhotel-Bernriederhof* (E), Von-Muller-Str. 12 (08821–71074). Enormous old farmhouse with 41 rooms, all tastefully furnished in regional style with real comfort—especially the marble bathrooms. Health cure facilities, restaurant. Centrally located with a splendid view across to the mountains. Also has vacation apartments. AE, DC, MC, V. *Obermühle (Silence Hotel)* (E), Mühlstr. 22 (08821–7040). 88 rooms, 6 apartments, 4 suites, most with bath. Five minutes from the center, in parkland. *Mühlenstube* rotisserie restaurant with international cuisine and rustic bar serving Bavarian specialties. Indoor pool, sauna, solarium. AE, DC, MC, V. *Partenkirchner Hof* (E), Bahnhofstr. 15 in Partenkirchen (08821–58025). 80 rooms with bath. A charming mix of first-class elegance and cozy Bavarian charm, located near the station. Pool, sauna, beauty farm, as well as 14 delightful apartments in *Wetterstein* annex. Well-regarded *Reindl Grill* restaurant. Closed Nov. 15–Dec. 15 AE, DC, MC, V. *Posthotel Partenkirchen* (E), Ludwigstr. 49 (08821–51067). 90 beds. Original stagecoach post. First-class service, good restaurant and wine tavern with music. AE, DC, MC, V.

Aschenbrenner (M), Loisachstr. 65A (08821–58029). Near the Kurpark. 24 rooms and 1 suite, most with bath. A mixture of modern comfort, *belle époque* furnishings and a noble country house. AE, DC, MC, V. *Buchenhof* (M), Brauhausstr. 3 (08821–52121). Comfortable house with 20 beds, some apartments, all rooms with bath or shower. Small indoor pool, sunbathing lawn, café. *Forsthaus Graseck* (M), Graseck 10 (08821–54006). Situated 900 meters (3,000 ft.) above Garmisch in idyllic surroundings. 74 beds. Indoor pool, restaurant and terrace with panoramic view. Reached by its own cable car. AE, DC, MC. *Garmischer Hof* (M), Bahnhofstr. 53 (08821–51091). 43 rooms with bath or shower. Right in the town center; no restaurant. AE, DC, MC. *Schneefernhaus* (M), on the Zugspitz, reached by cogwheel railway from Garmisch or cable car from Eibsee. 30 beds. The highest hotel in Germany (over 2,650 meters or 8,7000 ft.) with large public rooms and sun terraces. *Wittelsbach* (M), Von Brug Str. 24 (08821–53096). 100 beds, all with bath or shower, most with balcony and panoramic view. Beautifully situated in town center in its own grounds; indoor pool. AE, DC, MC.

Gästehaus Hohenzollern (I), Alpspitzstr. 6 (08821–2950). 19 beds, some with own bath or shower. No restaurant. *Gästehaus Kornmüller* (I), Höllental Str. 36 (08821–3557). 32 rooms, 8 apartments, 4 suites, most with bath. Friendly guesthouse in local style; three minutes by car from town center. AE, MC, V.

Restaurants. *Posthotel Partenkirchen.* (E), Ludwigstr. 49 (08821–2075). Bavarian dishes, Swiss and French regional specialties. Reservations advised. AE, MC, V. *Rotisserie Mühlenstube* (E), Mühlstr. 22 (08821–7040). Fresh salt-water fish thanks to specially built tanks. Reservations advised. AE, DC, MC, V. In addition to the high class restaurants in the main hotels: *Café Bauer* (M), Griesstr. 1 (08821–2109). Local atmosphere and music. *Gasthof Fraundorfer* (M), Ludwigstr. 15 in Partenkirchen (08821–2176). Typical Bavarian tavern with *schuhplattler* dancing, very popular with visitors. Reservations advisable. Some rooms, too. *Heuriger Zum Melber* (M), Ludwigstr. 37 (08821–2055). Rustic surroundings; also has a bowling (skittles) alley and dancing. *Isis Goldener Engel* (M), on Marktplatz (08821–56677). Café, bar, wine-tavern. *Werdenfelser Hof* (M), Ludwigstr. 58 (08821–3621). Opposite the *Drei Mohren* Hotel (see above). Particularly good game specialties. Reservations advised. Closed Thurs. DC, MC. *Stahl's Badstuben* (I), Klammstr. 47 (08821–58700). In the Alpspitz Wellenbad swimming and sports center. Good set menu and self-service. Reservations advised. No credit cards.

Grainau (Werdenfelser Land). *Alpenhof* (M), Alpspitz Str. 22 (08821–8071). 40 rooms. Pool. AE, DC. *Badersee* (M), Am Badersee 5 (08821–8685). On the lake, quiet with noted restaurant; boating. AE, MC.

Grainauer Hof (M), Schmolzstr. 5 (08821–50061). 52 beds, most rooms with own bath. Indoor pool, sauna, solarium. No restaurant. AE, DC, MC. *Post* (M), in the Obergrainau section, Postgasse 10 (08821–8853). 33 rooms and 7 apartments, with bath or shower. Restaurant. Closed Oct. 20–Dec. 20 and Jan. 10–Feb. 1. AE, DC, MC.

Grassau (Chiemgau). *Gasthof zur Post* (M), Kirchplatz 8 (08641–3113). 8 rooms. Cozy inn near the town center. Restaurant with local and international food, also a café. Terrace and outdoor pool. AE, MC. *Pension Gamsei* (I), Wöhrstr. 15 (08641–2749). 12 rooms. Very quietly located with beautiful views of the mountains from the garden. Heated outdoor pool; no restaurant.

Restaurants. *Gasthof Restaurant Fischerstüberl* (M), in nearby Rottau, Hauptstr. 5 (08641–2334). Locally-caught fish specialties; also some rooms. *Sperrer* (M), Ortenburgerstr. 5 (08641–5011). Bavarian fare, magnificent views. Reservations advised. Closed Mon. and Nov. No credit cards.

Herreninsel (island in Chiemsee). **Restaurant.** *Schlosshotel Herrenchiemsee* (M) (08051–1509). Open all year round, next to the castle. First-class restaurant serving fish specialties and home-made cakes and pastries. Also has its own beach. No accommodations.

Hindelang (Allgäu). *Prinz Luitpold* (E), Andreas-Gross-Str. 7 (08324–2011). 190 beds. Quietly-located on the southern slopes with a beautiful view. Bar, tennis court, swimming pool and health cures in the house; good food. Special arrangements for winter and summer packages, and *Alpengasthof Hirsch* (M), Kurzegasse 18 (08324–308). Rustic-style inn with good food. Both in the Bad Oberdorf section. *Alpengasthof Rosen-Stuben* (M), Jörg Lederer Str. 17 (08324–2370). Small, 10 rooms, most with bath. Fine view and restaurant. *Bären* (M), Bärengasse 1 (08324–2001). 47 beds, most rooms with bath or shower. Colorful traditional inn dating from 1812. Quietly-located on the southern edges of town. Rustic restaurant. *Kur und Sporthotel Haus Ingeburg* (M), eight km. (five miles) out of town, in Oberjoch, Am Prinzewald 3 (08324–7111). Bar, tennis court and small indoor pool. *Sonne* (M), in the town proper, Marktstr. 15 (08324–2026). 60 rooms, 46 apartments. Cozy restaurant and dance bar. AE.

Hintersee (Berchtesgadener Land), lakeside section of Ramsau. *Alpenhof Bartels* (I), Am See 27 (08657–253). 34 beds. On the lake in quiet location. Good restaurant with local specialties. *See-Hotel Gamsbock* (I), Am See 75, on the lakeside (08657–279). 34 rooms, all with bath or shower. Only a few minutes from start of the Berchtesgaden National Park, ideal for walking; also private fishing, and boating. Wonderful view, lakeside terrace, restaurant with game specialties from own hunting grounds.

Hohenschwangau (Allgäu). *Lisl und Jägerhaus* (E), Neuschwansteinstr. 1 (08362–81006). 57 rooms. Hunting-manor style building; outdoor pool and restaurant. AE, DC. *Müller* (E), Alpseestr. 14 (08362–81056). 46 rooms and four apartments. Attractive *Kutscherstube* restaurant. AE, DC.

Inzell (Chiemgau). *Dorint-Hotel* (E), Lärchenstr. 5 (08665–6700). 88 rooms, 130 apartments, all with bath or shower, radio, color T.V., telephone and balcony. Five minutes' walk from the town center. Bar, smart restaurants with international menu and Bavarian specialties. v. *Falkenstein* (M), Kreuzfeldsstr. 2 (08665–250). 66 beds, some rooms with own bath, most with shower; four apartments. Restaurant and cozy *Bauernstube*. AE. *Gasthof Schmelz* (M), in the Schmelz section, Schmelzer Str. 132 (08665–834). 35 rooms and apartments with bath or shower; eight holiday flats. Sauna, two solariums, indoor pool, massage and cosmetic treatment. Ponies for hire and winter sports on the doorstep. Restaurant. AE.

Kempten (Allgäu). *Fürstenhof* (E), Rathausplatz 8 (0831–23050). 300 year-old building with period furniture. All rooms with bath, three suites. Near the Town Hall. Fine restaurant serving French cuisine and rustic *Ratskeller* with Allgäuer specialties. AE, DC, MC. v. *Bahnhof Hotel* (M), Mozartstr. 2 (0831–22073). 40 rooms; newly renovated. Near the main station. Restaurant. AE, DC, MC. *Haslacher Hof* (M), Immenstädterstr. 74 (0831–24026). Near the station with view of the mountains. Good value. AE, DC, MC. v. *Peterhof* (M), Salzstr. 1 (0831–25525). A Ring Hotel. 51 rooms, all with own bath. In the town center, well known for good food in its *Peterhof Stüble*. AE, DC, MC. v. *Pension Haus Liesl* (I), Sängerstr. 13 (0831–23879). 20 beds. No restaurant.

Restaurants. *Sir Alexander* (M), Haslacher Berg 2 (0831–28322). Fine gourmet restaurant with international menu. *Café-Restaurant Hummel* (M), Immenstädter Str. 2 (0831–22286). Has own garden and home-made pastries. AE, DC, MC. *Weinhaus Winkel* (M), Fischersteige 9. (0831–22457). Historic wine tavern. Wholesome local specialties and fine international dishes on the menu. Good German wines and beer. DC, MC. *Goldene Traube* (I), Memmingerstr. 7 (0831–22187). Specialty gasthaus-restaurant serving large selection of fish dishes, international and local, as well as good game. Also some rooms. MC.

Kleinwalsertal (Allgäu). Actually in Austria, but it can only be reached by road from Oberstdorf. *Alpenhof Wildental* (E), Höfle 8 (08329–5611). 121 beds, all rooms with bath/shower. A modern I.F.A. hotel in the Mittelberg section. Quiet, sunny location amid fields and hills. Restaurant and bar, indoor pool and other first-class amenities. *Ifen Hotel* (E), Oberseitestr. 6 (08329–5071). In the Hirschegg section, a quiet location at the foot of the Ifen peak (2,000 meters or 6,600 ft.). Modern but in local rustic style. 67 rooms with large balconies, sauna, solarium massage, health facilities and large indoor pool. Fine restaurant with international cuisine. *Walserhof* (E), Walserstr. 11 (08329–5684). All rooms with bath or shower, also some apartments and hotel suites, also in the Hirschegg section. Modern, but in local style. Indoor pool, tennis courts, buffet and grill room, dancing.

Alpenrose (M), Walserstr. 46 (08329–5585). In Mittelberg section. Heated pool. *Alte Krone* (M), Walserstr. 87 (08329–5728). In Mittelberg section. Indoor pool. *Der Berghof* (M), Walserstr. 22 (08329–5445). In Hirschegg section. Traditional establishment with peaceful location and fine view. *Montana* (M), Schwarzwassertalstr. 13 (08329–5361). All rooms with bath or shower. Indoor pool, sauna. *Sporthotel Riezlern* (M), Schwendestr. 9 (08329–6652). 80 two-room apartments, all with bath or shower and some with kitchenette. In Riezlern section. Indoor pool, sauna, horseback riding.

Kochel (Walchensee). *Alpenhotel Schmied von Kochel* (M), Schlehdorfer Str. 6 (08851–216). 34 rooms, all with bath or shower. Bavarian inn with long, low wooden roof and brightly colored painted walls. Zither music every evening in the restaurant. MC, V. *Fischer am See* (M), in the Urfeld section, directly on the Walchensee lake (08851–818). Delightfully-located with a beautiful view. Lakeside terrace and openair pool. Good fish in the *Fischerstüberl* restaurant. *Grauer Bär* (M), Mittenwalder Str. 82 (08851–861). 26 rooms, some with balconies overlooking the lake. Located directly on the banks of the lake. Simple, tasteful hotel in cozy rustic style. Good wholesome local specialties in the restaurant, which has a lakeside terrace garden. AE, MC.

Konstanz (Bodensee). *Steingenberger Insel* (E), Auf der Insel 1 (07531–25011). A former monastery on a small island near the lake shore. 120 rooms, all with bath. Three restaurants and private park overlooking the lake. Own swimming beach. AE, DC, MC, V. *Barbarossa* (M), Obermarkt 8–12 (07531–22021). Historic inn with 100 beds. *Buchner Hof* (M), Buchnerstr. 6 (07531–51035). Neat, friendly and small hotel located in a residential area. 13 rooms, all with own bath. Sauna, solarium; good service but no restaurant. Closed Christmas–Jan. 10. AE. *Dom-Hotel St. Johann* (M), Brückengasse 1 (07531–22750). Built in the 10th century and looking like an old church. Has noted restaurant. *Seeblick* (M), Neuhauser Str. 14 (07531–54018). Second largest hotel with 86 rooms, most with own bath. Relatively simple furnishings, but comfortable. Indoor pool, solarium, sports room and tennis. Restaurant. AE, DC, MC. *Strandhotel Löchnerhaus* (M) (07534–411). 76 beds. On nearby Reichenau Island. Large hotel facing the lake with private swimming facilities. *Schiff am See* (I), in the Staad section, William-Graf-Platz 2 (07531–31041). Fine view. AE, DC, MC, V. *Zur Traube* (I), Fischerstr. 4 (07531–31317). Near the ferry boat landing stages.

Restaurants. *Casino* (E), in the Casino building, Seestr. 21 (07531–63615). Rustic-style, with pleasant terrace overlooking the lake, outstanding cuisine and dance bar. AE, DC. *Siber* (E), Seestr. 25, in Seehotel Siber (07531–63044). Best restaurant in town and among the finest in Germany. Closed second week in Feb. AE, DC.

Konzil (M), Hafenstr. 2, in the old Council Hall building (07531–21221). Has terraces and a lake view. *Zum Nikolai Torkel* (M), Eichhornstr. 83 (07531–64802). Fine cuisine, terrace with a pleasant view. *Zur Linde* (M), Radolfzeller Str. 27 (07531–77036). Also a café and Gasthof with pleasant comfortable rooms. *Engstler* (I), Fischmarkt 1 (07531–23126). At the lake corner of Marktstätte, with a large beer garden. Family restaurant. Game dishes. Closed Jan.–Feb. AE, DC, MC, V. *Terrine* (I), Bodanstr. 17 (07531–23718). For lovers of thick hearty soups; over 100 varieties. Open 11.30 A.M. to 9 P.M.

On the **Island of Mainau**, *Schwedenschenke* (M), (07531–303166). Swedish specialty restaurant inside an enormous wine barrel.

Kreuth (Tegernsee). *Zur Post* (E), Nördliche Hauptstr. 5 (08029–1021). 55 rooms, all with own bath. In the town center, with restaurant. Special weekend arrangements. *Bachmair-Weissach* (M), in the Weissach section, Tegernseer Str. 103 (08029–24081). 53 rooms, all with own bath and balcony; some apartments. Large indoor pool, sauna, solarium and massage, sunbathing lawn. Cozy, rustic wine tavern with first-class Bavarian dishes. **Restaurant.** *Gasthof Café Zum Batznhäusl* (M), Am Kurpark (08029–249). Near the river. Good Bavarian specialties and afternoon coffee and cake.

Landsberg Am Lech. *Goggl* (M), Herkomer Str. 19 (08191–2081). 49 rooms, most with own bath. Restaurant. AE, DC, MC. **Restaurants.** *Schmalzbuckl* (M), Neue Bergstr. 7 (08191–47773). Rustic style, atmospheric. *Historisches Wirtshaus Alt Landtsperg* (M), Alte Bergstr. 436 (08191–5838). Historic old inn with fine food. Reservations essential. Closed Wed., Sun. lunch, last 2 weeks in Feb., and Aug. AE, MC.

Langenargen (Bodensee). *Kurhotel Seeterrasse* (E), Obere Seestr. 52 (07543–2350). 80 beds, about half of the rooms with bath. Restaurant with lakeside terrace, heated pool and own beach. *Litz* (M), Obere Seestr. 11 (07543–2212). Rooms with bath and lake view usually higher. Lakeside terrace. *Löwen* (M), Obere Seestr. 4 (07543–3010). *Engel* (M), Marktplatz 3 (07543–2436). DC. *Seemann* (I–M), in town at Obere Seestr. 28 (07543–2579).

Lenggries (Upper Isar Valley). *Brauneckhotel* (M), Münchner Str. 25 (08042–2021). With all the facilities one would expect of an Arabella hotel. Rooms in Bavarian style. Good restaurant serving Bavarian and international specialties. AE, DC, MC, V. *Zum Papyrer* (M), Fleck 5 (08042–2467). 20 double rooms, some without bath in the old building. Located between Lenggries and the Sylvenstein lake. Traditional hotel-restaurant, much frequented by Munich citizens as an excursion trip. Idyllic position, typical Bavarian furnishings and character. First-rate restaurant serving Upper Bavarian specialties, with a good wine list and 11 different brands of beer. *Gästehaus Seemüller* (I), Oberreitrweg 3 (08042–2781). Small, all rooms with a bath or shower. Located in a quiet area at the foot of the Geierstein peak. Indoor pool.

Lindau (Bodensee). *Hotel Bad Schachen* (E), (08382–5011), in the Bad Schachen health resort in the western suburbs. A magnificent castle-like building in its own huge park right on the lakeside. 210 beds and all possible amenities, including beauty farm, tennis, water sports, health cure facilities and acupuncture. Has its own landing stage. AE, DC, MC, V. *Hotel Helvetia* (E), Seepromenade (08382–4002). 60 rooms, 2 apartments, all with bath. On the harbor. Canopied beds, TV, pool, sauna, restaurant, creperie-bistro, bakery. Closed Nov. 15–Feb. AE, DC, MC, V. *Bayerischer Hof* (M), Seepromenade (08382–5055). 172 beds, most with bath. Closed in winter. DC. *Goldenes Lamm* (M), Schafgasse 3 (08382–5732). Oldest and largest inn in Lindau. Restaurant. *Lindauer Hof* (M), Seepromenade (08382–4064). 23 rooms, 17 with shower, 6 with bath; 4 apartments. Stately hotel on the harbor. Indoor pool, sauna, solarium, restaurant. Closed Nov. 15–Mar. 15. AE, MC, V. *Reutemann* (M), Seepromenade (08382–5055). Most rooms with bath. Open all year. DC. *Seegarten* (M), on the Seepromenade (08382–5055). 50 beds. *Zum Stift* (M), Stiftsplatz (08382–4038).

In the market place next to the two churches in the middle of the pedestrian zone. 53 beds. Restaurant with Bavarian and Swabian specialties, as well as a good selection of Bodensee fish.

Restaurants. *Anton Lenz* (E), in nearby Stockenweiler (08388–243). Notable cuisine in country-house setting. Dinner only. *Hoyerberg Schoessle* (E), Hoyerbergstr. 64 (08382–25295). One of the culinary highspots of the Bodensee, with fish and game specialties, 6- and 8-course dinners. Stunning view. Dress is expected. Reservations necessary in summer. Closed Mon. and Feb. AE, DC, MC. *Lieber Augustin* (E), Augustin Arkaden, Ludwigstr. 29 (08382–5055). On the island peninsula, in the arcades. *Spielbank* (E), in the casino building in the city park (08382–5200). Has lakeside terrace. AE, DC, MC. V. *Walliser Stuben* (E), Ludwigstr. 7 (08382–6449). Good value, local style. AE, DC. *Weinstube Frey* (M), Maximilianstr. 15 (08382–5278). Old wine tavern dating from 1560. *Gasthaus Zum Sunfzen* (I), Maximilianstr. 1 (08382–5865). Former patricians' inn, now a local favorite with good regional specialties. Reservations accepted. Closed Feb. AE, DC, MC, V. *Schlechterbräu* (I), In der Grub (08382–5842). Large beer restaurant. Good sausages and Bavarian specialties. Reservations accepted. Closed end–Feb. and mid-Nov. No credit cards.

Meersburg (Bodensee). *Rothmund am See* (M), Uferpromenade 11 (07532–6054). 21 rooms, 3 apartments, 4 suites, all with shower. On the lake front. Perfect for families. Outdoor pool with garden. Closed Nov.–Mar. AE. *Strandhotel Wilder Mann* (M), also on lake front (07532–9011). Outdoor and indoor glassed-in terrace restaurant and café with music and dancing; closed in winter. *Terrassen-Hotel Weisshaar* (M), Stefan-Lochnerstr. 24 (07532–9006). On the hill above the lake, marvelous views. *Zum Bären* (I), Marktplatz 11 (07532–6044). 16 rooms with shower. Atmospheric old inn in center of Old Town. Beautiful restaurant/wine bar. Closed mid-Nov.–mid-Mar. No credit cards.

Restaurants. *Burgkeller* (M) (07532–6028). With garden and musical entertainment. *Winzerstube zum Becher* (M), Höllgasse 4 (07532–9009). Next to the Neuen Schloss; oldest wine tavern on Lake Konstanz, very atmospheric. *Ratskeller* (I), the vaulted Town Hall cellar (07532–9004). AE. *Vinothek Winzerstube* (I), Winzergasse 4 (07532–7510). Well-known and atmospheric wine tavern. *Winzertrinkstube* (I), Steigstr. 33 (07532–6484). Ample portions of Schwabish food. Terrace. Reservations accepted. Closed Dec.–Feb. No credit cards.

Mittenwald (Werdenfelser Land). *Post* (E), Obermarkt 9 (08823–1094). 90 rooms, 10 apartments, 4 suites, most with bath. Three restaurants, garden café, indoor pool, health cure facilities. No credit cards. *Wetterstein* (E), Dekan-Karl-Platz 1 (08823–5058). Indoor pool, health cure facilities, restaurant, bar and café. AE, DC, MC, V. *Wipfelder* (M), Riedkopfstr. 2 (08823 1057). 15 rooms, most with own bath. Riverside terrace. Breakfast only, but 100 meters away has separate first-class *Arnspitze* restaurant at Innsbrucker Str. 68 (08823 2425). *Hotel Rieger* (M), Dekan-Karl-Platz 28 (08823–5071). 46 rooms with bath or shower. Rustic hotel of great charm, with indoor pool, health-cure facilities, sauna, restaurant. Closed Nov.-3rd week of Dec. AE, DC, MC, V.

Alpenhotel Erdt (M), Albert-Schott-Str. 7 (08823–2001). Good food. DC, MC, V. *Gästehaus Franziska* (M), Innsbruckerstr. 24 (08823–5051). Garni.

Comfortable, with garden and good view. AE, DC, MC. *Jagdhaus Drachenburg* (M), Elmauer Weg 20 (08823–1249). View over the town; game specialties in restaurant. AE, MC.

Restaurant. *Alpenrose* (M), Obermarkt 1 (08823–5055). Hearty Bavarian fare, excellent venison dishes in the fall. Reservations advised.

About three km. (two miles) west of Mittenwald is *Sporthotel Lautersee* (E), Am Lautersee 1 (08823–1017). 50 beds. Near the lake of the same name. About five km. (three miles) north is *Tonihof* (M), Brunnenthal 3 (08823–5031). In lovely quiet location, indoor pool.

Murnau (Ammergauer Alps). *Alpenhof* (E), Ramsachsstr. 8 (08841–1045). 52 rooms, all with own bath and tastefully spacious; also some apartments. Near the end of the Munich–Garmisch autobahn and a short distance from Stafelsee. Heated pool, bar; first-class service. Restaurant *Alpenhof* (E) serves typical old Bavarian dishes and nouvelle cuisine. Regina Hotel (E), Seidlpark 2 (08841–2011). 60 rooms and 2 suites, with bath or shower. Quiet location with impressive view of the surrounding mountains from rooms on the south side. All first-class amenities including indoor pool, sauna, health cure facilities, sports room. Restaurant and café. AE, DC, MC. *Pension St. Leonhard* (I), Dorfstr. 3 (08841–1253). In the suburb of Froschhausen, on the lake of the same name. 19 rooms, some with bath. Nearby beach.

Nesselwang (Allgäu). *Bären* (M), Hauptstr. 3 (08361–3255). 25 beds. In the town center. Cozy, established, brewery-Gasthof. Good restaurant with Alpine specialties. DC, MC. *Brauerei-Gasthof-Post* (M), Hauptstr. 25 (08361–238). All rooms with bath or shower. Traditional Gasthof in Allgäu style. Local specialty restaurant, zither music once a week. Beer from their own brewery. *Kur und Sporthotel Alpspitz* (M), Badeseeweg 10 (08361–255). Comfortable rooms with own bath or shower. Health cure facilities. Good restaurant, bar, sun terrace, sports room, swimming pool across the road. AE. *Sportheim Böck* (I), on Alpspitz (1,500 meters or 4,900 ft.) (08361–3111). 30 beds in rustic-style rooms. Wonderful position above town; panoramic restaurant with good cooking. It can only be reached by cable car, followed by a two-minute walk. Baggage delivered separately. Hang-gliding instruction.

Nussdorf (Inn Valley). *Gästehaus Binder* (M), Hochriesweg 7 (08034–2919). 32 beds, all rooms with own bath. Quiet, atmospheric guest house. Terrace, sauna, solarium. No restaurant.

Oberammergau (Werdenfelser Land). *Alois Lang* (E), St. Lukasstr. 15 (08822–4141). 44 rooms with bath or shower. Sauna, solarium, cozy restaurant and bar. AE, DC, MC, V. *Böld* (E), König Ludwigstr. 10 (08822–520). Ring Hotel. 62 rooms, most with bath or shower. Panoramic views, bar, terrace and restaurant. AE, DC, MC, V. *Alte Post* (M), Dorfstr. 19 (08822–6691). Magnificent facade, garden and pleasant Ludwig-Thomas-Stube. AE, MC. *Friedenshöhe* (M), König Ludwigstr. 31 (08822–598). Small, all rooms with bath or shower. AE, MC, V. *Turmwirt* (M), Ettaler Str. 2 (08822–4291). 22 rooms with bath. Hotel band presents regular Bavarian folk evenings. Restaurant. Closed Jan. 10–Jan. 30. AE, DC, MC, V. *Wittelsbach* (M), Dorfstr. 21 (08822–4545). 100 beds. Beer tavern.

AE, DC, MC, V. *Wolf*(M), Dorfstr. 1 (08822–6971). 31 rooms with bath. Bavarian atmosphere. Outdoor pool, sauna, solarium, restaurant. AE, DC, MC, V. *Ambronia* (I), Ettaler Str. 5 (08822–532). 54 beds. Garden restaurant. AE, MC. *Gasthof zur Rose* (I), Dedlerstr. 9 (08822–4706). 29 rooms, most with bath. Lovely view. Restaurant. Closed Nov.–Dec. 15. AE, DC, MC, V. All these hotels offer special 6-day packages from May to Oct.; contact local tourist offices.

Oberstaufen (Allgäu). *Allgäu Sonne* (E), Am Stiessberg 1 (08386–7020). On the hillside with panoramic view. All modern comforts and health cure facilities in rustic surroundings. *Alpina* (E), Am Kurpark (08386–1661). Period furniture in the public rooms; indoor pool. *Löwen* (E), Kirchplatz 8 (08386–2042). Near the church. Colorful chalet-style building. Good restaurant. *Rosenalp* (M), Am Lohacker 5 (08386–7060). All rooms with bath or shower. *Traube* (M), (08325–451). Ring Hotel in nearby Thalkirchdorf. AE, DC, MC, V.

Oberstdorf (Allgäu). *Kurhotel Adula* (E), in Jauchen outskirts, In der Leite 6 (08322–7090). 130 beds, all rooms with bath and balcony. Indoor pool, cure facilities, rustic bar and restaurant. *Parkhotel Frank* (E), Sachsenweg 11 (08322–5555). One of the town's most comfortable hotels. AE, MC. *Alpenhof*(M), Zweistapfenweg 6 (08322–3095). 45 beds, built in Allgäu country style; indoor and heated outdoor pools. AE. *Filser* (M), Freibergstr. 15 (08322–1020). 150 beds. Excellent restaurant, indoor pool, cure facilities. *Wiese* (M), Stillachstr. 4A (08322–3030). Beautiful view; quiet and with a cozy atmosphere. Breakfast only. *Wittelsbacher Hof* (M), Prinzenstr. 24 (08322–1018). 115 beds, many rooms with bath. Noted restaurant, bar, heated pool (closed Apr. and May, Oct. to mid-Dec.).

Nine km. (5 miles) south of town in the Stillachtal valley is *Alpengasthof Pension Birgsau* (I), (08322–4036). Very quiet location, bus connection into town, all rooms with bath or shower. Short distance from Felhornbahn cable-car station, and ideal as a starting-out point for summer walking or winter cross-country skiing. Good food.

Pfronten (Allgäu). *Bavaria* (E), Kienbergstr. 62 (08363–5004). In the Dorf section. Luxurious; good view, convenient for hiking or skiing. *Flora* (M), Auf der Geigerhalde 43 (08363–5071). Quietly located in own grounds, in Weissbach; large terrace and sunbathing lawn. Fine view of the mountains from all rooms. AE, DC, MC, V. *Post* (M), Kemptener Str. 14 (08363–5032). 27 rooms, all those in the main building with own bath; some rooms in a connecting annex, where it is quieter and the mountain view better. Quaint, rustic-style restaurant. AE, DC, V. *Schlossanger-Alp* (M), in the Obermeilingen section, Schlossanger 1 (08363–381). 15 rooms, most with own bath, and 16 apartments. Indoor pool, sauna, solarium and cross-country skiing on the doorstep. Restaurant specializing in health foods. AE, DC, MC, V. *Haus Achtal* (I), in the Dorf district, Brentenjochstr. 4 (08363–8329). 16 rooms and one apartment. Indoor pool, sauna, solarium. No restaurant. *Pension Pfronter Blick* (I), Burgweg 25, in the Meilingen section (08363–8568). Very quiet location; rooms in rustic style, cozy lounge with open fireplace. Ski instructor in house.

Reit Im Winkl (Chiemgau). *Steinbacher Hof* (E), Steinbachweg 10, in the Blindau section (08640–8410). All rooms with bath. On hillside, with a ski lift. Quiet and luxurious with a fine view. Indoor pool. *Unterwirt* (E), Kirchplatz 2 (08640–8811). 69 rooms, most with bath. Pool, bar and restaurant. Open year-round. *Pension Sonnenblick* (M), Dorfstr. 49 (08640–8261). Indoor pool. *Post* (M), Kirchplatz 7 (08640–1024). Garden and sun terrace. *Alpengasthof Augustiner* (I) Klammweg 2 (08640–8235). 25 beds. At Winklmoosalm (1,158 meters or 3,800 ft.) about 11 km. (seven miles) southeast of Reit im Winkl; with restaurant.

Restaurant. *Kupferkanne* (I), Weitseestr. 18 (08640–1450). Good country fare with some interesting Austrian specialties. Reservations advised. Closed Sat. and Nov. DC, MC.

Rottach Egern (Tegernsee). *Bachmair am See* (E) Seestr. 47 (08022–2720). First class international complex on lakefront with 400 beds in its eight buildings; all rooms and apartments with bath. Seven restaurants, particularly good is the *Barthlmä-Stuben* for atmosphere. Dancing and entertainment in nightclub. Indoor and heated outdoor pools; also well known for its beauty farm. AE, DC. *Seehotel Überfahrt* (E), Uberfahrtstr. 7, also on lakefront (08022–26001). Nearly as large with indoor pool, lakeside terrace, nightclub. AE, DC, MC. *Bachmair-Weissach* (M), at Weissach, Tegernseestr. 103 (08022–24081). 35 rooms. Excellent Bavarian specialties in attractive restaurant. AE, DC, MC. *Hotel Jaedicke* (M), Aribostr. 17–23 (08022–2780). 45 rooms, individually decorated and offering the highest standard of comfort, but accommodations are mostly in large self-contained apartments with balcony or terrace; hotel service is optional. Set in its own beautiful park. Cozy café with superb home-made pastries, but no restaurant. AE, MC. *Wallberghotel* (I), at the top of the Wallberg cable car (08022–6800).

Restaurant. *La Cuisine* (E), Südliche Hauptstr. 2 (08022–24764). On the first floor of a shopping arcade in the town center. Splendid décor and first-class French cuisine and extensive wine list. Among the best restaurants on Tegernsee lake. AE, DC, MC, V. *Café-Restaurant Alpenwildpark* (M), at cable car departure station (08022–5832). With sun terrace.

Ruhpolding (Chiemgau). *Steinbach* (E), Maiergschwendterstr. 10 (08663–1644). Ruhpolding's largest hotel with 167 beds with bath or shower, balcony or terrace. Many rooms with hand-painted rustic furniture. Self-service breakfast buffet, *Pils* tavern and fine food in the *Hobelspan* restaurant. *Zur Post* (E), Hauptstr. 35 (08663–1035). 100 beds, most with bath. 650 year-old Gasthof, tastefully furnished in traditional style. Heated indoor pool, sauna, solarium, terrace. First-class restaurant and dancing every evening.

Ruhpoldinger Hof (M), Hauptstr. 30 (08663–1212). 76 beds, most rooms with bath or shower. Central position. Indoor pool with underwater massage. First-class food, particularly from own trout farm. Dancing. AE, DC, MC. *Sporthotel am Westernberg* (M), Am Wundergraben 4 (08663–1674). A Ring Hotel. 70 beds. On hillside with panoramic view. Indoor pool, thermal baths, sauna and fitness center and restaurant. AE, DC, MC, V.

Haus Heidelberg (I), Brettreichweg 4 (08663–9215). Particularly quiet and comfortable. *Hotel-Garni Alpina* (I), Niederfeldstr. 11 (08663–9905). Elegant, rustic. No restaurant.

Scheidegg (Allgäu). *Kurhotel Scheidegg (Silence Hotel)* (E), Kurstr. 18 (08381–3041). All rooms and apartments with bath and balcony. Beautiful view of the Alps. Indoor pool, tennis, ice-skating, Kneipp water cures. Restaurant, bar. Pension terms only. DC, MC. *Gästehaus Allgäu* (M), Am Brunnenbühl 11 (08381–5250). 14 rooms, all with own bath; one holiday flat. Quiet with a fine view. *Gästehaus Bergblick* (I), Am Brunnenbühl 12 (08381–7291). 14 rooms. Small and quiet with good view. No restaurant.

Schliersee (Schliersee). *Schliersee Hotel Arabella* (E), Kirchbichlweg 18 (08026–4086). 130 luxurious rooms, apartments and holiday flats, all with balconies or terraces. Indoor pool, sauna, solarium, cure facilities, bowling, rustic-style *St. Sixtus Stube* restaurant and cozy wine and beer taverns with open fireplaces. DC. *Hotel Reiter* (M), Risseckstr. 8 (08026–6010). 29 rooms, most with bath or shower; two apartments. Quietly-located (Silence Hotel) on hillside above the lake, with fine views of the lake and mountains. Indoor pool, sun terrace, cozy bar with open fireplace. *Schlierseer Hof-am See* (M) Seestr. 21 (08026–4071). 80 beds. Lakeside terrace, own lake facilities. AE, MC. *Haus Vogelsang* (I), Waldschmidtstr. 5 (08026–7308). 24 beds. Breakfast buffet, sauna, terrace. *Postgasthof-Café St. Bernhard* (I), Seeweg 1 (08026–71011). Terrace and lake swimming. V.

In the *Spitzingsee* section, high above Schliersee on the mountain lake of the same name: *Spitzingsee Hotel* (E), Spitzingstr. 5 (08026–7081). 84 rooms. A luxurious Arabella hotel right on the lakeside with a fine panorama of the surrounding mountains and forest. Two restaurants. AE, DC, MC, V.

Restaurant. *Ratskeller* (I), Rathausstr. 1a (08026–4786). A place to meet the locals. Wholesome Bavarian food. Closed Mon. and last 3 weeks in Nov. and Feb. No credit cards.

Schönau (Berchtesgadener Land). *Alpenhof* (E), Richard Voss Str. 30 (08652–6020). 80 beds, all rooms with own bath. First-class cure-hotel in the middle of the Alpine National Park. Indoor pool, sauna. *Stoll's Alpina* (E), Ulmenweg 14–16 (08652–5091). Two hotel buildings and some apartments in their own park. Indoor and outdoor heated pools, sauna. Fine rustic restaurant serving Bavarian and international specialties. *Zechmeisterlehen* (M), Wahlstr. 35 (08652–3897). 55 beds, most rooms with bath, seven apartments. Stands amidst its own meadowland, ideal for winter and summer sports. Indoor pool, restaurant. Generous breakfast buffet.

Schongau (Ammergauer Alps). *Alte Post* (M), Marienplatz 19 (08861–8058). In the town center with café and restaurant. *Holl* (M), Altenstädter Str. 39 (08861–7292). 50 beds, all rooms with own bath; one apartment and one holiday flat. Quiet location with a fine view. Restaurant serves fresh and imaginative fish dishes. AE, DC, MC, V.

Sonthofen (Allgäu). *Der Allgäu Stern* (E), Auf der Staiger Alp (08321–4012). 870 beds, 150 apartments. On the heights above the town with a wonderful view, set in its own park. Kingly establishment with every imaginable facility, including health cures. Three restaurants and nightclub entertainment. AE, DC, MC, V. *Sonnenalp* (E), outside and above the town at Ofterschwang (08321–720). 222 rooms and apartments. Cure hotel and paradise for sportsmen and women: 26 different sports to indulge in, including riding, golf, tennis, swimming and skiing. Three first-class restaurants; beer cellars and bars. Has one of the best breakfast buffets in Germany. Fine view. *Allgäuer Berghof* (M), also in Ofterschwang (08321–4061). 69 rooms, most with own bath. At 1,300 meters (4,200 ft.), it can be reached from Sonthofen and Bihlerdorf by a private toll road. Indoor pool, sauna, solarium, tennis, health cure facilities. Isolated location with a panoramic view.

Starnbergersee (Ammergauer Alps). In **Starnberg** itself— *Bayerischer Hof* (M), in front of the station (08151–12133). Has a garden restaurant, café and tennis. AE, DC, MC. *Seehof* (M), Bahnhofsplatz 4 (08151–6001). Has good *Ristorante Romagna* Italian restaurant, a lakefront café and a dance bar. AE, V. *Tutzinger Hof* (M), Tutzinger Hof Platz (08151–3081). 65 beds, all rooms with own bath. Terrace and restaurant noted for its Bavarian specialties. AE, DC, MC, V.

Restaurant. *Seerestaurant Undosa* (M), in Starnberg, right on the lakeside (08151–12144). Garden restaurant. Openair dancing in summer on Sunday afternoons. AE, MC.

In **Berg**—*Strandhotel Schloss Berg* (M), right on the lake. Seestr. 17 (08151–50021). 40 beds, ten baths. Grill specialties in the restaurant. Bar, tennis, lake swimming, ferry landing-stage.

In **Feldafing**—*Golf-Hotel Kaiserin Elisabeth* (M), Tutzingerstr. 2–6 (08157–1013). 125 beds. On golf course in lovely country surroundings. Outdoor dining terrace, bar, tennis, riding and swimming facilities. Schroth cures. Departure point for excursions by colorful old stagecoach. AE, DC, MC, V.

In **Tutzing**—*Hotel-Restaurant Café am See* (M), Marienstr. 16 (08158–490). 45 beds, including apartments, some self-catering. Good restaurant serving freshly caught fish. Lakeside.

Restaurant. *Forsthaus Ilkahöhe* (M), auf der Ilka-Höhe (08158–8242), with a superb view from the terrace or upstairs veranda. Excellent cuisine in typically Bavarian surroundings. Off the road to Weilheim.

Tegernsee (Tegernsee). *Bastenhaus am See* (E), Hauptstr. 71 (08022–3080). 36 beds. In the main street, but with a lakeside garden. Good food, particularly local fish. Own beach. *Haus Bayern* (E), Neureutherstr. 23 (08022–1820). On the slopes above the lake, in its own park. Indoor pool, sauna, fitness room, bowling. Restaurant with a terrace café. AE, DC, MC. *Fischerstüberl am See* (M), Seestr. 51 (08022–4672). In one of the most beautiful locations in the Schlossbucht Bay. A few minutes' walk from an outdoor pool; large sunbathing terrace. Well-known for the good food in its restaurant, particularly fish. *Luitpold* (M), Hauptstr. 42 (08022–4681). Also on the lakefront, all rooms have a view over the lake, balcony and bath or shower. Indoor pool and rustic restaurant. DC. *Seehotel zur Post* (M), Seestr. 3 (08022–3951). On the lakefront, all rooms with bath. Good terrace restaurant and café. AE, DC, MC.

Restaurants. *Weinstub'n "Zum Brendl"* (M), Hauptstr. 8 (08022–

4502). Cozy cellar-tavern with local and international dishes. Music until 1 A.M. *Berggasthof Lieberhof* (I), Neureutherstr. 52 (08022–4163). Quiet location above the lake. Small, colorful tavern. *Herzogliches Bräustuberl* (I), Schlossplatz 1 (08022–4141). Former monastery, now a popular brewery-restaurant. Beer brewed on the premises. Good views. No credit cards.

Traunstein (Chiemgau). *Parkhotel Traunsteinerhof* (M), Bahnhofstr. 11 (0861–69041). 62 rooms, most with own bath. Restaurant. AE, DC.

Restaurant. *Brauereigasthof Schnitzlbaumer* (M), Stadtplatz 13 (0861–4534). In the center of the market square. In addition to the traditional Bavarian dishes on the menu, a wide variety of international gourmet dishes are served, including fish from Chiemsee.

Überlingen (Bodensee). *Parkhotel St. Leonhard* (M), Obere-St.-Leonhard-Str. 83 (07551–8080). 158 rooms, 2 suites, all with bath or shower. Quietly located (Silence Hotel) on the slopes above the lake, with a lovely view from the sun terrace. Own park with a wild game reserve. Modern rooms, indoor pool, tennis courts and billiard room. Restaurant serving international and Swabian specialties. AE. *Ochsen* (M), Munsterstr. 48 (07551–4067). Excellent location for sailing; good facilities. AE, DC, MC, v. *Gasthof Engel* (I), Hafenstr. 1 (07551–63412). Wine tavern.

Restaurant. *Romantik Hotel Hecht* (M), Munsterstr. 8 (07551–63333). Has a fine restaurant in the 200-year-old *Weinstube.* Good value specialty is the eight-course meal. Reservations necessary. Closed Mon. and Feb. AE, DC, MC, V.

Wasserburg (Bodensee). *Schloss Wasserburg* (E), Hauptstr. 5 (08382–5692). 14 rooms, most with bath or shower. Hotel in 8th-century castle on an island peninsula; panoramic view, terrace, pool on the lakeside, restaurant. *Pfälzer Hof* (M), Hauptstr. 83 (08382–6511). Small, 13 rooms; garden restaurant. *Haus des Gastes* (I), Hauptstr. 12 (08382–24848). Pleasant Gasthof-restaurant with seven rooms, all with own bath or shower. Fine terrace view.

Wasserburg Am Inn (Inn Valley). *Fletzinger* (M), Fletzingergasse 1 (08071–8010). 30 rooms, about half with own bath. Restaurant. AE, DC, MC. *Paulaner Stuben* (I), Marienplatz 9 (08071–3903). 19 rooms, most with own bath or shower. Fine view from the terrace. Restaurant. AE.

Wendelstein (Schliersee). *Berghotel Wendelstein* (I), near the top of the 1,800-meter (6,000-ft.) mountain of Wendelstein. The oldest mountain hotel in the Bavarian Alps, built in 1833. 60 beds. Restaurant, bar, café. Rather crowded in summer.

CAMPING AND YOUTH HOSTELS. Camping. Campsites are plentiful throughout the region, most of them well equipped and picturesquely located with a large number also open throughout the winter. General information and free brochures may be obtained from the Camping Section of the *ADAC Auto Club,* Camping Referat, Hauptverwaltung, Baumgartnerstr. 53, 8000 München 70 (089–76761) or from the respective regional and local tourist offices:

For Munich and Upper Bavaria: *Fremdenverkehrsverein Oberbayern,* Sonnenstr. 10, 8000 München 2. For Lake Constance region: *Fremden-verkehrsverband Bodensee-Oberschwaben,* Schützenstr. 8, 7750 Konstanz (ask for brochure "Camping Baden-Wurttemberg"). For Berchtesgadener Land, write to: *Kurdirektion, Berchtesgadener Land,* Königsseer Str. 2, 8240 Berchtesgaden.

Youth Hostels. For general information on youth hostels in the region, inquire at the headquarters of the Bavarian. Section of the German Youth Hostel Association in Munich: *Landesverband des Deutschen Jugendher-bergswerkes,* Mauerkircherstr. 5, 8000 Munchen 80 (089–987451).

MOUNTAIN HUTS. There are many mountain huts and hostelries dotted all over the alpine region offering simple accommodation, with or without breakfast, for hikers and climbers. These *Berghütten* generally belong to the German Alpine Association (Deutsche Alpenverein) and are run by a landlord or innkeeper. For those huts which are not run by anyone and provide overnight accommodation only, keys must usually be picked up from an address in the nearest town or village, and returned afterwards. The local tourist offices can provide lists of available mountain hut accommodation, or, if you already belong to an alpine club of some kind, you can obtain a list of huts open to members of the German Alpine Association only. (See *Facts at Your Fingertips,* Addresses).

TOURIST INFORMATION. There are two regional tourist offices for the whole area: the *Fremdenverkehrs verein Allgäu Bayerisch-Schwaben,* Fuggerstr. 9, D-8900 Augsburg (0821–33335) and the *FVV Bodensee-Oberschwaben,* 8 Schützenstr. 7750, Konstanz (07531–22232) cover the Allgäu and Bodensee areas. In addition the *FVV München-Oberbayern,* Sonnenstr. 10, 8000 München 2, (089–597347) covers the whole of southern Bavaria and the Bavarian Alps. A selection of local tourist offices (some providing an accommodations booking service) is as follows:

Augsburg, *Verkehrsverein,* Bahnhofstr. 7, 8900 Augsburg (0821–502070). **Bad Reichenhall,** *Kur-und-Verkehrsverein,* im Hauptbah-nhof-Nebenbau, 8230 Bad Reichenhall (08651–3003). **Bad Tölz,** *Kurverw-altung,* Ludwigstr. 11, 8170 Bad Tölz (08041–70071). **Bayrischzell,** *Kuramt,* Kirchplatz 2, 8163 Bayrischzell (08023–648). **Berchtesgaden,** *Kurdirektion,* Königsseer Str. 2, 8240 Berchtesgaden, (08652–5011). **Gar-misch-Partenkirchen,** *Verkehrsamt der Kurverwaltung,* Bahnhofstr. 34, 8100 Garmisch-Partenkirchen (08821–18022). **Lindau,** *Verkehrsverein am Hauptbahnhof* (at main station), 8990 Lindau, (08382–5022). **Mittenwald,** *Kurverwaltung,* Dammkarstr. 3, 8102 Mittenwald (08823–1051). **Oberam-mergau,** *Verkehrsamt,* Eugen-Papst-Str. 9a, 8103 Oberammergau (08822–4921). **Prien am Chiemsee,** *Kurverwaltung,* Am Bahnhof 8210 Prien (08051–3031). **Reit-im-Winkl,** *Verkehrsamt,* Rathausplatz 1, 8216 Reit-im-Winkl (08640–8207). **Rottach-Egern,** *Kuramt,* Nördliche Haupt-tstr. 9, 8183 Rottach-Egern (08022–671341). **Wasserburg,** *Verkehrsverein,* im Rathaus, 8090 Wasserburg am Inn (08071–3061).

HOW TO GET AROUND. By air. The main airport for the region is, understandably, Munich, from where buses transfer you to the main railway station for connections to the rest of the region. If you are travelling with a package tour, the transfer buses will be at the airport to meet you and drive you to your holiday destination. Stuttgart is a connecting airport for the Friedrichshafen Delta airline serving the Bodensee, and there is also a direct express rail route from Zurich (Kloten) Airport to Lindau.

By train. Munich once again is the big rail center for southern Germany, with the main FD (Fern-Express) and Inter-City express lines running to Lindau, Kufstein (and on to Innsbruck) and through to Salzburg and Vienna. Four of the FD Express Trains, the *Berchtesgaden, Königsee, Chiemgau* and *Wörthersee,* connect the Rhine and Ruhr areas of northern Germany and Hamburg and Hanover respectively with the Berchtesgadener Land, as well as Inter City routes from Hamburg, Bremen, Dortmund, Hanover and Münster, and the new express (D-Zug) connection from Karlsruhe, in addition to the existing direct express lines from Kassel and Trier. Augsburg is the main rail terminus for the Allgau.

By bus. Augsburg and Munich are both main stops on the Europabus Romantic Road and other long-distance bus routes. The network of Bahn- and Postbuses (German Railways and German Post buses) is particularly far-reaching and connects all those resorts to which there are no, or only inconvenient, rail services. In Garmisch Partenkirchen, for example, there is a regular nostalgic post bus service throughout the summer months between the rail station and Badersee lake. In addition, private coach companies organize excursion tours from almost every town and these day trips are very good value for sightseeing. Inquire at local tourist offices and travel agents, such as the *ABR* (official Bavarian Travel Agent).

A good number of popular winter sports resorts have shuttle bus services to take skiers to and from the ski lifts. Also, in some places (such as Ruhpolding), buses connect the various outlying pensions with the town or resort center, free of charge for guests possessing a *Gästekarte* or *Kurkarte* pass (available from the Tourist Office for a small fee). Inquire at the Tourist Offices for "Pendelbusverkehr." There are also reductions on various trains and buses.

By bike. Cycling in the Alps is not quite as mad as it sounds; or, at any rate, cycling in the Alpine lowlands along the valleys of the rivers Isar, Mangfall, Loisach, Inn and Lech, and around lake Chiemsee and the east Allgaü. Many of these areas are both reasonably flat and, bizarre as it may at first seem, ideal for cycling, with good roads and a positive surfeit of magnificent scenery; plus plenty of strategically placed inns and gasthofs where you can quench your thirst and still your appetite. (There are even specialized cyclists' inns known as "Radler Einkehr," easily recognized by the bicycles propped up outside and the sportily-clad Bavarians inside or in the beer garden quaffing *Radler,* a mixture of beer and lemonade much favored by the experienced Alpine cyclist). One exceptionally pretty route is the 31-km. (19-mile) cycling path connecting the resorts of Reit im Wirkl, Ruhpolding, and Inzell, which goes through some of the beautiful scenery of the region's nature park.

The Bavarian Regional Tourist Office in Munich (see *Tourist Information* above) produces a good brochure detailing cycling routes and organizations in Upper Bavaria. While the Ammersee and Lech Tourist Office (Von Kühlmann Str. 15, 8910 Landsberg/Lech) also produces a brochure detailing 11 different cycling routes, all starting from an S-Bahn station and all taking in at least one bathing spot and one gasthof en route. The regional tourist office for the Bodensee area lists local resorts—52 in all—with bikes for hire.

As ever, bicycles can be hired from many rail stations and Tourist Offices.

Mountain railways and cable cars. Mountain railways, cable cars, chairlifts or cogwheel railways (*Seilbahn, Sessellift, Zahnradbahn*) serve practically all the major mountains in the Alps, affording easy access to vantage points with panoramic views, and high-altitude walking routes in summer, and of course skiing in winter. The Zugspitz at Garmisch-Partenkirchen (at almost 3,000 meters or 10,000 ft. Germany's highest mountain) is served by both a cogwheel railway from the Zugspitz Railroad Station, and a spectacular cable car from Eibsee. Both are rather expensive. The cogwheel railway departs from Zugspitz Station—connecting with main line trains—and travels via Grainau and Eibsee, costing a pricey DM.45 return (in winter 42 in conjunction with a ski-pass) through a tunnel, right to the summit of the Zugspitz. The journey takes just under an hour.

The other giant peaks in the same group—the Alpspitz (7,284 ft.), the Wank (5,840 ft.), the Hausberg and Kreuzeck (5,420 ft.)—are served by a further five cable cars: the *Osterfelderbahn,* up to the 6,150-ft. Osterfelderkopf on the Alpspitz; the *Wankbahn,* from the center of Partenkirchen up to 5,340 ft. on the Wank; the *Hausbergbahn,* up to 4,044 ft.; the *Kreuzeckbahn,* up to 4,041 ft.; the *Eckbauerbahn,* from the cable-car station next to the Olympic Stadium to the panoramic and sundrenched Eckbauer peak, 3,678 ft.

Other important mountain railways in the region are at: Aschau, Kampenwandbahn, 4,500 ft.; Bad Reichenhall, Predigstuhlbahn, 4,840 ft.; Bad Tölz, Blombergbahn, 3,650 ft.; Bayerischzell, Wendelsteinbahn, 5,170 ft.; Berchtesgaden, Jennerbahn, 5,400 ft.; and Obersalzbergbahn 3,060 ft.; Kleinwalsertal, Kanzelwandbahn, 6,000 ft.; Lenggries, Brauneckbahn, 4,650 ft.; Mittenwald, Karwendelbahn, 6,730 ft.; Oberammergau, Laberbergbahn, 5,040 ft.; Oberstdorf, Nebelhornbahn, 5,800 ft. and Fellhornbahn, 4,500 ft.; Pfronten, Breitenbergbahn, 4,500 ft.; Rottach-Egern, Wallbergbahn, 4,850 ft.; Ruhpolding, Rauschbergbahn, 4,900 ft.; Samerberg, Hochriesbahn, 4,650 ft.; Schliersee, Schliersbergbahn, 3,180 ft.; Schwangau, Tegelbergbahn, 5,160 ft.; Spitzingsee, Taubensteinbahn, 4,840 ft.

By car. The main autobahn routes into the Alpine region are the A7 from the northwest (Ulm and Kempsten); from the northeast the A95 (E6) via Munich; from the west via Lake Konstanz, the A96; and from the south the E533 from Innsbruck—the last two of these are still incomplete with long stretches of regular highway, the most important of which is the Lindau to Munich stretch, the B12 or B18.

One road of particular scenic interest is the Deutsche Alpenstrasse (German Alpine Road), which runs all the way from Lindau on the Bodensee to Berchtesgaden. It passes some of the most beautiful mountain scenery in Europe, but as it is still incomplete, some detours into the lowlands are necessary. Another scenic route that begins (or ends!) in this region is the Romantische Strasse (Romantic Road) running from Fussen, near the Royal Castles, north to Würzburg. Other scenic routes running through the Allgäu are: the Oberschwäbische Barockstrasse (of architectural interest); the Schwäbische Dichter Strasse (for lovers of poets and poetry); and the Schwäbische Bader Strasse (thermal spa tour).

Or you can take the B20 road—the Blaue Route (Blue Route)—which follows the valleys of the Inn and the Salzach east of Munich and takes

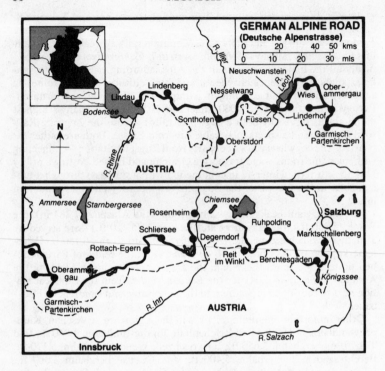

in some beautifully tranquil and unspoilt scenery such as the Waginger See and Abtsdorfer See, two little-known bathing lakes, the warmest in Upper Bavaria and a paradise for family excursions.

From Wasserburg on the River Inn to Traunstein on Chiemsee lake and on to Berchtesgaden is the southermost stretch of the long Deutsche Ferienstrasse (German Holiday Road) which runs the length of West Germany from Kiel on the Baltic coast to the Alps. The B304, 305 and 306 take in such towns as Amerang with its famous castle, Seebruck, Prien and Chieming on Chiemsee lake, the Chiemgau mountains, on through Inzell, Weissach, Schneizelreuth, Unterjettenberg and the Raumsau with its idyllic alpine scenery and past the magnificent Watzmann peak to its destination in Berchtesgaden.

It should be noted that some mountain roads in the Alps are toll-roads, usually forest roads, for which you must pay a fee at the start of the particular stretch where you see the sign *Maut.*

By boat. Try a trip on the Bodensee with the German-Austrian-Swiss Weisse Flotte (White Fleet) which has been ferrying passengers on Lake Constance for 120 years. There is a Bodensee Pass available for about DM.70, and valid for 15 days, on 7 of which free trips on all ferryboats and regular cruise ships, and on the remaining 8 days, a reduction of 50%. On all 15 days you are entitled to reduced fares on all excursion trips in the area, as well as local rail, bus and mountain railway services.

There are also good car-ferry services across the lake linking Germany, Austria and Switzerland.

Inquiries about cruises on Lake Chiemsee ("the Bavarian Sea") can be made at *Chiemsee Schiffahrt,* L. Fessler, Seestr. 108, 8210 Prien (08051–1510). Steamer services are also available on the Ammersee, Starnberger, Königsee and Tegernsee. Information from local tourist offices or the German railways.

Rowing boats, pedal, sail and electric boats may be hired at all of these large lakes. One of the main attractions of Fünf Seen Land (Five Lakes Land), as the lakes Ammersee, Wörthsee, Wesslingersee, Pilsensee and Starnbergersee southwest of Munich are known, is the hire of rowboats rented out by fishermen for about DM.6 an hour. Motorboats would cost between DM. 15 and 20 an hour.

SPORTS. There is pretty well every sport imaginable available in this region—something for everyone. Summer sporting activities include swimming, surfing, sailing, hiking, cycling, riding, mountain-climbing, hang-gliding or just plain sunbathing. Then there is the vast spectrum of winter sports activities: skiing, tobogganing, ice-skating, curling, sleigh-riding or just après-ski for the less sport-minded. The following is just a small selection of what sports you can take part in and where, but for more details inquire at the regional and local tourist offices (see *Tourist Information* and *Useful Addresses*). The Allgäu tourist association, for example, offer interesting sports packages as combination holidays, in particular at Fischen, Füssen, Lindau, Nesselwang and Oberstaufen.

Swimming. You can swim in all lakes. Modern indoor pools can be found in Garmisch-Partenkirchen (*Alpspitz Wellenbad,* with waves, is one of the finest swimming-pools and fitness centers in Europe), in Berchtesgaden, Bad Reichenhall (salt water), Bad Tölz (*Alpamare* with waves and fitness center), Oberammergau (Wollenberg, with waves) in Inzell and Kochel (*Trimini* fitness center), and the beautifully situated lake establishments near Füssen.

Sailing and Windsurfing. On all principal lakes. There are sailing and windsurfing schools at Füssen, Immenstadt, Nesselwang, Isny and Lindau in the Allgäu; on Chiemsee at Bernau, Chieming, Gstadt, Prien, Seebrück, Übersee and Waging am See; and on Tegernsee, Starnbergersee and Ammersee. One of the best lakes for windsurfing is the *Walchensee,* because of its good air currents, and on the same lake there is a recently opened diving school at Einsiedel for exploring the depths of the crystal clear waters on a sort of Alpine underwater safari. Information from the Kurverwaltung (Cure Offices) in Mittenwald.

Water-skiing. Possible at Immenstadt and Lindau on the Bodensee and on some parts of Starnberger and Ammersee. Best for **kayaking** are the Isar from Bad Tölz through Munich-Landshut to the Danube near Deggendorf; the Inn from the Austrian border at Kufstein through Rosenheim, Wasserburg, Neu-Otting and along the German-Austrian border to Passau (easy) and at Schleching near Reit im Winkl in turbulent mountain waters.

The Lech River is also good for kayaking; it is very scenic from Füssen to Schongau and difficult in some spots; from Schongau to Landsberg it goes through artificial lakes and dams (nine portages), and from Landsberg to Augsburg it is easy.

Tennis. There are courts in all spas and resorts, some indoor and open year-round. **Golf** courses can be found in Garmisch, Berchtesgaden, Bad

Tölz, Augsburg, Chiemsee, Bad Wiessee, Feldafing on Starnberger Lake, Wörthsee and Lindau, Ottobeuren and Bad Waldsee in the Allgäu. There are American-run golf courses at Gmund on the Tegernsee and at Obersalzburg, Berchtesgaden (9 holes, 3,300 feet up, with a distracting view of the Watzmann range). The latter is open for play from May through October; tel. 08652–2100 for information. A spectacular 18-hole course is located at Bad Wiessee, high above the Tegernsee; tel. 08022–8769.

Bowling. Many resort hotels have their own bowling alleys (usually English-style skittles; rarely 10 pin). The *Hotel Bayerischer Hof* in Bad Reichenhall (08651–5084) organizes skittle weeks from March to June. The DM.535 cost includes half-pension, unlimited skittling, and two competitions with prizes.

Horseback riding. There are schools and facilities in many areas, including Amerang, Aschau and Chieming around Chiemsee Lake, at Ruhpolding, Tittmoning and Traunstein in the Chiemgauer Land, in Berchtesgaden and Oberstdorf in the Allgau and in Augsburg. Prices for an hour or more's ride out are expensive, and if you are really keen on horseback riding as a holiday pastime it is better value to book one of the all-inclusive holiday-sport-packages, where the price includes bed and breakfast and riding lessons. The tourist office of the Allgäu has some attractive offers.

Hang-gliding. See the Alps from above. If hang-gliding's your thing, tel. 08822–520 or 08822–4470 in Oberammergau.

Fishing. Good in almost all the streams and lakes but you must have a permit, usually available from the tourist office or from the local gamekeeper. Once again, you can book all-inclusive angling holidays through the various tourist offices, where permit formalities are taken care of for you. The holiday region of East Allgäu between the River Lech and the Bodensee has some of the best stocked fishing waters. Such Allgäu towns as Immenstadt and Fischen offer seven-day packages for anglers for as little as DM.212, including bed and breakfast, a four-day angling permit and other extras. Inquire from the *Verkehrsamt Immenstadt,* Marienplatz 3, 8970 Immenstadt, *Verkehrsamt Fischen,* 8975 Fischen i. Allgäu, or for general information from the *Fremdenverkehrsband Allgäu Bayerisch Schwaben* (see *Tourist Information*).

Bicycling. Most local rail stations have bikes to rent at DM.10 per day; half that if you have a valid train ticket. Many local sports shops also have limited numbers of bikes for rent: Try *Sport Eich,* Fendtgasse 5, Oberammergau, and *Sport Bittner,* Andreas-Fendt-Ring 1, Bischofswiesen, near Berchtesgaden. The Bavarian regional tourist office in Munich (see Tourist Information) issues a regularly updated booklet on recommended cycling routes. A particularly striking route runs between the resorts of Reit im Winkl, Ruhpolding, and Inzell, and is 32 kilometers (19 miles) long. Bikes can be rented from the rail station at Ruhpolding.

Hiking and Mountain Walking. As indigenous a pastime to the Alps as the lederhosen-clad locals who participate almost every Sunday. Depending on your level of fitness, and your clothing and equipment, there are virtually unlimited possibilities for hiking and mountain walking tours. It would not be possible for us to name all the centers with starting points for Alpine walking tours here. Every local tourist office can supply you with a hiking-map (*Wanderkarte*) of the area, with suggestions for mountain tours according to the degree of difficulty you want to attempt. Every excursion by foot into the mountains should be undertaken with care and in accordance with a few simple rules: take note of weather-forecasts, advice and warnings from the locals and mountain guides. Never start a mountain tour without wearing sturdy, warm and heavy-soled (with a good tread) shoes and taking some kind of waterproof clothing with you. Mountain weather is very changeable. Before setting off, always leave details of your destination with someone in your resort, so that in case of accident, the Mountain Rescue Squad (*Bergwacht*) can search in the right area. Also, in summer and winter, check the daily avalanche report (*Lawinenbericht*) displayed in every winter sports center, usually at the ski-lift station or tourist office.

Hiking trails are well marked—in mountainous regions usually in red or blue—and usually lead to a panoramic viewpoint. Hiking round-trips are organized by most of the larger tourist centers. These can either be individual day trips along suggested routes, organized hikes with guide, or inclusive arrangements lasting two or more days with bed and breakfast accommodation.

Full information about all forms of mountain walking and hiking can be obtained from the *Deutsche Alpenverein* (German Alpine Association) at Praterinsel 5, 8000 Munchen 22 (089–293086). They can also issue you with lists of mountain huts, guides, routes, etc. Naturally, members of the Association are given preferential treatment, and quite often fill up the mountain lodges in advance.

Mountain Climbing. The Bavarian Alps are the most important climbing region in Germany. An efficiently-run net of mountain lodges provides direct access to rock faces and mountain guides are available at all important points of departure; Garmisch-Partenkirchen has a school (Bergsteigerschule Zugspitze) as does the Berchtesgadener Land in Straub. The principal valley bases are: Garmisch and Grainau for the Wetterstein group, which includes Zugspitze; Mittenwald and Krün for the Karwendel group; Rottach-Egern, Wildbad Kreuth, and Bayrischzell for the German offshoots of the Mangfall group, most of which is in Austria; Berchtesgaden, Ramsau, and Bad Reichenhall for the Berchtesgaden Alps; Hindelang and Oberstdorf for the Allgäu mountains. Rock-scaling tours in the Bavarian Alps, and thousands of easy hiking paths.

Mountain-climbing guides: Bayrischzell, inquire at Gustl Müller sports shop; Berchtesgaden, Hellmuth Schuster, Locksteinstr. 5. Heinz Zembsch, Burgergraben 11, 8244 Strub. Garmisch-Partenkirchen, (inquire at Deutschen Alpenverein, Bahnhofstr. 13), several in Grainau; Mittenwald, consult board showing names in Bahnhofstrasse; Bad Reichenhall, inquire at Sport-Noack, Innsbrucker Strasse 5; Oberstdorf at Bergsport Oberstdorf, Hauptstr. 6; Hindelang at Bergfuhrerburo at the Kurverwaltung (Cure Direction), tel. 08324–2061.

WINTER SPORTS. The Bavarian Alps constitute the principal winter sports region of southeastern Germany and of Germany as a whole. The skiing season lasts in the valley areas from December to early March, above 1,500 meters (5,000 ft.) until late April, and above 2,000 meters (6,500 ft.) from November until late May.

For cross-country skiing *(Langlauf)* all the main centers offer long stretches of prepared ski tracks or *Loipen,* through beautiful winter scenery. If you're a Nordic skier, match your speed against Bavaria's best in Oberammergau's annual King Ludwig race, the first weekend in February. The town also hosts events over distances of six kilometers (four miles) and 15 kilometers (nine miles) every Wednesday during the winter season.

Special winter sports trains run in the winter season between Munich and the principal skiing centers at reduced rates. The roads leading to various of the winter resorts have recently been improved considerably. There are even well equipped winter camping sites at Berchtesgaden, Königsee, Ruhpolding, Reit im Winkl and Mittenwald-Krün, as well as at Aschau, Ramsau, Sachrang, Seeshaupt, Königsdorf and Kreuth.

When deciding upon an area in which to ski, first consult the respective tourist office about the different prices and arrangements for ski-passes and season tickets. There is often quite a price difference between day tickets and two or seven-day passes. If you intend to stay a week or more in the same resort, these passes often include vouchers for indoor pools, saunas and car parking.

EAST BAVARIA

Germany's Last Frontier

In parts wild and rocky, in others fertile and productive, bordered by Czechoslovakia to the east and Austria to the south, East Bavaria is one of Germany's last frontiers, a land well off the beaten track, as rich in scenery as it is in history. It extends north as far as the Fichtelgebirge mountains east of Bayreuth and west as far as Ingolstadt, due north of Munich. But its most interesting areas are concentrated in its southeastern corner around Regensburg and along the Danube to Passau on the Austrian border; and between the Danube and the Czechoslovak border in and around the Bayerischer Wald, the Bavarian Forest, the largest unbroken stretch of forest in Central Europe.

Exploring East Bavaria

Regensburg is the principal city of East Bavaria and the fourth largest in Bavaria. It is the best point of departure for the exploration of this region. If you are coming from Munich, you may also like to stop off in Landshut on the way, although this route is a bit longer than the direct one.

Landshut is an interesting old city with gabled houses of the 14th and 15th centuries lining its central squarelike streets of Altstadt and Neustadt, and Dreifaltigkeit Square. It has been the seat of government of Lower Bavaria since 1839. The impressive Gothic Church of St. Martin, built in the early-15th century, has a richly carved portal, superb and very high interior vaulting, the high altar from 1424, and a 133-meter (436-foot) brick church tower supposed to be the highest in the world. Stadt-Residenz (City Residence Palace), once inhabited by the Dukes of Bavaria, contains Renaissance, Baroque and neo-Classical sections, and in addition contains a very fine painting gallery and several museum collections in addition to the period-decorated suites of the 16th and 18th centuries. Landshut is dominated by Burg Trausnitz, a powerful castle-fortress on the hill above it, with the 13th-century double chapel and Wittelsbach Tower, and with such interior details in the main building as the "Fools' Staircase," so called because it is decorated with scenes from Italian comedy.

The city has many other interesting buildings, such as the Rococo church of Seligenthal Abbey, but Landshut is just as renowned for its recollection of the very good times it once had at a wedding. That event took place in 1475, when Prince George, the son of the reigning Duke, married the Polish Princess Hadwiga. The feasters consumed 333 oxen, 275 hogs, 40 calves and 12,000 geese, with, it must be assumed, a few side dishes as well, and something to wash it all down. Landshut has never forgotten that celebration, and every three years it enacts the Princely Wedding all over again, with most of the population turning out in medieval costume.

Ancient Regensburg

Much bigger and older than Landshut, Regensburg was originally a Celtic town, taken over by the Romans about 2,000 years ago. Next to the Celtic settlement, to which the name Radasbona was given, the Romans built a military fortress town and called it Castra Regina. When the Bavarian tribes migrated to this area in the early 6th century, they occupied it, made it the seat of their dukes, and apparently on the basis of the Latin name, called it Regensburg. Later the city became the capital of the Carolingian monarchs and in the middle ages developed into a commercial center. Later it became a free imperial city and for some 150 years was the site of the Imperial Diet. An important archeological find was made at the end of 1982, when workmen in the Niedermünster Church in Regensburg stumbled across the remains of what must have been the house altar of the Roman Emperor Commodus, dating back to between 180 and 190 B.C. A 50–60 cm.-high stone plinth buried in clay beneath the church bears an inscription stating that the pillar was the altar for incense offerings to the house god of Commodus. The site is now open to the public as a museum.

To get a general view of Regensburg, walk to the far end of the Steinerne Brücke, the Stone Bridge. This early 12th-century structure was an engineering miracle for its time and is the oldest bridge in Germany. Penetrating into the city, keeping straight ahead from the bridge, you will come to the square where the magnificent St. Peter's Cathedral stands. It was built in its present form between the 13th and 15th centuries and rates among the finest examples of the German Gothic ecclesiastical architecture. In addition to works of art (the Gothic sculptures deserve special note), it has preserved some of the 14th-century stained-glass windows and its treasury contains valuable items from the late middle ages. For the next four or five years, unfortunately, the interior, the nave in particular, has been turned into a building site, while necessary renovation and restoration are carried out. The building of a Bishops' Crypt is also planned. For the duration of this work, large sections of the cathedral will be closed to the public, and church functions and concerts drastically reduced. The Cathedral's famous Regensburger Domspatzen (Regensburg boys' choir) can meanwhile be heard every Sunday in the nearby Niedermünster Church. The cathedral is connected by an arcaded courtyard with the early Romanesque St. Stephan's Church and the late Romanesque All Saints Chapel. Across the cathedral square is the 13th-century St. Ulrich's Church.

At the nearby Alter Kornmarkt is the Romanesque Alte Kapelle (Old Chapel), of which the earlier parts date from about 1000 and which was the church of the ducal castle that stood here in the Middle Ages. This is also the area where the Roman fortress was located and in a narrow street between the cathedral and the Danube you can still see the Porta Praetoria, constructed in 179, which was one of its gates. The continuation of the same narrow street towards the west is called Goliath Strasse because the Goliath House is located here, which in turn received its name from the giant 16th-century fresco.

Several other old patrician houses and narrow streets give this section of the city a truly medieval appearance; particularly interesting examples are the 13th-century Baumburger Turm on Watmarkt and the 9-story Goldener Turm in Wahlen Strasse, both built in the form of towers. Goliath Strasse ends at Kohlenmarkt and Rathaus Square, with the Old Town Hall built in 1350. Its star exhibit is the Reichstagssaal (Imperial Diet Hall), where the Diet sat, but it also boasts dungeons, instruments of torture, and some fine, richly medieval rooms.

Continuing in the same westerly direction and crossing the Haidplatz, which was a tournament field in the middle ages, you come to the twin squares of Arnulfsplatz and Bismarckplatz, separated by the city theater. At the Jakobstrasse corner is Schottenkirche St. Jakob, a 12th-century Romanesque church built by Scottish and Irish monks, particularly known for its north portal, on which Christian and pagan sculptural motifs are curiously intermixed. Not far from it, in Beraiterweg, is Dominikanerkirche, a noted 13th-century Gothic basilica, with some murals of the 14th and 15th centuries.

One other particularly important sight in Regensburg is the palace of the Princes of Thurn and Taxis, their residence since 1748, set in a pleasant park not far from the railroad station. This was originally the Abbey of St. Emmeram, and the adjoining St. Emmeram's Church, a Romanesque basilica parts of which go back to the 8th century (St. Emmeram's tomb, over which it is built, is even earlier, since he was buried there in 652), is one of the most interesting of this group of buildings.

Excursions from Regensburg

There are two particularly notable excursions (which can be made by boat if you like) from Regensburg. One is southwest along the Danube to Kelheim, an old town formerly belonging to the Wittelsbach family and located where the Altmuhl flows into the Danube. Its two principal sights are the Befreiungshalle, an impressive rotunda commemorating the wars of Liberation against Napoleon, and the Benedictine monastery of Weltenburg, which was founded shortly after the year 600, where there is a splendid Baroque church built in the early 18th century by the Asam brothers and containing a magnificent figure of St. George on horseback above the altar. In good summer weather, this can be made a delightful trip by walking from the Befreiungshalle to the monastery, which will take you about an hour, by a lovely clearly-marked forest path which takes you past the pre-Roman ramparts, and returning to Kelheim by motorboat, through a spectacular piece of the Danube Valley, known as the Donaudurchbruch, where the river narrows as it forces its way between limestone cliffs which run up to some 122 meters (400 feet). Every year on the first Saturday in July at Kelheim there is a spectacular illumination of the gorge known as "Flammende Donau" (Danube in Flames).

The other classic excursion from Regensburg is along the Danube in the opposite direction, to the east, and takes you to Donaustauf, where there is a remarkable view from the ruins of the Romanesque castle of the Bishops of Regensburg, and from Walhalla, the Hall of Fame, a somewhat incongruous neo-Classical temple designed by the architect Leo von Klenze spurred on by King Ludwig I, and containing marble busts and memorial plaques of some 200 famous Germans.

Proceeding farther downstream along the Danube, we enter the pleasant town of Straubing, also a Celtic and a Roman settlement, whose chief landmark is the 16th-century city tower crowned by several pinnacles. Straubing lies in the middle of a particularly fertile plain stretching between the mountains of the Bayerischer Wald north of Regensburg southwards to the hilly region of lower Bavaria around Passau. As far back as historical records go, this region has been famous for its agriculture and cattle rearing and became the granary center of Bavaria. Every year in mid-August the traditional Gäuboden (Fertile land) Folksfest takes place, the second largest folklore festival in Bavaria after the Oktoberfest, when the town of Straubing celebrates with folklore processions, music and country fare from its rich "Gäuboden." The town's Gäuboden Museum is also worth a visit with its prehistoric collection, including the world-famous Römischen Schatzfund (Roman Treasure Trove) excavated in 1950 and comprising golden masks, armor, harnesses and bronze figures.

Straubing is also the city of Agnes Bernauer, accused of sorcery in the year 1435 by Duke Ernst of Bavaria, who could see no other reason to explain why his son had married her, and so had her thrown into the Danube. Her tombstone is in the graveyard of the 12th-century Peterskirche; every four years Straubing gives summer performances in the Ducal Palace of Friedrich Hebbel's tragedy which recounts the story of Agnes Bernauer. The next performance will be in July 1989.

Still farther down the Danube is Deggendorf, another ancient town, founded around 750, which has also preserved its 14th-century city tower. The 16th-century Rathaus (Town Hall) stands alone in the center of the wide Luitpoldplatz square. Also of interest in the town is the Heimatmuseum (Local Museum), in Oberen Stadtplatz, with a rich collection of ecclesiastical art, local handicrafts, clocks, weapons and paintings. The prehistoric section illustrates the history of the early inhabitants of the Danube Valley.

Deggendorf is known as the "Gateway to the Bayerischer Wald," whose hills rise immediately to the north. In the vicinity of Deggendorf are several interesting excursion spots. The Kloster Metten is a Benedictine abbey dating back to the 8th century. The present church was built in 1720 with a sumptuous Baroque interior and magnificent wood carvings. It contains a valuable library. Not far from Metten is the Schloss Egg, a 12th-century castle, and a little further down the Danube is another Benedictine abbey at Niederalteich and the Baroque and Rococo Altenmarkt monastery church, with interiors by the Asam brothers. Another city tower, this time dating from the Renaissance, can be seen in Vilshofen, also an old town on the Danube. From here to Passau, about 24 km. (15 miles) away, the road on the left bank of the river is very scenic but before visiting that city we shall explore the area north of the Danube.

Oberpfalz and Bayerischer Wald

About 72 km. (45 miles) north of Regensburg is Amberg which refers to itself as "the Rothenburg of Oberpfalz" because, like that famed town on the Romantic Road, it has preserved its old walls, with their sentry walk and their four gates. In addition, there are many buildings of interest—the 15th-century Gothic St. Martin's Church, the unusual 14th-century Gothic St. George's Church, and the 17th–18th-century Baroque Mariahilf pilgrimage church on the outskirts; the 13th–14th-century castle of the Counts Palatine, with its fine Gothic chapel and 15th-century glass, and the 17th-century Elector's Palace; the 14th–16th-century Gothic Rathaus and the 17th-century building of the Knights of Malta.

Near Amberg, at Hirschau there are huge hill-like piles of white kaolin sand—Monte Kaolino—where skiing can be practised in summer. This is a porcelain-making area and kaolin is used for porcelain paste.

On to Weiden, in the valley of the River Naab and the cultural and commercial center of the northern Oberpfalz, with its four-yearly Music Festival, next to be held in April 1988. We then proceed southeast, following the Ostmark Road along the Oberpfälzer Wald and through the Bayerischer Wald, the largest stretch of unbroken mountainous forestland in Germany, with the first German National Park, covering over 777 square km. (300 square miles) of idyllic wildlife reserve.

Shortly after Weiden you come to Leuchtenberg Castle ruins on a wooded hill, easily reached from the road and worth walking up for the view from its top. A little beyond it, the road connecting Nürnberg with Prague takes you to the idyllic village of Waidhaus near the Czech border. From Waidhaus a very scenic road—though in poor condition—runs through Oberpfälzer Wald near the Czech border, passing through Schönsee and Tiefenbach to the small 1,000-year-old town of Waldmünchen, on Perlsee Lake, which can be reached more directly from Rötz on the parallel Ostmark Road. A net of rewarding hiking paths surrounds Waldmünchen which, however, is better known for its annual Trenck-the-Pandour Pageant in July and August, named in memory of the terrible occupation it endured in the 18th century at the hands of Baron Trenck and his wild Croatian pandours (mounted constabulary).

Dragons and Castles

Furth im Wald, some 16 km. (ten miles) southeast of Waldmünchen, has been a border town since the middle ages, for crossing into Czechoslovakia. It is noted for its "Drachenstich," the "Dragon-Sticking" pageant which takes place on the second and third Sunday in August every year.

A most realistic dragon is done to death in the streets of the town, and there is a procession with costumed groups, horses, musicians and decorated floats. Places of interest in the town include the Heimatmuseum (Local Museum), inside the city wall's tower, and the Pfarrkirche (Parish Church). The best way to reach Furth im Wald from Ostmark Road is via Cham, idyllically located on the Regen River. In Charlemagne's day, Cham was the commercial and cultural as well as geographical focal point of the region. Today it is still the commercial and transit center of the upper Bavarian Forest. There is an impressive city gate on the bridge over the Regen with distinctive, ochre-colored twin towers. This gate, the Biertor (Beer Gate) or Burgtor, is the town's symbol, and dates back to the 13th century. Also worth seeing are the late Gothic-style City Hall, the 13th-century St. Jacob's Church and the former Gasthof Krone, an old lodging house of knights and princes.

We are now in the Bayerischer Wald, along the Czech border, one of the most densely-forested areas of the country. The Regen flows into the Danube at Regensburg. In the section of the Bayerischer Wald between the Regen and Danube are many old castles and quiet villages offering simple vacations. Farther along the Ostmark Road is Viechtach, an unpretentious summer and winter resort, and the town of Regen with the nearby Pfahl ridge of natural rocky towers and the ruins of Weissenstein Castle.

The Regen River that flows through the town of Regen is actually the Black Regen and joins the White Regen—which passes through the folk-costume-conscious village of Kötzting—shortly below the Höllensteinsee into the Regen River proper. The Black and the White Regen form a giant pair of pincers that include in their grip Arber, the highest mountain of the Bayerischer Wald (1,458 meters, 4,780 ft.), whose top can be reached by a chair lift and you can drive up to the lower station. This is a skiing and hiking area with several pleasant winter and summer resorts dotted around the mountain, such as Bayerisch-Eisenstein, Lam, Grosse and Kleine Arbersee. Bodenmais is another of these resorts, with a museum of precious stones, minerals and fossils from all over the world, and geological specimens from the region, together with articles from the silver- and bronze-mining days of Bodenmais in the 18th and 19th centuries. There is also an abandoned ore mine shaft nearby, which can be visited on guided tours.

Passau

The old city of Passau lies on land which narrows to a point as the Inn and the Danube come together on either side of it (the little Ilz, dwarfed by the other two, enters modestly from one side, opposite the point) and on the two flanking banks across from the city, on both rivers, rise wooded heights. Its old buildings lining the waterfront, the varying levels of the streets rising to the hill in the center of the old city, and picturesque architectural details such as the archways joining one house with another all combine to make it a thoroughly delightful city—Humboldt called it one of the seven most beautiful cities in the world.

It is the 15th-century St. Stephan's Cathedral that dominates Passau, situated as it is on the highest point in the town. It is of rather unusual appearance, with an octagonal dome built over the point where the transept and nave roofs cross, as well as the more conventional two towers of the west façade. In it is the largest church organ in the world—17,000 pipes, 208 stops—which you may hear played at noon every day during the summer, with an additional recital at 6 P.M. in July and August. On the choir side of the cathedral is the Residenzplatz, surrounded by fine old patrician houses, a testimonial to the wealth of Passau in the past centuries. On Residenzplatz also stands the Baroque 18th-century New Residence Palace of the Prince-Bishops (hence the name of the square),with beautiful staircase, hall and Rococo interiors. Passau—which in Roman times was called Castra Batava and was a Roman military town—has been the seat of a bishop since 739. At that time the bishopric was set up mainly for the support of the missionary activities in the eastern territories. Later Prince-Bishops ruled Passau for many centuries. From summer 1987 a new Cathedral and Diocesan Museum can be visited in the "Hofsaal" and library of the Residence.

Among other outstanding buildings in the central section of the town are: the Gothic Rathaus on Landeplatz near the Danube with two large halls containing murals that depict the scenes of Nibelungen sagas; nearby in the 11th-century house Hotel Wilder Mann, the fascinating Glass Museum, exhibiting over 10,000 superb pieces of 19th and 20th-century glass from Bavaria, Bohemia and Austria; the Old Residence of Prince-Bishops, now Law Courts, in Zengergasse; the former Niedernburg Abbey (now a girls' school) with Holy Cross Church, founded in the 8th century as a convent, rebuilt in Baroque style—in the church is the grave of Abbess Gisela, the sister of Emperor Heinrich II and the widow of St. Stephen, the first Hungarian King (the cathedral is named after him). Across the Inn River, on a hill with a fine view of the city, is Mariahilf pilgrimage church.

You cross the Danube by the Luitpoldbrücke for the second most important building of Passau, the Veste Oberhaus, also on a dominating position on the heights. This is a great fortress, started in the early 13th century by the Prince-Bishops, and continually added to for the next seven and a half centuries.

Excavations in 1974 on the south bank of the Inn River revealed the long-sought Roman town of Boiotro, where St. Severin was known to have lived in the 5th century, when he undertook the Christianization of the Germanic tribes. Although the archeological work is not completed, to date they have unearthed the remains of the Roman fortress, with walls four meters broad, five defense towers, and a well, which is still full and fresh.

There are many excurisons which start from Passau. One would be a visit to the 11th-century Schloss Neuberg, about 11 km. (seven miles) south on the River Inn. The castle is built on a cliff high above the river, and, as a border fortress, was frequently the object of feuds between the Wittelsbachs and the Habsburgs. On the ground floor it houses the charming little St. Georgs Kapelle, dating back to the 14th century. Buses belonging to German Railways (Bahnbus) take in parts of the Bayerischer Wald, such as the regular service to Bayrisch Eisenstein in the National Park, and Dreisessel on the Arber mountain. You can also take a motorboat at the Rathausplatz or the Inn Promenade for a river ride.

In fact a boat trip on the Danube is a must for any visitor to Passau. Fast, comfortable cruise steamers of the Danube Steamship Company with first-class restaurants, sun decks and cabins on board leave the Rathausplatz daily for excursions to Regensburg, the Austrian Danube Valley, an afternoon's "Three Rivers Tour" (*Dreiflusserrundfahrt*) around Passau on the Danube, Inn and Ilz or directly to Vienna from where passenger steamers of Austrian, Hungarian, Czech or Russian shipping lines offer exciting tours of the Danube ports in five different countries on the way to the Black Sea.

PRACTICAL INFORMATION FOR EAST BAVARIA

TELEPHONES. We have given telephone codes for all the towns and villages in the hotel and restaurant lists that follow. These codes need only be used when calling from outside the town or village concerned.

HOTELS AND RESTAURANTS. There are many unpretentious, but nonetheless charming, summer and winter resorts. Accommodations are for the most part in the lower price categories, especially in the low season or April/May and Sept./Oct. Hotels remain open all year round, and most of them have restaurants. There are also a great many inexpensive bungalow villages and vacation apartments and houses available, particularly in connection with the increasingly popular farmhouse holiday program for family accommodation—*Ferien auf dem Bauernhof.*

Abensberg. *Klosterhotel Biburg* (M), Eberhardplatz 1 (09443–1427). In the old monastery in the town of Biburg; period furnishings, own brewery.

Aicha Vorm Wald. *Aichacher Hof* (I), (08544–283). *Gasthaus zur Linde* (I), Hofmarktstr. 20 (08544–283).

Altötting. *"Zur Post"* (M), Kapellplatz 2 (08671–5040). Renowned tavern dating back to 1280. 92 rooms. Contains *Jägerstuberl* tavern and *Postkeller* cellar-bar and Baroque banqueting hall. DC, MC, V. *Schex* (M), Kapuzinerstr. 11–13 (08671–4021). 55 rooms, half with own bath. Restaurant and garden. Quiet location, but still in easy reach of the center. DC. *Plankl* (I), Schlotthamerstr. 4 (08671–6522). 65 rooms in two modern inns next door to each other.

Amberg. *Bahnhof–Hotel* (M), Batteriegasse 2 (09621–12178). Near station, with garden. *Brunner* (M), Batteriegasse 3 (09621–23944). Breakfast only. DC. *Goldenes Lamm* (M), Rathausstr. 6 (09621–21041). In pedestrian zone. DC.

Restaurants. *Casino Altdeutsche Stube* (M), Schrannenplatz 8 (09621–22664). AE, DC, MC. *Churpfälzer Stuben* (M), Obere Nabburger Str. 28 (09621–12218).

Bayerisch-Eisenstein. *Berggasthof Brennes* (M), Brennes 14 (09925–256). On Arber. 33 rooms with bath, solarium, restaurant, terrace with excellent view. Closed Nov.–mid.-Dec. and Mar.–Apr. AE, DC, MC, V. *Waldspitze* (M), Hauptstr. 4 (09925–308). 50 rooms and 100 apartments with bath. Indoor pool, sauna, steam room, games room, restaurant. No credit cards. *Pension am Regen* (I), Anton-Pech-Weg 21, (09925–464). 16 rooms and 6 apartments with bath, indoor pool, sauna; quiet and comfortable small hotel. Closed mid-Mar.–mid-May and mid-Oct.–mid-Dec. MC.

Bierhütte. *Romantik Hotel Bierhütte* (M), (08558–315). Located high up on the borders of the Bavarian Forest, in building dating back to 1545, and centrally-located for visits to Passau and the Danube Valley. Bohemian decor and antique furniture; excellent cuisine and wines. AE, DC, V.

Bischofsmais. Near Regen in Bayerischer Wald. *Wastlsäge* (M), Lina-Muller-Weg 3 (09920–170). 86 rooms, 5 apartments with bath or shower. In a beautiful, isolated location. Good cross-country skiing and walking trails. Indoor pool, sauna, solarium, masseur, tennis, games room, cozy restaurant, bar. AE, DC, MC, V. *Pension Berghof-Plenk* (I), Oberdorf 18 (09920–442). 17 rooms with bath or shower. No credit cards.

Bodenmais. *Atlas Hotel Sonnenhof* (M), Rechensöldenweg 8 (09924–7710). All rooms with shower. Apartments, 2 restaurants, tavern-bar, nightclub and cure treatment. AE, DC, MC, V. *Silence-Hotel-Andrea* (M), Hölzlweg 10, Am Sonnenhang (09924–386). First class, most rooms with shower; on edge of forest. A few apartments. MC. *Zum Hofbräuhaus* (M), Marktplatz 5 (09924–7021). Indoor pool, sauna, 2 apartments. *Fürsten-bauer* (I), Kötztinger Str. 34 (09924–7091). 21 rooms, 1 apartment, all with bath or shower; five minutes from center. Breakfast buffet. AE, DC, MC.

Cham. *Hotel–Restaurant Ratskeller* (M), Kirchplatz (09971–1441). 11 rooms, with bath or shower. Good restaurant. AE, DC, MC. *Randsbergerhof* (M), Randsberger-Hof-Str. 15, near Grasselturm (09971–1266). 65 rooms, modern. Lovely garden cafe, weekend dancing and good restaurant. AE, DC, MC. *Gästeheim am Stadtpark* (I), Tilsiter Str. 3 (09971–2253). Breakfast only. *Gasthof Pension Steif* (I), (09461–235). In nearby Obertraubenbach, a farmhouse pension. *Hotel Sonnenhof* (I), Am Fuchsbühl 14 (09975–30398). In Schlondorf, on edge of forest. Restaurant and cafe; bicycles for hire.
Restaurant. *Burgerstuben* (I), Furtherstr. 11 (09971–1707). In the city hall, an authentic Bavarian dining experience. Reservations advised on weekends. DC.

Deggendorf. *Central Hotel* (E), Östliche Stadtgraben 30 (0991–6011). Modern, centrally-located hotel with indoor pool, sauna and fitness center. Restaurant with Bavarian and international food. AE, DC, MC, V. *Schlossho-tel Egg* (E), 8351 Schloss Egg (09905–289). 19 rooms with bath. Atmospheric rooms in a castle and adjoining guesthouse, 3 miles outside of town. Excellent restaurant. AE, DC, MC, V. *Berggasthof Rusel* (I), 8351 Schaufling, on B-11 road north (09920–316). 35 rooms, 20 with bath. Mountainside inn, hiking trails, ski lift, nearby golf course, restaurant. Closed Nov. AE, DC, MC, V.
Restaurant. *Ratskellar* (M), Oberer Stadtplatz 1 (0991–6737). In the town hall. Good Bavarian menu. Closed Fri. MC. *Zum Burgwit* (I), Deggendorfer Str. 7 (0991–32236). In Natternberg section. Cozy, typical Ba-

varian hotel-restaurant. 18 rooms. *Zum Grafenwirt* (I), Bahnhofstr. 7 (0991–8729). Filling Bavarian dishes and Danube fish. Reservations advised on weekends. Closed Tues. and late-May–early June. AE, DC, MC.

Falkenfels. About 19 km. (12 miles) north of Straubing in the Bavarian Forest. *Burghotel Falkenfels* (M), Burgstr. 8 (09961–6385). Originally medieval castle-fortress, first mentioned in 1100. Heated outdoor pool, fishing, good food.

Furth Im Wald. *Hohenbogen* (M), Bahnhofstr. 25 (09973–1509). 23 rooms, restaurant and cafe with dancing. Special diet meals. DC. *Bayerwald* (I), Bahnhofstr. 21 (09973–1888). All rooms with shower, garden, breakfast only. *Gastehaus Kolbeck* (I), Wutzmühlstr. 1 (09973–1868). Restaurant closed Fri.

Grafenau. *Parkhotel am Kurpark* (M), Freyungerstr. 51 (08552–2444). 50 rooms with bath. Cozy, rustic interior. Indoor pool, sauna, solarium, restaurant. AE, DC, MC, V *Säumerhof* (M), Steinberg 32 (08552–2401). Small, quiet and comfortable. First class restaurant. *Steigenberger Sonnenhof* (M), Sonnenstr. 12 (08552–2033). 196 rooms with bath or shower. Indoor pool, sauna, solarium, indoor/outdoor tennis courts, mini-golf, restaurant. AE, DC, MC, V.

Kelheim. *Ehrnthaller* (Ring Hotel) (M), Donaustr. 22 (09441–3333). 67 rooms, most with own bath. AE, MC, V. *Aukoferbräu* (I), Alleestr. 27 (09441–1460). 54 rooms, about half with own bath, terrace and restaurant. AE.

Kellberg. Near Thyrau. *Pfälzer Weinstube* (M), Kurpromenade 11 (08501–1315). Quietly-located with beautiful view. 26 rooms, terrace, sauna, solarium, tennis court and restaurant. DC.

Lalling. Resort in the Bavarian Forest national park, in a particularly favorable climatic area known as the "Lallinger Winkel." *Thula Sporthotel* (M), (09904–323). 17 rooms, all with own bath, 1 apartment. Quiet and scenically located, with indoor pool, sauna and tennis courts. Cafe and restaurant.

Landshut. *Romantik Hotel Fürstenhof* (E), Steinhamerstr. 3 (0871–82025). Modern hotel in a former "art nouveau" house; very tastefully furnished with every comfort. Attractive old Bavarian country-styled *Herzogstuberl* restaurant with small but good selection of dishes. AE, DC, MC. V. *Goldene Sonne* (M), Neustadt. 520 (0871–23087). Garden restaurant. *Hotel-Garni Bergterrasse* (I), Ger.-Hauptman-Str. 1. (0871–89190). Small and quiet. No restaurant. *Peterhof* (I), Niedermayerstr. 15 (0871–50113). 11 beds.

Restaurants. *Klausenberg* (M), (0871–41477). On the hill of the same name, with fine view of city from its terrace. *Bergcafe* (M), (08702–2285). Located in Niederaichach; hard to find, but has excellent food and view. DC.

Passau. *Passauer Wolf* (E), Rindermarkt 6/8 (0851–34046). 43 rooms. In the heart of the old town on the waterfront. First class restaurant. AE, DC, MC, V. *Wilder Mann* (E), Am Rathausplatz (0851–35071). 60 rooms with bath. Class and comfort in this 11th-century patrician house, furnished with antiques. Indoor pool in the vaulted cellars. First-class restaurant. AE, DC, MC, V. *Schloss Ort* (M), am Dreiflusseck (0851–34072). At the confluence of the rivers Danube, Inn and Ilz. The hotel is a 13th-century castle, converted to a hotel at the turn of the century. 58 rooms, all with own bath or shower, restaurant, sun terrace and garden, directly next to the river promenade and ferryboat pier. No credit cards. *Zum Laubenwirt* (M), Am Dreiflusseck, Ort 14 (0851–33453). Also on the point where the three rivers join. Small, with good terrace restaurant. AE, DC, MC, V.

Restaurants. *Blauer Bock* (M), Fritz–Schäffer–Promenade (0851–34637). Waterfront terrace, music. *Heilig Geist Stifts-Schänke* (M), Heilig Geist Gasse 4 (0851–2607). Founded in 1358; garden, good wines. Reservations advised. Closed Wed. and Jan. 6–30. AE, DC, MC. *Gasthof Andorfer* (I), Rennweg 2 (0851–51372). One of the finest wheat beers in lower Bavaria is brewed here. Fine views and a few rooms. No credit cards. *Ratskeller* (I), Rathausplatz (0851–34686). In the Rathaus, with terrace on the Square.

Regen. *Pension Panorama* (M), Johannesfeldstr. 27 (09921–2356). 17 rooms, all with own bath; indoor pool. *Wieshof* (I), Poschetsriederstr. 2 (09921–4312). 15 rooms, with bath, pool, bowling, restaurant. No credit cards. *Burggasthof Weissenstein* (I), Haus No. 32 (09921–2259). In suburb of same name. Located directly beneath the castle. 15 rooms, with bath, fine view and restaurant. Closed Nov. No credit cards.

Regensburg. *Avia* (E), Frankensstr. 1 (0941–4300). 95 rooms, garden, good restaurant, bar. Situated in the suburbs across the river; good value. AE, DC, MC, V. *Kaiserhof am Dom* (E), Kramergasse 10 (0941–54027). Just west of the Cathedral. All rooms with shower, half with own bath. Separate *Taverne* restaurant (M). AE, MC. *Park Hotel Maximilian* (E), Maxstr. 28 (0941–51042). 52 rooms, all with own bath, very comfortable. Elegant, first-class establishment. Rustic *Jägerstube* restaurant. AE, DC, MC, V. *Münchner Hof* (M), Tändlergasse 9 (0941–58262). 65 rooms, almost all with own bath/shower. Located in the heart of the Old Town, near the pedestrian zone. Good restaurant. AE, DC, MC. *St. Georg* (Ring Hotel) (M), Karl Stieler Str. 8 (0941–97066). Located halfway between the autobahn and the city center. All rooms with bath or shower; restaurant, beer tavern and open fireplace, terrace. AE, DC, MC, V. *Weidenhof* (M), Maximilianstr. 23 (0941–53031). 50 rooms, some with own shower. Three minutes' walk from the main station. Standard comfort. Breakfast only. AE, DC, MC. *Peterhof* (I), Fröhliche Türkenstr. 12 (0941–57514). Modern, with good-value restaurant.

Restaurants. *Historisches Eck Zur Stritzelbäckern* (E), Watmarkt 6 (0941–52966). *Alte Munz* (M), Fischmarkt 7 (0941–54886). Historical tavern serving local specialties. *Leerer Beutel* (M), Bertholdstr. 9 (0941–58997). Next to the Minoriten Church. *Zum Krebs* (M), Krebsgasse 6 (0941–55803). Small and atmospheric, in the old town. Reservations advisable. *Historische Wurstkuche* (I), Weisse-Lamm-Gasse 3 (0941–59098). Next to the Steinernen Brücke (Stone Bridge). *Kneitinger*

Garten (I), Müllerstr. 1 (0941–86124). Typical old beer tavern with lots of dark wood and nostalgic wall decorations. Plenty of good-value, tasty Bavarian specialties.

Inexpensive beer restaurants. *Brandl-Bräu-Gastätte,* Ostengasse 16 (0941–51487). *Hofbräuhaus,* Rathaus Platz (0941–51280). *Spitalgarten,* Katharinenplatz 1 (0941–52300). Serving beer since 1300.

Wine taverns. *Alt Regensburger Weinkeller,* Fischgassl 4 (0941–54747). Well-known wine tavern/restaurant. AE, MC. *Bastei,* Hinter der Grieb 5–7 (0941–51463). Rustic tavern with open fireplace. *Zum Steidlwirt,* Am Ölberg 13 (0941–52618).

St. Englmar. *Aparthotel Predigstuhl* (M), (09965–81). 400 self-catering apartments, also hotel rooms. AE, DC, V. *Berghotel Maibrunn* (M), in Maibrunn section (09965–292). 22 rooms and indoor pool. *Kurhotel Gut Schmelmerhof* (M), Rettenbach (09965–517). Rustic decor, all rooms with bath or shower. Restaurant, indoor and outdoor pools, sauna. *Kur-und Sporthotel* (M), (09965–312). On the Predigstuhl. Especially equipped for tennis and riding holidays. AE, DC, MC.

Straubing. *Heimer* (M), Schlesische Str. 131 (09421–61091). Small, all rooms with bath or shower. AE, DC, MC, V. *Motel Lermer* (M), Landshuterstr. 55 (09421–3485). Small, all rooms with bath or shower. DC, MC, V. *Seethaler* (M), Theresienplatz 25 (09421–12022). Bavarian cooking. All rooms with bath or shower.

Vilshofen. *Parkhotel* (M), Furtgasse 2 (08541–8037). 31 beds; garden restaurant. DC, MC. *Bayerischer Hof* (I), 8358 Vilshofen (08541–5065). 31 rooms, half with bath or shower. Comfortable, park-like setting, with beer garden and restaurant. Closed Dec. 27–Jan. 10. MC.

Waldmünchen. *Post* (I), Marktplatz 9 (09972–1416). DC. *Schmidbräu* (I), Marktplatz 5 (09972–1349). With annexe and local specialty restaurant. DC. *Pension Gruber* (I), Herzogau 19 (09972–1439). Located in Herzogau, four km. southeast of town, in a quiet position near the forest.

Weiden. *Europa* (M), Frauenrichterstr. 173 (0961–25051). All rooms with shower. AE, DC, MC. *Hotel am Tor* (M), Hinterm Wall 24 (0961–5014). 33 rooms, all with bath; quiet and romantic; in the old town next to the city gate. Rustic *Turmkeller* bar and *Turmstuberl* restaurant. AE, DC, MC. *Stadtkrug* (M), Wolframstr. 5 (0961–32025). 52 rooms, all with own bath. Restaurant with garden. AE, DC, MC, V.

Restaurant. *Zum Heindlwirt* (M), Pfarrplatz 2 (0961–44705). Also some rooms.

Zwiesel. *Kurhotel Sonnenberg* (M), Augunstinerstr. 9 (09922–2031). 19 rooms with bath or shower, 1 apartment. Comfortable, quiet, modern hotel with fine view. Indoor pool, sauna, solarium, fitness room, restaurant. No credit cards. *Linde* (M), Lindenweg 9 (09922–1661). Located outside the town on the south slopes of the Hennenkobels peak above Zwiesel, in the Rabenstein section. Directly on the edge of the forest. Modern hotel with rustic interiors. 74 beds, all rooms with own bath, balcony and panoramic view over the town and Bavarian Forest. Indoor pool, sun terrace and fine restaurant with Bavarian and international specialties. *Waldbahn* (M), Bahnhofsplatz 2 (09922–3001). 28 rooms with bath or shower. Opposite the station, with a beautiful garden and good-value restaurant. Closed Nov. No credit cards.

Restaurants. *Gasthof Deutscher Rhein* (M), Am Stadtplatz (09922–1651). Rustic restaurant serving Bavarian and Bohemian dishes. Live music on Tues., Wed., and Sat. Reservations advised. DC. *Braustuberl* (I), Regenerstr. 9 (09922–1409). Sample the beers of one of the oldest and best breweries in the Bavarian Forest. Basic Bavarian fare. No credit cards.

YOUTH HOSTELS. Youth hostels are well distributed throughout the whole region. For a complete list of addresses and telephone numbers write to the Regional Tourist office. See below for address.

CAMPING. East Bavaria offers a wide selection of campsites for tents and caravan trailers, including camping on farms. For a full list, also including separate lists of sites especially run for young people, write to the Regional Tourist Office in Regensburg for their informative brochure *Camping*.

MOUNTAIN HUTS. A full list of addresses of self-catering huts can be obtained from the Regional Tourist Office in Regensburg. (See *Tourist Information*). Other huts open to the public, and serving meals include: **Bayerisch Eisenstein.** Arberschutzhaus (09925–242). **Bischofsmais.** Landshuter Haus in Unterbreitenau (09920–255). **Ludwigsthal.** Falkensteinschutzhaus (09925–313). **Sankt Oswald.** Lusenschutzhaus (08553–1212). In summer reserve beds in advance.

TOURIST INFORMATION. The main regional tourist office for East Bavaria is the *Fremdenverkehrsverband Ostbayern,* Landshuter Str. 13, 8400 **Regensburg** (0941–57186). The region around the southern Bavarian Forest (Bayerischer Wald) between the Rivers Danube and Inn is covered by the *Fremdenverkehrsgemeinschaft Passauerland,* Domplatz 11, 8390 **Passau** (0851–3971) and for the nature park region of the upper Bavarian Forest around Cham, write to *Gemeindeverwaltung, Verkehrsamt Landkreis Cham,* Postfach 154, 8490 **Cham** (09971–781).

Information about Bavarian Forest National Park is available from *Nationalparkverwaltung,* 8352 Grafenau (08552–2077), or *Direktion für Tourismus,* 8393 Freyung (08551–4455).

Information about the southern Bavarian Forest is available from *Fremdenverkehrsgemeinschaft Passauer Land,* Domplatz 11, 8390 Passau (0851–3971). For holiday centers in the Bavarian Forest, write *Ferienzentrum Bayerwald,* Gottsdorf, 8391 Untergriesbach (08593–444).

The following are area tourist offices. When writing to them, address your letters to the *Verkehrsamt.*

Bayerisch Eisenstein. Schulbergstr. 8371 Bayerisch-Eisenstein (09925–327). **Bodenmais,** Bergknappenstr. 10, 8373 Bodenmais (09924–214). **Cham,** Rosenstr. 1, 8491 Cham (09971–4933). **Deggendorf,** Oberer Stadtplatz 4, 8360 Deggendorf (0991–380169). **Freyung,** Rathausweg 1, 8393 Freyung (08551–4455). **Fürth-im-Wald,** Schlossplatz 1, 8492 Fürth-im-Wald (09973–3813). **Grafenau,** Rathaus, 8352 Grafenau

(08552–2085). **Kelheim,** Neues Rathaus, 8420 Kelheim (09441–3012).
Lalling, Verkehrsamt "Lallinger Winkel", 8351 Lalling (09904–374).
Landshut, Altstadt 315, 8300 Landshut (0871–23031).
Passau, *Tourist Information,* Am Rathausplatz, 8390 Passau
(0851–33421). **Regen,** Stadtplatz 1, 8370 Regen, (09921–2929). **Regensburg,** Altes Rathaus, 8400 Regensburg (0941–5072141). **St. Englmar,**
Rathausstr. 6, St. Englmar (09965–221). **Straubing,** Rathaus, Theresienplatz, 8440 Straubing (09421–16307). **Tittling,** Marktplatz 10, 8391 Tittling (08504–2666). **Viechtach,** Rathaus, 8374 Viechtach (09942–1622).
Vilshofen, Rathaus, Stadtplatz 29, 8358 Vilshofen (08541–8022). **Waldkirchen,** Hauzenberger Str. 1, 8392 Waldkirchen (08581–665). **Zwiesel,**
im Rathaus, 8372 Zwiesel (09922–1308).

HOW TO GET AROUND. By car. The region is quiet and generally
empty. However, the Autobahn A3 (Frankfurt–Nürnberg–
Regensburg–Passau) is open all the way, linking Germany's southeastern
city directly with the cities of the north such as Hamburg, Hannover,
Dortmund, Köln and West Berlin. The scenic holiday route, *Ostmark
Strasse,* from Bayreuth to Passau (roads B22 and B85) traverses the Oberpfälzer and Bavarian forests from northeast to southwest.

By train. The whole region is well-served with rail connections, the
main rail stations being Regensburg, Landshut and Passau on the Frankfurt–Vienna, Oostende–Nürnberg–Passau–Linz–Vienna and Munich–Berlin lines. To these, many smaller towns are linked by rail and post
buses.

There are five through trains daily to Passau from Munich, calling at
Landshut, Dingolfing, Landau, Plattling, Osterhofen, Wilshofen and Passau, and two daily on the Munich–Passau–Bayerisch Eisenstein express
route, which continues from Passau via Deggendorf into the Bavarian Forest, terminating at Bayerisch Eisenstein.

By bicycle. There is delightful cycling countryside in and around the
Bavarian Forest, the National Park, the Oberpfälzer Wald and in the river
valleys. The Regional Tourist Office for East Bavaria, *Fremdenverkehrsverband Ostbayern,* Landshuter Str. 13, 8400 Regensburg, publishes the
cycling brochure *Radeln in Ostbayern* (Cycling in East Bavaria), describ-
ing the most suitable areas, suggested routes, places with bicycles for hire,
cycle tracks, and interesting sights en route.

By bus. The whole of East Bavaria is covered with a dense network of
bus routes. Timetables of municipal bus lines are available from railway
stations or the local tourist offices, although bus connections into the Bavarian Forest are not particularly good. However, from Passau there are
several regular services of the German Railway buses to places of interest
in the Bavarian Forest and surroundings. These buses, connecting with
trains, are usually listed in rail timetables; further information is available
from the bus terminus in front of the main rail station in Passau
(0851–501357).

Furthermore, all major towns throughout the region possess bus companies offering organized trips and day-excursions into the surrounding
countryside, including into Austria and Czechoslovakia, for which the
tour organizer takes care of the necessary visa formalities.

By boat. Throughout the summer months (May to Sept.) regular motorboat services operate between Regensburg and Passau calling at Straubing,

Deggendorf and Vilshofen. The return journey can also be by rail from Passau's main station. Information and timetables from *Donauschiffahrtsgesellschaft Wurm & Koch,* Bräugasse 8, 8390 Passau (0851–2065 or 2066).

Numerous other boat excursions by various shipping lines include trips to the romantic Wachau wine growing region of Lower Austria; day or week-end trips to Linz in Austria; cruises from Regensburg into the valley of the Altmühl to visit the beautiful castle Schloss Prunn; evening dance-cruises from Passau. In addition, there are passenger steamers to Vienna and the Black Sea run by Austrian, Hungarian and Russian shipping lines, which all call in at Passau, or the new, super *Donauprinzessin* belonging to the Deilmann Line of Germany which operates a luxury cruise from Passau to Budapest and back every Saturday.

There are also various shorter round-trips to places of interest, departing from Kelheim, Regensburg, Straubing or Passau, and inter-town ferry services all along the Danube. The tourist offices supply information about the various private shipping companies operating ferry services and boat trips.

SPORTS. Hiking tops the list of pastimes in East Bavaria (see below for more details) but in addition there is **swimming** in the Ilz and Danube rivers and in many outdoor and indoor pools, such as in Regensburg (*Westbad,* Messerschmittstr. 4) or in Passau (*Schwimmbad "Bschütt,"* an openair pool near the Ilz bridge, and the *Hallenbad Passau* in Neuburgerstr.). There is also bathing in the lakes of Pocking and Hartkirchen near Passau. **Water sports,** including **motorboat hire** (from Regensburg) and **water-skiing,** forbidden on many other lakes, are allowed on the Danube near Obernzell; **rowing** and **canoeing** on the Altmuhl. **Sailing** and **windsurfing** on the lakes of Perisee near Waldmünchen, Badesee at Eging, Rannasee near Wegscheid and the Höllensteinsee near Viechtach. There is a **squash court** in Pocking, south of Passau; **golf courses** at Regensburg, Furth-im-Wald, Eggenfelden, Schmidmühlen (which offers combined package deals with instruction), Schwarzenfeld, Lallinger Winkel, and Waldkirchen in the Bavarian Forest. **Tennis courts** can be found in most towns.

There is **horseback riding** in 46 resorts throughout the Bavarian Forest. In most of the riding stables, covered waggons and carriages can also be hired. The cost of hourly riding instruction ranges from DM.7 to DM.16, and carriages and waggons about DM.20 for up to four passengers.

Fishing is generally good in the rivers of the Bavarian Forest and the Oberpfalz, particularly for trout. A specialty of the area is *Huch* (huck), a large and savage river salmon, caught in the Danube and its tributaries, as well as eel and sheathfish. Day permits must be purchased, and vary from about DM.7 to DM.10. Lists of places issuing permits can be obtained from the local tourist offices, the town hall or from the booklet published by the Regional Tourist Office for East Bavaria in Regensburg, entitled *Angeln in Ostbayern.*

HIKING. Hiking is a favourite pastime in East Bavaria, especially around Waldmünchen in the Oberpfälzer Wald and the Arber mountain area. You can follow the historic Pandurensteig trail, one of the most beautiful hiking paths in Germany, which stretches from Waldmünchen to

Passau for 150 km. along the ridge in the center of the Bavarian Forest National Park. The trail can be hiked in stages, with 10 overnight stays in the *Wandern ohne Gepäck* (Hiking without Luggage) program where accommodation and transfer of luggage is arranged in advance from Gasthof to Gasthof. Contact the regional Tourist Office in Regensburg for information and reservations. Sturdy mountain walkers and those in search of real wildness will find the mountains of the Bavarian Forest southeast of the Arber along the Czech border and their approaches particularly challenging. There are also several mountain lodges here belonging to the Bavarian Forest Trust where you can stay overnight. Some also offer meals. It's advisable to telephone in advance in the high season as dormitories quickly get filled. (See below).

The whole of the Bavarian Forest contains a dense network of hiking trails, all well-marked with a numbering system. A word of warning, however: take great care when walking in the areas near the Czech border not to cross over the border itself, marked with red and white poles.

For less strenuous walking and in less rugged surroundings, try the four nature parks of the Oberpfälzer Wald.

Three resorts of the Bavarian Forest—Kellberg, Hauzenberg and Büchelberg—have joined forces to offer a good-value hiking holiday called *Wandern mit Tapetenwechsel* ("Hiking with a Change of Scene"). The all-in package includes 14 days' hiking, bed and breakfast, guided hiking tour, luggage transportation for around DM.450. Information from the *Verkehrsamt Kellberg,* 8391 Thyrnau (08501–320).

WINTER SPORTS. Next to the Black Forest East Bavaria is the most important winter sports region in Germany outside the Alps. There are still excellently prepared facilities for both downhill and crosscountry skiing. In addition to long stretches of marked crosscountry *(Langlauf)* tracks, ski-lifts, floodlit pistes, etc., there are facilities for skating, curling and tobogganing. The best winter sports centers are in the Bayerischer Wald, where the skiing season lasts from December until early March. World Cup downhill ski championships take place on the Arber mountain in January and February, as well as international crosscountry competitions. The main winter sports regions are: Arber-Osser-Falkenstein (includes towns of Bayer, Eisenstein, Bodenmais, Zwiesel, etc.); Rachel-Lusen (includes Frauenau and Grafenau); Freyung-Mitterfirmiansreut (includes Freyung); St. Englmar-PröllerPredigstuhl (includes St. Englmar and Viechtach); Gibacht-Voithenberg-Hoher Bogen (includes Furth-im-Wald, Grafenwiesen and Waldmünchen). Details of resorts offering winter sports facilities in East Bavaria are available in the booklet *Winter Information fur Ostbayern-Urlauber* issued by the Regional Tourist Office. Look too for special winter packages *Pauschalangebote,* also available from the tourist office.

EATING IN GERMANY

A Guide to German Food

There's just no getting around the fact that the staple diet of practically the entire German nation revolves around starch. In fact, that's just the starting point. Combine the two words "food" and "German" and immediately a splendid caricature of a red-faced, knee-slapping, endomorphic specimen tucking into a giant sized plate of *Eisbein mit Sauerkraut,* frothing stein of beer close at hand, leaps to mind. One has only to realize that there are 200 different types of bread alone baked in Germany—most of it delicious, by the way—or to consider the veritable tons of *Knödel* (dumplings) consumed in Bavaria, swimming in gravy and accompanying the obligatory *Sonntagsbraten,* or Sunday roast, and it doesn't take too long to begin to feel that perhaps our jovial German isn't such a cliche. Similarly, the predominance of thick, rich soups, the platefuls of pasta, the many hundreds of different cakes and pastries, and the beer—above all perhaps, the beer—all seem to point to the fact that the guzzling German is not such a mythical figure after all.

Unfortunately, however, he is. Up to a point anyway. German food if it is anything is unquestionably *deftig,* literally "heavy." But the Germans today are probably every bit as health-conscious as their counterparts in California. The statistics show that every third German has an almost fanatical dedication to some species of *Diät,* or diet, while sports and every type of fitness and body-care facility under the sun abound. You have only to step onto a tennis court or go to a swimming pool in Germany to realise that the all-so-obvious evidence of a surfeit of bread, *Knödel* and beer is generally not on show.

So what then do the Germans eat? The immediate answer is certainly not as much as most visitors imagine, or indeed eat themselves while in Germany. But, beyond this simple fact, the question becomes much harder to answer than one might at first sight imagine.

The basic complication is that German cuisine as such does not really exist. That is, there is no readily identifiable body of cooking in Germany that one can point to and confidently label as such, unlike French cuisine, for example, or Italian. There are, it is true, certain general characteristics that can be indentified, particularly the emphasis on starch. But for the most part German cooking consists of an amalgam of regional dishes that are not generally found outside their own areas. Of course you will find specialty restaurants throughout the country that serve dishes from other regions, much as you might find a Chinese restaurant in Italy or even an English restaurant in France. And it's important also to realize that many regional dishes represent no more than local variants of foods found in other parts of Germany. Yet for the most part, it has to be admitted that German cuisine as such does not really exist.

Say It with Sausages

There is, however, one very important exception. It may not quite rate with the soufflé or *turbot à la reine* in terms of delicacy, finesse or sophistication, but it *is* found all over Germany. This is the sausage, the ambassador of German cooking and the one universal foodstuff over which the Germans can claim undisputed mastery.

The most famous German sausage is the Frankfurter, found throughout the world and so well-known that it is doubtful whether more than a tiny percentage of the hundreds of thousands who eat them daily pause to think that its name derives from the city where they originated. Frankfurt sausages should be cooked in hot water, but must never be boiled, only allowed to cook through gently. They are then eaten with bread and mustard or horseradish. A smaller variety of the Frankfurter found in southern Germany and made from identical ingredients is called, perversely, a *Wienerwurst.* In the U.S. and Britain they are known as Wieners or Vienna sausages, while in Austria itself they're known as frankfurters!

A quick lunchtime snack in Bavaria is *Ein Paar Wiener mit Kartofelsalat,* which means a "pair" of Wienerwurst sausages. These are sold only in multiples of two: "ein Paar, dwei Paar, drei Paar" and so on. Anyone who asks for them in any other way immediately identifies himself as either a foreigner or a "Prussian."

The number and variety of other types of German sausage are immense. There is *Fleischwurst, Gelbwurst, Rindsbratwurst,* and *Wollwurst,* not to mention the typical Munich specialty, *Weisswurst,* a delicate white sausage made from veal, calves' brains and spleen, and traditionally eaten only between midnight and noon. Small wonder that it's a favorite breakfast for Carnival revelers returning home in the early hours after a *Faschingsfest.* Everyone has heard of *Leberwurst;* it is a specialty of Hesse (they call it *Zeppelinwurst* in Frankfurt). *Nürnberger Bratwurst,* the pork sausage of Nürnberg, usually served fried or, better still, grilled, is similarly famous, so much so in fact that you will find restaurants all over the country called

Bratwurststube that specialize in them. A favorite between-meal snack in Mainz is *Weck, Worscht und Wein,* a roll, sausage and wine. Coburg serves sausages roasted; Soest in Westphalia bakes them in dough. Westphalia is the place for *Rinderwurst* and *Blutwurst,* beef sausage and blood sausage (which unappetizing as it may sound is really very tasty). The *Bouillonwurst* of Hannover is served with mustard and horseradish; *Milzwurst,* a spleen sausage found along the Danube, is very good sliced and fried in golden breadcrumbs. Stuttgart has the *Saiten,* a juicy sausage served with lentils. Braunschweig has a whole army of sausage specialties. This is the city that gave cervelat sausage to the world, along with *Mettwurst* and *Knackwurst.*

But, as we say, the sausage aside, German cooking really means regional cooking. So the best and most convenient way to arrange our overview of German food is by region.

Bavaria

Our gastronomic tour begins in Bavaria. Traditionally a poor area of the country, the Bavarians have always taken pride in using simple ingredients and making them decidedly appetizing. The best known example of this labor of love is the dumpling, a humble dish raised to something approaching an art form. The array of dumplings is positively stupendous. The basic dumpling is the *Kartoffelknödel* or *Kartoffelkloss,* the classic version of which is made from roughly one-third boiled potatoes and two-thirds raw potatoes. But in addition there are also *Leber-* (liver), *Semmel-* (bread), *Böhmische-* (dough) and *Speck-* (bacon) dumplings, the last two having their origins in Czechoslovakia and the Austrian Tyrol respectively. The dumpling is most often served with *Schweinebraten,* roast pork, which all Germans love, though perhaps none more so than the Bavarians. Also popular in Bavaria is *Schweinshax'n,* roast knuckle of pork, and *Kalbshax'n,* veal shank, both of which are served with dumplings—of course—or potato salad. Other Bavarian specialties include *Leberkäs,* pork roast loaf, particularly popular in Munich and served piping hot like *Weisswurst* with sweet mustard and crisp pretzels or rolls. The natural accompaniment to all these dishes, needless to say, is a large glass of cold beer.

Before leaving central southern Bavaria, a mention should also be made of the excellent trout, *Forelle,* most usually caught in mountain rivers, the freshwater salmon-trout, *Lachsforelle, Bachsaibling* found throughout upper Bavaria, and the Chiemsee *Renke,* a type of whitefish from the Chiemsee.

Among East Bavarian specialties that shouldn't be missed is the *Regensburger,* a short, thick, spicy sausage made in Regensburg and comparable to Nürnberg's famous *Bratwurst.* (Like them, they should be grilled.) Another local sausage specialty is the *Bauernseufzer,* the "farmer's sigh," which hails from Amberg. The Danube also provides a number of tasty fish, among them the *Donawaller,* or Danube sheatfish, served *blau* (boiled) or *gebacken* (breaded and fried). Carp, or *Karpfen,* are found in abundance in Tirschenreuth, slightly farther to the north. East Bavaria also boasts a fine radish, the *Weichser Rettiche,* again best when washed down with the good locally-produced beers.

Passing westwards across Southern Bavaria and heading into the Allgäu, you'll find that cows and cheese are as integral a part of the region as mountains and meadows. Surprisingly, the art of cheesemaking in the Allgäu does not date back all that far, only about 150 years when an enterprising Allgäuer brought the secret of the famous Swiss cheeses to the region, subsequently called *Allgäuer Emmantal.* Kempten, the capital of the Allgäu, is the home of the Cheese Exchange *(Käsebörse),* and in numerous cheese dairies, or *Käskuchä,* you can watch top cheese-masters at work. Another Allgäuer import, introduced to the region by French soldiers, is *Böfflamott,* a German corruption of *Boeuf à la mode.* It's a form of marinated beef casserole cooked in red wine and lemon, served with lettuce and potatoes. A genuinely local Allgäu dish, both popular and delicious, is *Kässpatzen,* cheese noodles; not recommended for those on a stricter *diät,* however.

Continuing westwards again toward Bodensee, or Lake Constance, you'll find that fish specialties top the list. There are 35 different types of fish in the lake, the *Felchen* being the most highly prized. It belongs to the salmon family and is best eaten *blau* (poached) in rosemary sauce or baked in almonds *(Müllerin)* and accompanied by a top quality Meersburg white wine.

Swabia and Franconia

We are now in Swabia, the land of the *Pfannkuchen* and the *Spätzle,* both flour-and-egg dishes, and both essentially rather thrifty dishes, as is only appropriate to a region known for its economizing inhabitants. Hence the various noodle dishes. *Pfannkuchen,* pancakes, are generally filled with meat, cheese, jam, or sultanas, or chopped into fine strips and scattered in a clear consommé soup known as *Flädlesupp. Spätzle,* golden-yellow egg noodles, are the usual accompaniment for the Swabian Sunday roast beef lunch of *Riderbraten.* Perhaps one of the best known dishes is the Swabian version of ravioli, *Maultaschen,* again usually served floating in a broth strewn with chives.

Everyone has probably heard of the delicious Black Forest Cherry cake, *Schwarzwälderkirschtorte,* and certainly at some time or another have sampled the *Kirschwasser,* Black Forest cherry brandy. Locally it is called *Chriesewässerle,* which comes from the French *cerise* (cherry), proof of the region's culinary affinity with nearby France. The region also has a number of excellent brandies, or *Schnaps,* made from plums, raspberries and pears, all identified by the name *Schwarzwälder,* followed by the kind of fruit "water" *(Wasser).*

But the inhabitants of the Black Forest don't just eat cake and drink *Schnaps.* They also have delicious smoked bacon or *Speck* known as *Schwarzwaldgeräuchertes,* the genuine article being smoked over Black Forest fir cones. This, together with a hearty chunk of farmhouse bread and a glass of chilled white wine, constitutes the local farmers' "second breakfast" (served at around 9 A.M.!) and known as *z'Nuni.*

Heading northeast towards Franconia, a visit to Würzburg must, necessarily, put wine before food. The delicious dry white wines from the river Main in their specially-shaped bulbous green bottles known as *Bocksbeutel* number among the finest in Germany. The people of Franconia like good, strong food so plain homely fare is much in demand. *Schlachtplatte* consists of several types of fresh sausages, meat and *Leberwurst,* and it may be served with *Fränkische Klösse*—yet another type of dumpling. *Bamberger Krautbraten* is a white cabbage stuffed with meat filling, served with—you guessed it—potato dumplings and washed down with a glass of good Franconian beer such as *Kulmbacher* or the smokey *Rauchbier* from Bamberg.

Central Germany

Proceeding northwest, we enter Hesse. Although the region has no local specialties as such, fine dishes are made with simple ingredients such as bacon, pork, potatoes, turnips, leeks, apples or pears. *Weckewerk,* for example, is pork mixed with softened bread-rolls and baked in a mould, while *Sulperknocken* is made from pickled and boiled pigs' ears and trotters served with sauerkraut and a puree of green peas. And you really cannot say you have been to Hesse, or indeed to nearby Mainz as well, without trying the *Hankäs mit Musik. Handkäs* is a Mainz cheese, which is round and rather waxlike in appearance. It should only be eaten when fully ripened, the ripe cheese being distinguished principally by its extreme smelliness. In the Rheingau it is eaten with potatoes in their jackets, and in Rheinhesse it is accompanied by white wine from the local vineyards. The *Musik* is a liberal portion of sliced onions in a mixture of oil and vinegar which is poured over the cheese.

The Saarland borders directly onto France, giving rise to a distinct French influence on Saarland cuisine. However, while the region's very high standard of cooking is undeniable—the number of three-star restaurants makes this only too clear—Saarland haute cuisine should not be confused with everyday Saarland specialties, most of which are based on potatoes. In addition, Saarland also produces excellent cider made from wild apples and pears shaken from the trees, traditionally drunk with *Stinkes,* an exceedingly aptly-named Limburg cheese served with onions that outdoes even the *Hankäs* for sheer odor impact.

Higher up in the Palatinate, the people are reputed to have a particular weakness for sausage—even more so than other Germans—the herb-flavored *Pfälzer* being a special favorite. The basic reason for this sausage mania is believed to be that sausages are an excellent way of building up a thirst, the Palatinate being of course one of the very best wine-producing areas of Germany. The ideal combination of wine and sausage is found at the annual *Dürkheimer Wurstmarkt* (Dürkheim Sausage Fair) held each September.

Entering the Rhineland, look out for *Hase im Topf,* a delicious and highly-flavored rabbit pâté made with port, Madeira, brandy and red wine, baked for hours in an earthenware pot. A specialty of the Lower Rhineland and the Bergisch Land is *Panhas,* a meat paste prepared with sausage gravy, blood and buckwheat meal.

But it is Rhenish pickled beef, or *Sauerbraten,* one of the most popular dishes in Germany, that is perhaps best known of all the Rhineland specialties. It's marinated for at least three days in spiced vinegar, then simmered in red wine. Traditional accompaniments are stewed apples, Brussel sprouts, or *Rotkohl* (red cabbage), plus *Knödel*—dumplings—and local beer.

Continuing on again, be on the look-out for Westphalian ham, famous for more than 2,000 years. The hams can weigh as much as 33 pounds and are considered particularly good for breakfast, when a huge slice is served on a wooden board with rich, dark pumpernickel bread baked for 20 hours (and tasting considerably better than its reputation), and, for the sturdy, a glass of strong, clear *Steinhäger Schnaps.* A favorite main course is *Pfefferpothast,* a sort of goulash with lots of pepper and heavily browned. The "hast" at the end of the name is from the old German word *Harst,* or roasting pan. In Hameln and its surroundings, home of the famous Pied Piper and, further into the Weserbergland, setting for the Grimms' fairy-tales, you will come across rivers and streams abundant with trout and eels.

Traveling through the Weserbergland, you must sample some *Göttinger Speckkuchen* from the town of the same name. It's similar to the southern German *Zwiebelkuchen,* or onion tart, and unquestionably numbers among the more *deftig* lunchtime dishes.

Heading up into the mountainous Harz, you'll find an abundance of fresh-water fish and excellent game dishes, particularly venison. However, the Harz is probably best known for its cheese—*Harzer,* to be exact—a round, sharp-tasting cheese seasoned with caraway seeds and covered in a bluish mould. It is best eaten with black bread spread with *Gänseschmalz,* goosefat.

Lower Saxony and the North

The Lüneberger Heide, a vast area of rolling heathland between Celle and Lüneberg in Lower Saxony, is particularly famed for the delicious lamb it produces from the small sheep that roam the great heath in their thousands. The best known of the area's many lamb dishes is *Heidschnückenbraten,* roast lamb with an unusual flavor halfway between mutton and game. It is a delicacy which on no account should be missed when you are in this area. Other specialties of Lower Saxony include the strange-sounding and originally Frisian *Grünkohl mit Pinkel.* It consists of kale or cabbage with *Pinkelwurst,* the local sausage made out of finely-chopped fatty pork. In order to digest the fat, you should wash the whole lot down with a measure of ice-cold *Korn Schnaps,* traditionally drunk out of a pewter spoon.

Approaching the coast, German gastronomy undergoes a radical change. In Bremen, for example, a must in summer is *Aalsuppe grün,* eel soup seasoned with dozens of herbs. Smoked eel, *Räucheraal,* is equally delicious, while in the fall you should try *Bunte oder Gepflückte Finten,* a wonderful dish of green and white beans, carrots and apples. A dish available at any time of year is *Bremer Küken ragout,* a fabulous concoction of sweetbreads, spring chicken, tiny veal meatballs, asparagus, clams and fresh peas cooked in a white sauce.

Along the popular resorts of the East Frisian Islands, fish—boiled, fried, baked or smoked—reigns supreme. In addition there is fresh crab galore, *Granat* or *Garnelen* (shrimp), and even seagulls' eggs.

Schleswig Holstein is also a paradise for seafood. A particular regional specialty is *Labskaus,* much favored by sailors. This is a stew made from pickled meat, potatoes, herring (sometimes) and garnished with a fried egg, sour pickles and lots of beetroot. *Holstein Schnitzel,* found throughout

Germany but invented and best in Schleswig Holstein, is a golden-fried, breaded veal cutlet, somewhat like the Austrian *Wienerschnitzel,* the whole topped with a fried egg and anchovy. A much more unusual regional specialty, however, is *Gefüllte Schweinerippchen,* pork chops stuffed with toast, raisins, apples, and laced with rum. In Büsum you should try *Krabben,* a sort of tiny shrimp, while Lübeck is famous for its marzipan.

We have now reached the most northerly point of Germany—Flensburg—home of Schleswig Holstein rum. Why this most unlikely spot should be famed for rum of all unlikely drinks is easily explained by the fact that until the mid-19th century Flensburg belonged to Denmark, whose merchant fleets then spread far and wide around the world bringing back, among their varied cargoes, large quantities of Caribbean rum. But rum, famous and delightful though it is, is by no means the extent of Flensburg's specialties. *Schweinebauch,* roast belly-pork, *Schweinebacken,* pigs cheek, *Speck,* bacon, and *Schinken,* ham, are all commonly found here. There is also a local ham, *Holstein Katenschinken,* that is a real delicacy. And in addition to rum, try the *Holsteiner* beer, best drunk with juniper-scented *Korn* or *Bommerlunder* brandy; it should see you through nobly.

There is just one corner of the Federal Republic whose cuisine we have not yet considered: Berlin, home of the infamous and fabled German national dish—*Eisbein mit Sauerkraut.* This is a heavily-spiced pork shank, served with Sauerkraut and mashed potatoes or pease pudding, a very thick pea puree. This dish—along with *Bockwurst,* a chubby Frankfurter, and *Bockwurst,* usually served with *Erbsensuppe* (yellow pea soup)—form the Berliner's staple diet, and you will find them on menus throughout the city. In fact, *Bockwurst* stands are as common as hotdog stands in the States. But Berliners also like *Schlesisches Himmelreich,* roast goose or pork with potato dumplings, cooked with fried fruit in a rich gravy. *Königsberger Klopse,* and *Berliner Bouletten,* the former a small meatball with herring and capers, the latter Berlin's variant of the Hamburger—the American rather than the German version—are also common and very popular. Finally, look out for *Kasseler Rippenspeer,* not a dish from the town of that name in Hesse, but salted pork, fried golden in butter then slowly cooked, the recipe concocted originally by a Berlin butcher named Cassel.

Last but Not Least

This gastronomical tour should not be concluded without a bow to the herring. If you are fond of herring, Germany will make you very happy. Herrings are eaten here in every imaginable way: there's "Green" herring, fried fresh; rollmops, or "Bismarck" herrings, rolled up around pickles, gherkins, and onions; *Brathering,* sour, pickled herring; *Matjeshering,* herring with potatoes boiled in their skins, plus lots of butter; and even a herring salad with diced cucumber potatoes and much seasoning. In Emden, in fact, they'll give you a whole herring lunch, with hors d'oeuvre, main dish and salad all provided by this protein-rich fish.

A couple of final tips should also be noted. Wherever you go in Germany, sooner or later you will be confronted with a *Brotzeit*—an in-between or second breakfast, and as important a meal to the Germans as any other. As they start their day relatively early, usually around 7, by about 10 most Germans' thoughts begin to turn toward their stomachs. Out come the rolls and sausage, a piece of cheese or *Leberwurst,* a slice of *Sulze* (chopped meat in aspic) or a piece of *Kasseler,* washed down with—no, not always beer, more often than not it's mineral water, of which there are almost as many kinds as there are wines, or *Apfelsaft* (apple juice). But as a visitor you can *Brotzeit* whenever you feel like it. Many taverns and restaurants have a special *Brotzeitkarte* supplement to their menus, or serve a *Brotzeit-teller,* a platter of cold meat with cheese and bread and a glass of *Schnaps.*

And finally, if, after lunch, you are still hungry, there is always the oblig-atory *Kaffee und Kuchen,* coffee and cake taken in one of the many cafes found in all towns. A cup of fresh ground coffee is accompanied by a por-tion of one of the mouth-watering cakes like *Schwarzwalderkirsch* or *Käsekuchen,* though the Germans are also very fond of less elaborate cakes such as Madeira cake, known variously as *Englischer Kuchen, Mar-morkuchen,* or even *Sandkuchen.*

At the end of the day it's onto the bathroom scales again and time to start thinking about *abspecken,* literally, if rather bluntly, "getting the fat off." As a tourist, however, when you have completed your typical Ger-man gastronomic day, whether in the north, south, east or west, with or without *Knödel, Eisbein, Würst, Pumpernickel* or *Schwarzwälderkirsch-torte,* you will just have to forget the excess pounds. Tomorrow will bring more opportunities for sampling Germany's culinary delights. You can always *diät* when you get home.

GERMAN WINE

Weinfests and Carousels

by
PAMELA VANDYKE PRICE

*Pamela Vandyke Price is a noted British writer on wine. She has pub-
lished 21 books on the subject. Her writing, broadcasting and lecturing on
wine and wine-related subjects have won her several awards, both French
and British.*

Germany produces some of the most famous, and indeed most expensive, wines in the world. Moreover, her wine-producing regions are among
the most beautiful in the country, with imposing castle ruins on rocky
crags, black-and-white gabled houses filling the villages, and elegant spas
abounding. You need only sit on a terrace overlooking a river and a vineyard and sample the local wine for the romantic magic of Germany and
her wines to become dreamily clear.

Yet there's a paradox here, for Germany doesn't, or at any rate
shouldn't, seem an obvious wine producing country. For one thing, the
wine regions are relatively far north, on the same latitude as Vancouver
and Winnipeg, with cold winters and unreliable summers. To this extent
the existence, and, even more to the point, the quality of German wines
is in large measure a tribute both to the high caliber of the vines and the
skill and dedication of those who devote their lives to making fine wine.

The paradoxes do not end here, however, for the curious seeker after German wine is in for a couple of further surprises. The first is that, unlike in France for example, the very finest wines are seldom drunk with meals. Rather, they are reserved for leisurely sipping in appreciative company, often with no food at all or perhaps just a few biscuits or plain sponge cake. The delicacy and complexity of these great wines is such that they deserve the whole attention of the drinker in a clean and fresh atmosphere. This isn't affectation. Their wonderful bouquet and lingering flavor merit the sort of attention that you simply can't give them in a crowded dining room, particularly when they have to compete with the conflicting smells of food and, likely as not, smoke. Of course, there are plenty of pleasant wines you can, indeed should, drink with meals, especially carafe wines or *offener weine* (literally, "open wines"). But even then it's not necessary to order a meal if you want to try a selection of open wines; you need merely order a range of glasses and then compose a mini-tasting of your own.

The second surprise concerns Liebfraumilch. Though unquestionably the best-known German wine, you'll seldom see it on a wine list in Germany itself. The reason is simply that although the original Liebfraumilch came from the vineyard surrounding the Liebfraukirche (the Church of Our Lady) at Worms, it has long since been a general term, used to describe a style of German wine. Though subject to legislation, and a "quality" white wine, it was originally created as a general *type* of wine, intended specifically for export, as the ambassador of German wines if you like. So don't expect to find it in Germany itself; instead make the most of the chance to try other wines in their birthplace. Not only will they be less expensive here, but some, produced only in small quantities, will never be found outside the country.

2,000 Years of Wine

The history of Germany's wines begins with the Romans, whose armies placed a high priority on their wine ration, using it for disinfectant and medicinal purposes—wine was often used to make a doubtful water supply safe—as well as for refreshment. How much of the wine consumed by the Romans in Germany was actually produced there is unknown, and it seems likely that it was only in the reign of Charlemagne in the 9th century that significant quantities of wine began to be produced in Germany itself. It was Charlemagne, or so the story goes, who noticed that certain south facing slopes shed their winter snows early and who suggested that vines be planted on them. The success of these early wine-producers, and the importance of the rivers along which all the important vineyards were situated, is made clear by the famous medieval relief of a wine ship in the Landesmuseum in Trier transporting wine casks along the Mosel.

Later, the great medieval monasteries, who needed wine for sacramental as well as medicinal purposes, were to exert a significant influence on the development of German wines, not least by introducing more systematic methods of cultivation. But in addition, merchants, bankers, scholars, diplomats and the nobility all helped promote German wines, which by the Renaissance had become not only an important export but had improved dramatically in quality. By the 19th century, the fame of German wine had spread even farther afield, even to the New World, with political and religious refugees and the hoardes of immigrants who settled in America all helping to spread the message abroad. Queen Victoria, who loved everything German, also helped boost the reputation of the country's wines, and following a visit to Hocheim in 1850 even permitted the use of her name for the Königin Viktoria-Berg site.

By the middle of the 19th century, German wine production had become significantly more scientific and exact, a process that has continued and accelerated throughout the 20th century. Much of this work has been carried out by the world-famous German Wine Institute at Geisenheim, which has played a vital role in evolving new strains of vines, improving fermentation techniques, soil analysis, and the like. In addition, they have advised many of the great estates on the laying out of their vineyards. A great many wine producers have also helped in the ever more precise and productive methods used in Germany today, not least by banding together to form winegrowers' co-operatives—there are several hundred today—and pooling their resources and expertise. The most modern and expensive equipment is now commonplace, and the co-operatives supply wine to hundreds of outlets.

BASIC WINE FACTS

German wine means, first and foremost, white wine. There are a number of pale wines (generally very pale in color), some sparkling wines, and even a few red wines, but essentially the vast bulk of German wines—almost 90%—and all the really great ones, are white. Secondly, like all wines, particularly the very finest, an almost infinite number of factors can influence the final product. Even supposedly similar wines can vary tremendously. Every bottler, shipper and importer, every change in the weather, every different type of grape, every tiny difference in the soil, all these factors and many more beside influence and alter every bottle of wine in a thousand subtle ways. The difficulties facing the would-be connoisseur are made all the more extreme by the fact that tastes also vary greatly, and that one man's "dry" can easily be another's "medium dry," to take just one simple example.

So short of going out and actually drinking the stuff, which is of course the ultimate object of the exercise, what do you need to know to guide you through the initially daunting world of German wines? Below we list the salient facts.

Bottles and Glasses

There are five basic types of bottle. Mosel wines come in slender, dark green bottles, Rhine wines in slender brown bottles. Red wines come in slightly fatter, sloping-shouldered bottles. Franconian *steinwein* is bottled in dumpy flagons of green glass known as a *bocksbeutel.* Its origins can be traced back to the Middle Ages when leather skins, hung from a saddle or belt, were used to transport wine. Finally, sparkling wines come in a traditionally-shaped Champagne bottle.

The standard German wine glass has a long stem, to ensure that your hand does not warm the wine, and a bowl shaped somewhat like an onion with the top cut off. This inward curving shape catches the bouquet and directs it to the drinker's nose. There are also a number of variations on this standard type. Mosel glasses, for example, often have green stems, while Rhine glasses can have brown stems. Similarly, the finest Mosel wines are sometimes drunk from a glass known as a "Treviris," after Trier, whose bowl is cut with a special pattern. You may also find that the very best wines of all, from whatever region, are drunk from a smaller glass so that more can be shared around. Sparkling wines are served in a deepish, triangular-shaped stemmed bowl. At wine festivals and some tastings, a miniature tumbler is used. Finally, you may also encounter all or any of these types in tinted glass. These were very much more common in the last century and owe their existence to the same mock-modesty that led the Victorians to put petticoats on piano legs so as not to offend, the offending article in this case being the "flyers," or little bits of cork, grit or grape that are occasionally found in wine and which, it was felt, affronted the gaze of the drinker.

Tasting

Although many inexpensive German wines are very pleasant to drink, and can be swallowed casually for the immediate enjoyment they afford, the finer wines should be sampled in a much more deliberate way. First, look at the color; for most of the young white wines it will be a light, lemony-gilt. But for all white wines it should be brilliantly clear. Then sniff the wine as you twirl it around in the glass. If you fill your glass to the brim you won't be able to do this and will cheat yourself of the bouquet. The fragrance of German wine is usually quite marked: wafting, delicate, and charming, tempting you to drink . . . and then drink more. The flavor tends to be light, the dry wines refreshing the palate, the sweeter wines appealing by the luscious way they linger, trailing slowly away so that the final impression is enchanting.

The finest wines should be drunk at leisure. Sample them with deliberate care. They are masterpieces of the wine makers' art and deserve your undivided attention, even for a short time, and should not be drunk at meals.

Label Language

German wine labels are often magnificent specimens of intricate design, delightful in themselves. They provide detailed information about the contents of the bottle and everything on them is strictly controlled by law. Understanding them is an essential step in coming to grips with German wine. Unfortunately, they can also often appear difficult to decipher, in some cases positively impenetrable. Names can be disconcertingly long, and the famous Gothic script apparently used specifically to obscure.

In fact most labels are much easier to read than they might seem. Long names are often only those of growers and shippers run together. The monster "Winzergenossenschaft," for example, only means "Wine Growers' Co-operative." Similarly, the suffix "er" is often attached to place names, meaning "of," thus Oppenheim becomes Oppenheimer—of Oppenheim— Rüdesheim becomes Rüdesheimer. Anything appearing after "Schloss" is just the name of a castle, while "Graf von Hatushka-Greiffenclau" means no more than the "Count of Hatushka-Greiffenclau." The secret is not to panic but to sort out the different names calmly. You'll find everything falls into place surprisingly quickly.

A Typical German Wine Label

Wine region —— RHEINPFALZ —— Vintage

1982

Site name —— **Winzerdorfer Rebberg** —— Grape name

Riesling

Halbtrocken

Taste or style —— Qualitätswein b.A. A.P.Nr. 5 16 98 7 83 —— A P # (see below)

Erzeugerabfullung Winzer Bacchus, Winzerdorf

Wine Quality —— Grower and bottler

Amlitiche Prüfungsnummer

5	16	98	7	83
# of testing station	# identifying location of bottler	bottler's identification #	# of a particular lot or bottling	year of test

General Label Terms. Grape names. A number of different grapes are used in Germany. For white wine, the most important are: Riesling, specifically Rheinriesling which should not be confused with certain other wines from other countries that may be labeled Riesling; Muller-Thurgau; Sylvaner, which makes some of the finer Franken wines; Traminer; Scheurebe; Sigerrebe; Morio-Muskat; Ruländer, also known as Pinot Gris; Kerner; Trollinger; Gutedel.

For red wines, the principal grapes are: Portugieser; Blauer Trollinger; Blauer Spätburgunder, also known as Pinot Noir.

Don't forget that Riesling should be pronounced so that the first syllable rhymes with "geese" rather than "rice." The prestige of the Riesling is such that, though it will have been used on the very finest Rhine and Mosel wines, its name will not appear on the label. Confusingly, on cheaper bottles you will also find that no grape name appears.

Vintage dates. Everyone can read a date, but if no date appears it should be assumed that the wine should be drunk soon.

Trocken and **Halb Trocken.** These mean that the wine will be dry or medium dry respectively.

Site names. These will appear on quality wines, such as the "Goldtröpfchen" at Piesport, the "Doktor" at Bernkastel or the "Gutes Domtal" at Nierstein. The situation is slightly confused, however, by the fact that even a small site may be owned by several concerns—there are three owners of the Doktor site for example—but at the same time the particular owner's name will always appear on the label. Similarly, one owner may also have sites in a number of different vineyards.

A.P. This is an abbreviation of *Amlitiche Prüfungsnummer,* meaning that the wine has met with the approval of a qualified body of authorities. Once the wine has this official approval, it is issued with a number which appears on the label. Two sealed bottles are then deposited with the authorities who, in the event of any dispute as to the authenticity or quality of the wine, are able to trace the history of the wine and, if need be, sample the bottles. See our specimen label for a breakdown of these numbers.

Erzeugerabfüllung or **Aus Eigneneum Lesegut.** This means that the wine was produced and bottled on the same estate where the grapes were grown.

Süssreserve. A system whereby unfermented grape juice can be added, under strict control, to wines that are otherwise tart or too sharp. It may not be used for any of the finer wines. It should also not be confused with the French system of *chaptalization,* the addition of sugar to the unfermented grape juice to promote the action of the yeasts.

Oechsle. A system of measuring grape sugar in the "must," the unfermented grape juice. For the sweetest German wines, the higher the percentage the better, and if a grower announces the percentage his wine has reached, congratulate him.

Wine Quality.

Wine Quality. All German wines fall into two basic categories— *Deutsche Tafelwein* or *Deutsche Landwein* and *Qualitätswein*—both strictly monitored. In either case, all relevant information detailing the wine will appear on the label.

Deutsche Tafelwein. Essentially a simple table wine, for the most part drunk only in Germany, made from a blend of different wines from one of the four Tafelwein regions.

Tafelwein. A blend of simple everyday wines from other EEC countries which may or may not contain German wines, but generally bottled in Germany.

Deutsche Landwein. A category of Deutscher Tafelwein introduced after the 1982 vintage and made with rather more ripe grapes than those used for simple Deutsche Tafelwein. It is usually dry or medium dry and the grapes must come from one of the 15 Landwein regions.

Qualitätswein bestimmer Anbaugebiete. Usually shortened to "QbA," this category comprises the bulk of Germany's wines and represents something of a halfway house between the cheapest and the finest wines. It must come from one of the 11 specified wine regions (see below) and the grapes must have been allowed to ripen fully. These wines are best consumed young.

Qualitätswein mit Prädikat. Usually shortened to QmP, meaning "quality wine with a special attribute." This is the top category of German wine. It is divided into one of six types. In ascending order of quality these are:

—*Kabinett:* generally the driest of the QmP wines and made from fully ripened grapes; the label will normally mention the specific plot in the vineyard in which the grapes were grown.

—*Spätlese:* literally, "late harvest," that is the grapes have been picked late, though the wine is not necessarily particularly sweet. However, it will have an intense flavor.

—*Auslese:* the grapes will have been picked late and selected bunch by bunch with only the finest going into the vat; generally very sweet and very special.

—*Beerenauslese:* not only will the grapes have been picked very late, they will have been selected grape by grape; moreover, they will also have been subjected to the fungus *botrytis cinerea* (*edelfaüle* or "noble rot") which makes the flavor more intense still. This is a very fine wine.

—*Eiswein:* made from Beerenauslese grapes that are frozen at the moment of picking and go into the vat with a coating of ice; very sweet, very fine, and very expensive.

—*Trockenbeerenauslese:* Beerenauslese grapes that have been left on the vine until they dry and shrivel, leaving no more than a single drop of intensely luscious juice in each grape; this wine is very sweet and rich, and very, very rare.

The Wine Regions

As we have already mentioned, there are 11 officially-designated wine-producing regions in Germany, each producing wines typical of their own area (i.e. similar in taste) and different from wine produced elsewhere in the country. All are located along rivers or around lakes, the importance of which are vital to successful wine production. The presence of water helps temper the climate in the immediate area by providing generally less variable day- and night-time temperatures than in other parts of the country, as well as reflecting the rays of the sun and helping the grapes to ripen. Moreover, the fogs and mists that rise from the waters in the fall protect the precious crop from frost at its most vunerable moment, most German grapes being picked relatively late (October and November) to let them ripen fully.

Particularly outstanding years for German wines were 1983 and 1985 for Southern Baden and Alsatian wines, and 1985 for Franken (Bocksbeutel), Palatinate and North Baden (Bergstrasse region) wines. 1983 was also a good year for Moselle, Rhine, Saar/Ruwer, Ahr and Nahe wines.

Bus tours and other sightseeing trips can be easily arranged through all the main regions—contact local tourist offices for details—while for the less active there are ferries and steamers that journey from vineyard to vineyard, many providing refreshments of one sort or another.

It is not normally possible to visit the great estates without having made prior arrangements, but all wine villages have plenty of *weinstube,* cafes and delightful restaurants where the local produce can be sampled in appropriate surroundings. There are also a number of important wine museums, while tourist offices can provide excellent guides and brochures to their own regions. They will also be able to advise on the all-important matter of wine tasting, though note that we give details of this in the *Practical Information* for each chapter.

Remember that in high season and during local festivals, accommodations can be very difficult to arrange and that roads and transport will be crowded.

We list the wine regions by size (area under cultivation), beginning with the largest.

Rheinhessen. This is the largest wine-producing area in Germany. It is bordered on the west by the river Nahe and on the north and east by the Rhine. The two largest towns here are Mainz and Worms, the latter the site of the Liebfrauenkirche, the Church of Our Lady.

Wines from here are generally rather full and fruity, and for the most part are pleasant and inexpensive, though a number of quality wines are also produced.

Rheinpfalz. Though smaller than the Rheinhessen, the Rheinpfalz nonetheless produces more wine than any other area of the country. The region runs along the west bank of the Rhine for 80 km. (50 miles) to Neustadt and the French border, with the Deutscher Weinstrasse (the German Wine Road) running its length. It is also one of the most attractive of Germany's wine regions, with an abundance of little villages dotting the countryside, their buildings sporting traditional black-and-white gables.

The wines here are generally fairly robust and are particularly good with many of the local specialties, particularly sausages, to which whole festivals, notably that at Bad Durkheim, are devoted. Weinstube here also commonly have a "carousel," an iron frame holding six, nine or 12 glasses in numbered slots. Fill them up and sample as many as you can manage.

Detour if possible to Speyer where, opposite the Cathedral, there is an important museum, a large section of which is devoted to wine and where the oldest wine in the world, dating from the third century A.D., is preserved in an amphora.

Baden. The southernmost of the wine regions and the most diverse, both in landscapes and wines. The region extends from near Heidelburg in the north to Bodensee (Lake Constance) in the south. Local wine consumption is significantly higher than in other regions of the country, with the result that very little wine is exported.

Much pink wine is made, produced by fermenting white and black grapes together. It's known as Schillerwein, though it has nothing to do with the 19th-century Romantic writer of that name, being derived instead from the word "schillern," meaning to shimmer or glitter. An unusual white wine from here, Weissherbst, is a white wine made from black grapes, whose skins—which provide the color—are removed early in the fermentation.

Mosel-Saar-Ruwer. The wine-growing regions of the Mosel, with its tributaries the Saar and the Ruwer (pronounced "Roover"), run from just south of Trier to Koblenz on the Rhine. They produce some of the most famous wines in Germany: crisp, fresh and charming, with a glorious bouquet. They are also often highly individual, the result of the extraordinary meanderings of the Mosel, so that even neighboring plots face in quite different directions and produce quite different wines. The banks of the river are also extremely steep, and you'll often see no more than a single row of vines on a precipitous ledge apparently accessible only to a mountain goat.

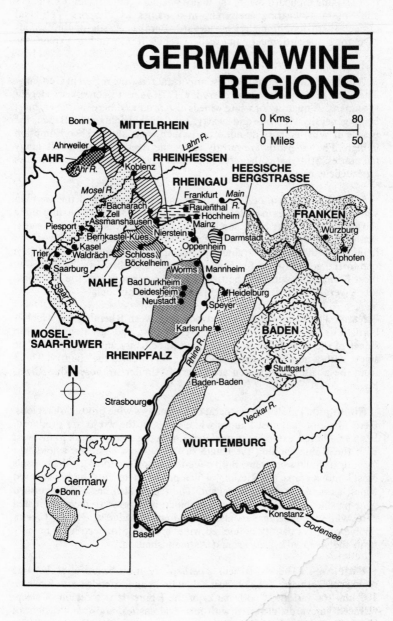

GERMAN WINE REGIONS

The famous sites are generally clearly marked, even from the river, so that relaxing on board one of the many steamers you can identify villages and vineyards bearing such renowned names as Piesport, Zell, and Graach, with its Nimmelreich vineyard. Bernkastel, site of the famous "Doktor" vineyard, makes an excellent center from which to explore the region.

Württemburg. This is the most important red wine region in Germany. These range in quality from everyday Tafelweins to some very elegant specimens. A quantity of white wine is also produced here, however, most being generally vigorous and hearty. Like their neighbors in Baden, the people of Württemburg do not export much wine, and local consumption is high. The vineyards are mostly along the river Neckar and its many tributaries. Stuttgart is the most important town in the region and makes an excellent base.

Franken. Franken, or Franconia, is the most easterly of the German wine regions, and lies in undulating countryside, its vineyards strung along the length of the river Main and its tributaries. The region's wines are generally earthy and rather dry, even "masculine." Franconia also boasts the famous "Stein" site at Würzburg, principal city of Franconia, which gave rise to the general term for Franconian wines, Steinwein. Traditionally, most Franconian wines are bottled in a squat, green flagon, the bocksbeutel. A very little red wine ia also produced in Franconia.

Nahe. The Nahe region is sandwiched between Rheinhessen, which it borders to the west, and the Mosel, to the east, and lies along the steep slopes of the river Nahe. Its wines tend to be fruity and slightly "fat" or spicy, with a number of them among the very best in the country. Those from the north of the region are generally similar to those from Rheinhessen.

Rheingau. This is the aristocrat of Germany's wine producing regions. Here, some of the most famous white wines in the world are produced. It's a small area, extending from Hocheim in the east to Lorch in the west with the Rhine running the length of its southern side, the whole area forming a shallow crescent. Both climate and soil are ideal for the region's most famous grape, the Riesling, which produces delicate, highly flavored wines, as noble as they are elegant. The region also has a distinguished wine-producing history. The term Kabinett is believed to have originated here, while the Rheingauers also discovered the value of *Botrytis Cinera*, "noble rot." A quantity of fine red wines are also produced here, notably from the steep vineyards around Assmannshausen.

Mittelrhein. The Mittelrhein is perhaps the most beautiful of the wine regions of Germany. It begins just below Bonn and extends south for some 100 km. (60 miles) on both banks of the Rhine. It is a region of steep, terraced vineyards, crowned with medieval castles, and many delightful little villages. The famed Lorelei, a lonely rock in the middle of the Rhine said to lure fishermen to their death, is also in the Mittelrhein, at Kaub at the southern end of the region. The wines here, very little of which are exported, are generally pert and fresh and rather fruity.

Ahr. This is the most northerly wine region in Germany. It produces predominantly red wines that are both light and fruity, the bulk of which is consumed locally. Charming, winding roads and pleasant scenery make this a delightful region to explore.

Hessische Bergstrasse. The literal translation of this, the smallest of the wine regions, is the Hesse Mountain Road, and the area, bordered by the Rhine to the east and the Odenwald Forest to the east, is delightful. Its wines tend to be rich and fragrant, verging on the hearty. Practically none is exported, giving a visit here added purpose.

Sparkling Wines

In addition to the vast quantities of ordinary wine—white, pink and red—produced in Germany, the Germans are also exceedingly fond of Schaumwein, or Sekt as it is more commonly known. Some of this could accurately be described as Champagne, though it may not legally be labeled as such (only French sparkling wines have that honor, a peculiarity made all the more bizarre for having been written into the Treaty of Versailles in 1919). However, much of the German variety is not made according to the Champagne method, but follows a slightly less time-consuming and hence more inexpensive process known as "sealed vat," or *Tank Vergämung.*

The name Sekt apparently owes its origins to the great early-19th-century actor Ludwig Devrient. Echoing his stage character, he would habitually call for "A cup of sack," in his favorite weinstube after performances when playing Falstaff. The nickname, suitably Germanized, caught on.

As with all German wines, the production of Sekt is strictly controlled. Bottles labeled Sekt, or even Deutscher Sekt, may be made from grapes grown outside Germany, though they must have been produced and bottled in Germany. However, bottles labeled more specifically, Mosel Sekt or Rhein Sekt for example, will be the genuine article, in these instances coming from the Mosel and the Rhine respectively. If the name of a particular estate, such as Schloss Saarfels in the Mosel, is used, then only wine from that estate may be in that bottle.

In addition to Sekt, there is also a semi-sparkling wine called Perlwein. This is distinguished also by the fact that it comes in bottles made of thicker than normal glass to resist the pressure inside.

Wine Festivals

Throughout the summer and fall, numerous wine festivals are held in the wine-producing regions. Complete lists are available from the *Deutsche Wein-Information,* Postfach 1707, D–6500 Mainz 1. The German National Tourist Office and regional tourist offices are also able to provide information on these festivals.

The term *weinfest* is self-explanatory. However, a *winzerfest* is a growers' festival; a *weinmarkt* is an occasion when both the trade and the public may sample wines from stalls; a *weinlesefest* is a vintage celebration; a *weindorf* is a wine village *en fête;* a *weinblütenfest* is a festival celebrating the flowering of the vines in early summer.

Wine Courses

A number of courses on wine are arranged in the various regions, most in German. However, the German Wine Academy arrange a program in English for both beginners and the more advanced. Contact the German Wine Academy, Postfach 1705, D–6500 Mainz 1, or the German National Tourist Office for details.

INDEX

Index

**The letter H indicates Hotels and other accommodations.
The letter R indicates Restaurants.**

Fodor's Travel Guides

U.S. Guides

Alaska
American Cities
The American South
Arizona
Atlantic City & the
  New Jersey Shore
Boston
California
Cape Cod
Carolinas & the
  Georgia Coast
Chesapeake
Chicago
Colorado
Dallas & Fort Worth
Disney World & the
  Orlando Area

The Far West
Florida
Greater Miami,
  Fort Lauderdale,
  Palm Beach
Hawaii
Hawaii *(Great Travel
  Values)*
Houston & Galveston
I-10: California to
  Florida
I-55: Chicago to New
  Orleans
I-75: Michigan to
  Florida
I-80: San Francisco to
  New York

I-95: Maine to Miami
Las Vegas
Los Angeles, Orange
  County, Palm Springs
Maui
New England
New Mexico
New Orleans
New Orleans *(Pocket
  Guide)*
New York City
New York City *(Pocket
  Guide)*
New York State
Pacific North Coast
Philadelphia
Puerto Rico *(Fun in)*

Rockies
San Diego
San Francisco
San Francisco *(Pocket
  Guide)*
Texas
United States of
  America
Virgin Islands
  (U.S. & British)
Virginia
Waikiki
Washington, DC
Williamsburg,
  Jamestown &
  Yorktown

Foreign Guides

Acapulco
Amsterdam
Australia, New Zealand
  & the South Pacific
Austria
The Bahamas
The Bahamas *(Pocket
  Guide)*
Barbados *(Fun in)*
Beijing, Guangzhou &
  Shanghai
Belgium & Luxembourg
Bermuda
Brazil
Britain *(Great Travel
  Values)*
Canada
Canada *(Great Travel
  Values)*
Canada's Maritime
  Provinces
Cancún, Cozumel,
  Mérida, The
  Yucatán
Caribbean
Caribbean *(Great
  Travel Values)*

Central America
Copenhagen,
  Stockholm, Oslo,
  Helsinki, Reykjavik
Eastern Europe
Egypt
Europe
Europe *(Budget)*
Florence & Venice
France
France *(Great Travel
  Values)*
Germany
Germany *(Great Travel
  Values)*
Great Britain
Greece
Holland
Hong Kong & Macau
Hungary
India
Ireland
Israel
Italy
Italy *(Great Travel
  Values)*
Jamaica *(Fun in)*

Japan
Japan *(Great Travel
  Values)*
Jordan & the Holy Land
Kenya
Korea
Lisbon
Loire Valley
London
London *(Pocket Guide)*
London *(Great Travel
  Values)*
Madrid
Mexico
Mexico *(Great Travel
  Values)*
Mexico City & Acapulco
Mexico's Baja & Puerto
  Vallarta, Mazatlán,
  Manzanillo, Copper
  Canyon
Montreal
Munich
New Zealand
North Africa
Paris
Paris *(Pocket Guide)*

People's Republic of
  China
Portugal
Province of Quebec
Rio de Janeiro
The Riviera *(Fun on)*
Rome
St. Martin/St. Maarten
Scandinavia
Scotland
Singapore
South America
South Pacific
Southeast Asia
Soviet Union
Spain
Spain *(Great Travel
  Values)*
Sweden
Switzerland
Sydney
Tokyo
Toronto
Turkey
Vienna
Yugoslavia

Special-Interest Guides

Bed & Breakfast
  Guide: North America
1936...On the
  Continent

Royalty Watching
Selected Hotels of
  Europe

Selected Resorts
  and Hotels of the U.S.
Ski Resorts of North
  America

Views to Dine by
  around the World